A FLY Guide to Real Estate: Owning and Managing Property When You're Under 25

By Mike Nie · Chris Nie · Kevin Nie

Board of Directors, SMART Life Family Foundation

GIFTED BOOKS

A FLY Guide to Real Estate: Owning and Managing Property When You're Under 25 with a Parental Guide to Financial Freedom

ISBN:

978-1-966261-14-8 Ebook

978-1-966261-15-5 Paperback

978-1-966261-16-2 Hardcover

Contents

Disclaimer

The Securities and Exchange Commission disclaims responsibility for any private publication or statement of any SEC employee or Commissioner. This book expresses the authors' views and does not necessarily reflect those of the Commission, the Commissioners, or other members of the staff.

This book is intended for educational and informational purposes only. It reflects the authors' personal experiences and interpretations and should not be construed as specific tax, legal, financial, or investment advice for any individual situation. Readers should consult with qualified tax, legal, and financial professionals before applying any strategies discussed herein.

While every effort has been made to ensure accuracy as of the date of publication, laws and regulations are subject to change, and the authors assume no responsibility for errors, omissions, or changes in applicable laws.

The book mentions well-diversified broad-based stock index (such as S&P 500 index), well-diversified, broad-based stocks with zero dividends, whole life insurance policies, crypto, real estate, or other financial assets. The authors advise the reader to seek help from licensed professionals regarding these financial assets. These licensed professionals have their respective expertise to suggest and design your personal portfolio based on your financial, liquidity, tax, and other specific situations.

The rate of return, yield and dividend ratio are as of year-end 2025. Past data does not guarantee future performance. Readers bear their investment risk. The authors, SMART Life Family Foundation, and Smart 1040 LLC are not responsible for such investment-related risks or losses.

The IRS tax forms are as of 2025, or the latest version is available at the IRS.gov website. The tax code-related dollar amounts are as of 2025, many of which are adjusted annually by the IRS. This book also addresses new tax law changes in the One Big Beautiful Bill Act (OBBB), which adjusts certain limits, caps, or phase-out amounts. The book has incorporated these new tax law changes. Many tax rule changes will require the readers to re-evaluate their tax planning strategies.

The hyperlinks used throughout the book may not work if the content owner removes or edits the post. All names and stories have fictional elements and are designed for illustration purposes only.

This book and its contents may not be used for training, developing, or enhancing any artificial intelligence (AI) model without the express written consent of the authors.

Author Content Responsibility Acknowledgment

The Authors have elected not to include endnotes, citations, or reference sources in the manuscript. The Authors confirm that the book is intended for general readers and reflects the Author's professional knowledge and personal experience.

The Authors represent and warrant that all content in the manuscript, including statements, opinions, financial explanations, and advice, is accurate to the best of the Authors' knowledge and does not knowingly contain false or misleading information.

The Authors acknowledge and agree that Gifted Books and its representatives act solely as a publishing service provider and do not independently verify the factual accuracy of the manuscript.

The Authors therefore assume full responsibility for the content of the work, including any claims, errors, omissions, or disputes arising from the publication.

The Authors agree to indemnify and hold harmless Gifted Books, its owner, and its service providers from any legal claims, liabilities, or damages related to the content of the book.

Preface

"The best inheritance a parent can give their children is a few minutes of their time each day and the tools to build their own future."—O.A. Battista

This book is the first in the *FLY Financial Literacy for Young People* series. It explores the *how*, *why*, and *what* behind teaching young people to achieve homeownership—and financial independence—by age 25 and beyond. I feel compelled to write this one with my sons Chris and Kevin as the first of our FLY series for a few reasons:

- Young people today are stepping into the most complex financial environment in modern history. Housing prices are rising faster than wages, student debt continues to soar, and the path to financial independence feels impossible and overwhelming for many teenagers.
- Various studies show that one in five young people (25-35) live with their parents for different reasons. The ratio for men is even higher. I see the urgency of resolving this "lifetime dwelling with parents" social issue.
- The advent of artificial intelligence poses unprecedented challenges in the entry-level job market. Many young people, after fruitless job searches during college and beyond, are forced to return to their parents' home.

As a father, Christian believer, CPA, professional tax advisor, and author of the *SMART Family Tax Guide*, I have witnessed both the successes and struggles of families raising the next generation. In my view, parenthood can be measured by three simple principles: raising children who are (1) responsible and accountable, (2) financially independent, and (3) contributing members of society. If our children embody these three values, we have succeeded as parents.

This book is a true story shared between me and my two sons. Both achieved homeownership at the age of 18 just as they were preparing for college. Through our journey, we learned not only how to make ownership possible, but also how to communicate, cooperate, and build together, even as a divorced family. It took collaboration, faith, and shared purpose from both parents to turn this goal into reality.

The book is more than a story; it is a mission. It demonstrates how early financial education and homeownership can empower young people to become responsible, resilient, and self-reliant. It also reflects my lifelong passion for family-centered tax and financial planning, as seen in my previous book, *The SMART Family Tax Guide.*

I am deeply grateful to the mortgage lenders, home builders, real estate agents, real estate investors, and contractors, and most importantly, my family, especially my ex-wife (Yuqin Ding), whose financial, emotional, and spiritual support made this dream possible. Together, we proved that when families work together with shared intention, they can raise children who build stronger futures for themselves and their communities.

As the Chinese proverb says, *"Rather than giving your child a fish, teach them how to fish."* My hope is that this book inspires parents and young people alike to take action, dream boldly, and pursue homeownership as early and wisely as possible.

—**Mike Nie, CPA · Chris Nie · Kevin Nie**

PART 1: Real Estate Introduction

Chapter 1

Four Pillars of Wealth: FLY Vision Board and Why Real Estate

"Ninety percent of all millionaires become so through owning real estate."—Andrew Carnegie

When you are young, particularly between the ages of 18 and 25, the choices you make about money shape your entire financial life. This chapter provides a 30,000-foot view of why real estate stands as one of the four pillars of long-term wealth building, and why it is a cornerstone for Generation Z investors looking to build financial freedom early.

Having seen my children grow into adulthood, I have witnessed firsthand how early planning changes the game. Starting early does not just give you a start: it multiplies your opportunities through compounding and diversification.

Part 1: The Four Pillars of Wealth

Every FLYer should have a strong financial plan that is built on four essential pillars:

1. **Real Estate**
   The focus of this book, and for good reason. Real estate is tangible, easily leveraged, tax-favored, a historically strong appreciating asset. The 2025 landmark court case hands a win to FLYers who want to control the commission fee and brokerage fee charged by the National Association of Realtors (NAR).

2. **Equity (Stocks & Brokerage Accounts)**
   This includes your 401(k), IRA, and general brokerage accounts. Over time (1975-2025), the S&P 500 index has averaged around 10–11% annual returns, tripling the historical inflation rate of 3–4%. Most importantly, the expense ratio can be as low as 0.015%, i.e., $1.5 index fee per $10,000, much lower than 99% of target date funds, ETFs, or mutual funds.

3. **Cash Value Life Insurance**
   Properly structured whole life or indexed universal life insurance policies can yield 4–6% tax-free after expenses, while providing liquidity, protection, and loan options. FLYers should seek the best insurance agent to maximize cash value and minimize whole life insurance premium. Steve Parisi, the CEO of IBC Global, and James Barber, the owner of Oregon Cash Flow Pro, LLC are two leading industry experts and agents.

4. **Exotic or Speculative Assets**
   Think crypto, pre-IPO stocks, or private credit. These can make, or break, fortunes. Keep them as "fun money," or "dumb money," limited to 5–10% of your net worth. Use due diligence to find the most reputable and safeguarding crypto exchange.

These pillars ensure your portfolio stays low-fee, inflation-beating, and tax-advantaged. I envision a five-book series to serve FLYers (book series subject to change):

- FLY #1: real estate investment under 25
- FLY #2: ten tax free or tax deferred investment accounts for young people
- FLY #3: cash value life insurance for young people
- FLY #4: small business and entrepreneurship by young people
- FLY #5: crypto and alternative assets for young people

The Asset Type Yield Table on the next page explains the power of compounding interest, and diversification.

- Real estate has maintained nearly 5% annual return in the past 50 years (1975-2025). Given the leverage factor (3-20% down payment plus 80-97% mortgage), the amplified return could be at an impressive range of 20-30%.
- With the scarcity of land and population growth, real estate will continue as a strong asset, not susceptible to AI technology threats.
- The stock market index (S&P 500) has an impressive 10% annual return, but it has been more volatile than the real estate market. The advantage of a stock index asset type is its high liquidity (compared with real estate), and one can access cash through a security-backed line of credit.
- Cash value in whole life insurance has the lowest return, but it has wide exposure to the fixed income market, and the annual return is very stable.

Asset Type Yield Table

Year	House Price Index (1)	Berkshire Hathaway (BRK.B) (2)	S&P 500 Index (3)	Guardian Life Gross Yield (4)
1975	4.7%	2.5%	37.2%	5.2%
1976	10.5%	129.3%	23.6%	5.5%
1977	14.5%	46.8%	-7.4%	6.1%
1978	14.9%	14.5%	6.4%	6.4%
1979	9.4%	102.5%	18.2%	6.5%
1980	5.2%	32.8%	32.3%	7.1%
1981	0.9%	31.8%	-5.0%	7.2%
1982	7.8%	38.4%	21.4%	7.5%
1983	4.4%	69.0%	22.4%	7.7%
1984	4.6%	-2.7%	6.1%	12.3%
1985	6.3%	93.7%	31.6%	13.3%
1986	7.3%	14.2%	18.6%	13.3%
1987	5.0%	4.6%	5.1%	12.5%
1988	5.2%	59.3%	16.6%	12.0%
1989	5.0%	84.6%	31.7%	11.5%
1990	1.5%	-23.1%	-3.1%	11.0%
1991	3.1%	35.6%	30.5%	10.5%
1992	1.7%	29.8%	7.6%	10.3%
1993	3.2%	38.9%	10.1%	9.8%
1994	1.5%	25.0%	1.3%	9.0%
1995	5.2%	57.4%	37.6%	8.5%
1996	2.2%	6.2%	23.0%	8.0%
1997	5.1%	34.9%	33.4%	8.5%
1998	4.6%	52.2%	28.6%	8.8%
1999	5.8%	-19.9%	21.0%	8.8%
2000	7.7%	26.6%	-9.1%	8.5%
2001	6.0%	6.5%	-11.9%	8.5%
2002	6.5%	-3.8%	-22.1%	8.0%
2003	7.4%	15.8%	28.7%	7.0%
2004	11.1%	4.3%	10.9%	6.6%
2005	10.5%	0.8%	4.9%	6.8%
2006	3.3%	24.1%	15.8%	6.5%
2007	-2.2%	28.7%	5.5%	6.8%
2008	**-5.8%**	**-31.8%**	**-37.0%**	**7.3%**
2009	-7.0%	2.7%	26.5%	7.3%

	Real Estate	ESV / UTMA / Roth IRA / Solo Roth 401(K) / HSA / FF / Family Bank	Brokerage Account / Trump Acct / State 529 / Employer 401(k)	Cash Value Whole Life Insurance	Crypto Account
Year	House Price Index (1)	Berkshire Hathaway (BRK.B) (2)	S&P 500 Index (3)	Guardian Life Gross Yield (4)	Bitcoin (5)
2010	-3.4%	21.4%	15.1%	7.0%	385.4%
2011	-1.6%	-4.7%	2.1%	6.9%	1437.4%
2012	2.2%	16.8%	16.0%	7.0%	193.3%
2013	4.7%	32.7%	32.4%	6.7%	5463.0%
2014	5.4%	27.0%	13.7%	6.3%	-57.6%
2015	4.9%	-12.5%	1.4%	6.1%	34.4%
2016	5.3%	23.4%	12.0%	6.1%	123.8%
2017	6.2%	21.9%	21.8%	5.9%	1369.0%
2018	4.6%	2.8%	-4.4%	5.9%	-73.5%
2019	5.1%	11.0%	31.5%	5.9%	92.0%
2020	7.5%	2.4%	18.4%	5.7%	303.1%
2021	19.6%	29.6%	28.7%	5.7%	59.7%
2022	8.1%	4.0%	-18.1%	5.7%	-64.3%
2023	5.5%	15.8%	26.3%	5.8%	155.4%
2024	4.0%	25.5%	25.0%	5.9%	121.0%
2025	1.6%	10.9%	17.9%	6.1%	-6.3%
Compounded Annual Return (1975-2025)	**4.90%**	**19.60%**	**10.30%**	**7.80%**	**142.30%**

Sources:

(1) Real estate returns, computed by the authors based on The S&P CoreLogic Case-Shiller Home Price Index (HPI) at https://fred.stlouisfed.org/series/csushpinsa

(2) S&P 500 index yield, available at https://www.stern.nyu.edu/~adamodar/pc/datasets/histre401(k).xls

(3) Berkshire Hathaway Class B rate of return, available at https://www.berkshirehathaway.com/reports.html

(4) Guardian life insurance yield, available at https://topwholelife.com/whole-life-insurance-dividend-rate-history/. Note: yield disclosed as gross number. Policyholders may receive lower ones after the cost of insurance and other overhead expenses.

(5) Bitcoin rate of return, available at https://www.slickcharts.com/currency/BTC/returns. The earliest data available is 2010 return.

The Long View: Compounded Wisdom from 1975 to 2025

Asset Type	Compounded Annual Return	Risk	Leverage	Tax Advantage	Liquidity
BRK.B	19.6%	Medium	Moderate (SBLOC)	Zero dividend. No kiddie tax Tax-free loans	High
S&P 500 Index	10.3%	Medium	Moderate (SBLOC)	Tax-deferred Tax-free loans	High
Whole Life Insurance	7.8% gross (~5-6 % net)	Low	High (Policy Loans)	Tax-free loans	High
Real Estate	4.9% unleveraged 18-20% leveraged	Medium	Very High	Excellent (Depreciation, §1031, and §121)	Medium
Bitcoin (Crypto)	142.3% (short history)	Very High	Limited	Not subject to the wash sale rule	Low

FLY Tip: The S&P 500 Index is like the squad of the 500 biggest U.S. companies that run the economy such as Apple, Microsoft, and Amazon. If Wall Street were a group chat, these 500 would be the main characters.

Since 2020, the index has increasingly shifted toward technology and AI stocks. The so-called "Magnificent 7" (giants like Apple, Microsoft, Nvidia, Amazon, Meta, Tesla, and Alphabet) are so massive that they make up 30%–35% of the entire index. They have more market shares than the bottom 400 S&P 500 companies combined.

In other words, any AI bubble burst would cause a significant correction of this tech-heavy stock index. FLYers should diversify their investment into nonstock assets such as real estate or cash value whole life insurance.

FLY Tip: A Securities-Backed Line of Credit (SBLOC) is a way to borrow money using the investments (like stocks, or S&P 500 index funds) in your brokerage account as collateral without selling them. Think of it like a home equity line of credit, but instead of using your house, you use your investment portfolio as the collateral to guarantee the loan repayment.

You can usually borrow 50% to 70% of the value of your eligible investments, and you only must make interest payments on what you borrow, not on the entire credit limit. There is no fixed time to repay the loan, so you can pay it back and borrow again as needed.

If structured properly, your interest in SBLOC may be treated as business expense and deductible from your rental, small business tax forms. It is called the IRS Interest Tracing Rule. Consult a tax pro for details. But you need to report interest income as "other income" in Schedule 1 of tax return 1040.

I suggest you borrow up to 50% to avoid any surprising or dismal market downturns that may trigger a forced selloff by the SBLOC lender, i.e., the brokerage firms.

FLY Tip: IRS rule 1031 exchange can be deemed a real estate's no-tax teleport. Normally, when you sell an investment property and make a profit, the IRS will tax you on the capital gains, which is not cool. But a 1031 exchange (from IRS Code §1031) is a tax-deferral strategy, in which you can sell one property and roll the profit into another without paying taxes now. Several criteria (time and dollar amount) are critical to satisfy.

FLY Tip: IRS Section 121 exclusion allows you to sell your primary home and keep a large portion of the profit tax-free. In simple terms: You don't have to pay capital gains tax on up to $250,000 of profit ($500,000 if married) when you sell your main home.

Analyzing the Investment Yield of Four Core Assets

Financial literacy for youth is not about chasing the next hot stock or crypto trend; it is about understanding how the world's wealthiest families build and preserve their fortune over decades. That strategy can be distilled into four timeless asset pillars:

1. Real Estate
2. Stock Market (S&P 500 Index or long-running, broad-based, and zero-dividend stocks)
3. Cash Value Whole Life Insurance
4. Crypto or Speculative Assets

Together, these four categories form what I call the FLY Vision Board, a visual framework for young investors under age 25 to see how financial freedom works through an entire lifetime.

I use the term *Vision Board* intentionally, because when you see these assets side-by-side (their returns, risks, and rewards) you begin to understand how wealth grows quietly and predictably in the background.

1. Real Estate, the Leverage Multiplier

The real estate pillar bridges the gap between paper wealth and tangible assets. The Case-Shiller House Price Index averaged 4.9% annual return from 1975 to 2025, but its real power lies in *leverage.*

If you put 3% down on a $300,000 home and it appreciates 4.9% a year, your equity grows over the investment, a 30:1 leverage ratio. That is the magic of using other people's money (OPM).

$9,000 down payment; annual appreciation $14,700. Return on equity = $14,700 / $9,000 = 163%

FLY Tip: OPM means other people's money. It is how smart investors grow fast without using much of their own cash. Instead, they borrow money from banks, SBLOC or IBLOC to buy rentals that appreciate. Note: SBLOC stands for securities backed line of credit, and IBLOC is life insurance backed line of credit. They are covered later in this chapter.

Why Real Estate Matters

- It is real: Unlike crypto or stocks, it is backed by physical land, walls, and value-producing assets. Real estate has *never* gone to zero.
- It is leveraged: Mortgage loans amplify returns. A 3% down payment controls a six-figure asset.
- It is tax-favored: Depreciation, ordinary and necessary rental expense deductions, like-kind exchanges (§1031), primary home sale exclusions (§121), and cost-segregation studies make real estate one of the most tax-efficient vehicles in existence.
- It is localized: Every market behaves differently since growth follows jobs, infrastructure, and demographics.

Practical Example

When my son Kevin signed his first purchase contract at 18, he put down $14,000 on a pre-construction home. Within two months, the property appreciated $45,000, which was a 320% ROI without taking much risk. That early start snowballed his financial base.

Cautions

Transaction fees average 6%, and property taxes run around 1% annually. Leverage amplifies gains *and* losses. Always keep reserves. But long-term data show real estate recovering more after every correction, including the 2008 housing crash.

For FLY readers: Real estate is how ordinary people build generational wealth. Start small—a duplex, a campus rental, a first-time FHA home. Let time and leverage do the heavy lifting.

2. The S&P 500 Index, The Growth Engine

The second pillar is your brokerage account, typically invested in the S&P 500, the 500 largest publicly traded companies in the United States. From 1975 to 2025, this index delivered an impressive 10.3% compounded annual return, proving that disciplined investing works even through recessions, wars, and crises.

Think about what that means: if you invested $10,000 in 1975 and simply left it alone, no trading, no timing, no panic selling, you would have more than $3.9 million today. That is the quiet miracle of compound growth.

Why It Works

- Low Fees: Fidelity's low-expense index fund charges only 1.5 basis points, $1.50 per $10,000 invested. In contrast, most actively managed mutual funds charge 100 times more. Over 30 years, that difference can eat half your gains.
- Automatic Ownership: Each share gives you exposure to America's largest companies, such as Apple, Microsoft, Amazon, and Nvidia, which together account for over one-third of total U.S. market capitalization. In addition, study shows that S&P 500 companies accounted for over 80% of the U.S. equity market capitalization.
- Liquidity and Flexibility: You can sell or borrow against your portfolio using a securities-backed line of credit (SBLOC), giving you flexibility without forced liquidation. If you use the loan to buy rental or lend to your entrepreneurship, you may deduct the interest expense from the business or real estate tax returns.

Risks and Lessons

The dot-com crash (2000–2002), the 2008 financial crisis, and the recent AI-stock bubble show that even strong markets can fall 30–50%. But history also shows recovery. Every downturn was followed by new highs within five years.

For FLY readers: start early, stay invested, and remember: the biggest risk is not market volatility; it is sitting on the sidelines with idled cash.

3. Cash Value Whole Life Insurance: The Financial Safety Vault

The third pillar is often misunderstood. Whole life insurance is not just about death benefits; it is about *living benefits*. It is the only financial product that compounds steadily and sustainably, can be borrowed tax-free, and pays out death benefits that are income tax-free to your family. If structured correctly, death benefits can be estate tax free (both federal and state level). Consult a tax pro or legal expert for further details.

The four companies I personally trust—i.e., Guardian, MassMutual, Northwestern Mutual, and New York Life, have survived the Civil War, two World Wars, the Great Depression, the Great Recession, and COVID-19. None have merged or been acquired. They have high credit ratings (up to AAA, even above U.S. Treasury bonds).

The table below highlights key figures of these Big Four whole life insurance companies.

Company	Year Founded	Credit Rating (A.M. Best / S&P / Moody's / Fitch)	Total Assets (Approx. 2025)
Guardian Life Insurance Company of America	1860	A++ (A.M. Best), AA+ (S&P)	$189 billion
Massachusetts Mutual Life Insurance Company	1851	A++ (A.M. Best), AA+ (S&P)	$366 billion
Northwestern Mutual Life Insurance Company	1857	A++ (A.M. Best), AAA (Fitch), Aa1 (Moody's)	$399 billion
New York Life Insurance Company	1845	A++ (A.M. Best), AAA (Fitch), Aaa (Moody's)	$259 billion

Note: S&P, Moody's, and Fitch are three major credit rating agencies. A.M. Best is the main insurance company rating firm.

FLY coach suggests these long-standing whole life insurance companies because they have a much longer proven business success record than the high-tech or AI companies (mostly in business for a few decades). Diversify some assets into cash value whole life to form a natural hedge against the stock market gyrations (which happened frequently based on history record).

Historical Return and Structure

Guardian Life's historical gross yield averaged 7.8% from 1975 to 2025. After accounting for internal costs, policyholders typically receive around 5–6% net.

I recommend a 10-10-80 structure:

- 10% in whole life (for guarantees)
- 10% in a one-year term rider (for cost efficiency)
- 80% in paid-up additions (PUA) to maximize compounding cash value.

I recommend FLYers to read Steve Parisi's book on this subject, *Whole Life Insurance | Unlocking the Secrets About Cash Value: How Banks, Corporations, and the Wealthy Use Cash Value Life Insurance.* Watch his YouTube channel too for hundreds of powerful and informative videos.

Benefits Beyond Yield

- Stability: Cash value continues to grow even during recessions. When the S&P 500 lost –37% in 2008, policyholders still earned dividends.
- Liquidity: You can borrow up to 95% of the policy's value for anything (tuition, a home down payment, or seeding your first business) without triggering taxable events.
- Tax Advantage: Loans are not taxable income; death benefits are income tax-free. In addition, the OBBB makes the lifetime estate exemption amount at $15 million, indexed with inflation. In other words, most taxpayers will not be subject to the estate tax

consequences when they die, at least at the federal level. Loan interest can be deducted as business expenses subject to the interest tracing rule and business interest limitation rule.

For FLY readers: Think of it as your *personal bank*. During downturns when banks tighten credit, you can borrow from yourself at predictable rates and keep your financial life moving forward.

4. Crypto and Bitcoin: The Frontier of Speculation

The youngest asset class, crypto, has existed only since 2009. Yet, its returns are astonishing. Bitcoin's compounded annual return since inception is 142%. In 2013 alone, it soared 5,463%, while in 2018 it crashed –73%.

Why It Excites Investors

- Decentralization: No central authority controls it; blockchain technology records every transaction transparently.
- Liquidity: Trades 24/7 worldwide.
- Low Fees: Typically, 1–2% per trade.
- Potential: Early-stage innovation often yields outsized returns, like internet stocks in the 1990s.
- No wash sale rule, yet.

Tax term: For stocks and securities, the **wash sale rule** says: If you sell an investment at a loss and buy it back within 30 days, you cannot deduct the loss. In other words, the IRS prevents people from "creating" tax losses while keeping the same investment.

Why Is Crypto Different (for now)?

- Cryptocurrency is treated as "property," not a security.
- The IRS wash sale rule (IRC §1091) applies only to stocks and other securities. Crypto is not explicitly covered.
- Result: You can sell crypto at a loss, deduct the loss, and buy it back immediately—without violating the wash sale rule.

This is often called crypto loss harvesting.

Why It Worries Regulators

Crypto lacks intrinsic value anchors. Prices move on sentiment, algorithms, and speculation. When markets correct, investors can lose half their portfolio overnight. Regulatory uncertainty, security breaches, cyber threat, and tax complications make it unsuitable for large holdings.

For FLY readers: Treat crypto as "fun money or dumb money." Limit exposure to 5–10% of your total portfolio. If it becomes the next technological revolution, you will benefit. If it collapses, your foundation (stocks, insurance, and real estate) keeps you secure.

Key Takeaways from 50 Years of Data

1. Duration matters. Stocks, insurance, and real estate have five decades of proof; crypto has only one.
2. Fees destroy wealth. Keep expense ratios below 0.015% for index funds and under 5% for insurance and real-estate transactions.
3. Leverage magnifies results. Real estate and life insurance both use leverage, either through mortgages or policy loans, to compound faster.
4. Tax strategy is the quiet partner. The richest families do not just earn more; they pay less taxes legally by using deferrals, exclusions, and loans.

Part 2: Why Real Estate Is So Important to FLYers

1. Tangibility and Stability

Unlike paper assets, real estate is backed by something real: land, walls, roofs, and systems you can see and touch. Real estate expert Brett Korade once said, *"Real estate has never fallen below zero."* That is what separates it from stocks or crypto: you cannot lose everything overnight.

2. Leverage: Other People's Money (OPM)

Real estate allows you to control large assets with small down payments. A first-time buyer can often buy a $500,000 property with just 3–5% down, leveraging 30:1 or more. No other investment class offers that kind of safe leverage.

For example, when Kevin signed his first purchase contract at age 18 with $14,000 down, the home appreciated $43,000 in a mere three months. His ROI exceeded 300% in just a few months. That is the power of leverage in action.

3. Depreciation and Tax Benefits

Real estate offers unmatched tax advantages. The IRS allows investors to claim depreciation, i.e., a non-cash expense that shelters rental income from taxes. Combine that with 1031 exchanges, cost segregation, and the "Buy, Borrow, and Build" strategy, and you can build and transfer wealth tax-efficiently across generations.

4. Diversification and Non-Correlation

Real estate moves differently from the stock market. The S&P 500's top seven tech companies drive most of its volatility, but local real estate depends on population, jobs, and other socioeconomic factors. This lack of correlation means when one market dips, the other often stays stable or even rises, creating balance in your financial life.

Part 3: Diversification is the 9th World Wonder

Diversification is the heart of the FLY strategy, and this updated correlation table highlights why allocating across four key asset pillars (S&P 500 index funds, Guardian Whole Life Insurance, House Price Index (real estate), and Bitcoin) can enhance portfolio resilience in all weathers.

The table below demonstrates that these assets do not move in lockstep. Most notably, Guardian Whole Life Insurance shows almost no correlation with the S&P 500 (2.2%) and is negatively correlated with the housing market (-14.4%), creating a stabilizing effect during market turmoil. Bitcoin introduces a new dimension, with moderate correlations to both equities (33.3%) and insurance (38.5%), but a negative correlation with real estate (-11.5%). Such relationships mean that downturns in one market are frequently offset by stability or growth in another.

Investment Return Correlation Table (1975-2025)

Correlation	BRKB	S&P 500	Guardian Whole Life Insurance	House Price Index	Bitcoin
BRKB	100%	43.9%	12.7%	27.3%	32.5%
S&P 500	43.9%	100%	2.2%	12.3%	33.3%
Guardian Whole Life Insurance	12.7%	2.2%	100%	-14.4%	38.5%
House Price Index	27.3%	12.3%	-14.4%	100%	-11.5%
Bitcoin	32.5%	33.3%	38%	-11.5%	100.0%

Note: Calculation by the authors.

By distributing family wealth and tax-advantaged accounts among these five types of assets, a FLYer maximizes the likelihood of capturing at least one source of positive returns in any given year, even through crises. During the worst year in the last five decades, 2008, cash value whole life insurance policies still delivered a 7.3% annual return, underscoring its enduring stability compared to other asset classes.

This balanced allocation fosters financial durability, reduces volatility, and positions families to benefit from the complementary strengths and risk profiles of each asset group. The FLY approach's power is shown through the lens of correlation: if assets do not rise or fall together, diversification provides not just peace of mind, but measurable results over time.

Weathering Crises with Diversification

When we look back into history, diversification is not just smart, but crucial. It is about *survival.*

- When the dot-com bubble burst (2000–2002), the S&P 500 lost –43 %, yet life insurance and housing stayed positive.
- During the 2008 recession, real estate crashed 7%, but life insurance policyholders could borrow from cash value to survive or buy discounted properties.
- In 2022, crypto collapsed 64%, showing why it must remain a small slice.
- When AI stocks dominated 2024–2025, concentration risk returned with seven companies controlling one-third of the index.

Every decade brings a new lesson, yet the four-pillar system endures because each asset moves differently. When one falters, another shines.

The Allocation Framework

A balanced portfolio for a young investor might look like this:

Asset Type	Allocation	Key Benefit
Stocks (401(k), Roth IRA, HSA, 529, Brokerage)	40-60%	Liquidity & compounding
Real Estate	20-30%	Leverage, appreciation, tax shelter
Cash Value Life Insurance	20-30%	Safety, liquidity, tax-free growth
Speculative ("Fun Money")	5–10%	High risk, high potential return that is suitable for risk-taking FLYers

🔍 **Tax term: Individual Retirement Arrangement (Roth IRA)** is a retirement savings account where contributions are made with after-tax dollars, meaning you do not get a tax deduction up front. The money grows tax-free, and qualified withdrawals in retirement are also tax-free. It is especially beneficial for young income earners or those expecting to be in a higher tax bracket in the future.

The Roth IRA is named after Senator William Roth, who created this type of account as part of the Taxpayer Relief Act of 1997.

🔍 **Tax term: Health Savings Account (HSA)** is a tax-advantaged savings account available to individuals enrolled in a high-deductible health plan (HDHP). Contributions are tax-deductible, grow tax-free, and withdrawals are also tax-free when used for qualified medical expenses. Unused funds roll over each year and can be invested, making the HSA a powerful tool for both healthcare and long-term savings. HSA tax provisions were effective in January 2004.

A **High-Deductible Health Plan (HDHP)** is a health insurance plan with lower monthly premiums but higher deductibles than traditional plans. To qualify as an HDHP in 2025, it must have a minimum deductible of $1,600 for individuals or $3,200 for families. HDHPs are required to contribute to a Health Savings Account (HSA).

A FLY can open and fund an HSA under his or her own name if he or she

(1) Is covered under parent's HDHP (a family plan);
(2) Is Aged between 18 and 26; and
(3) Files his or her own tax return.

How Young Investors Should Apply This

1. Start early, even small. Compounding rewards time, not size.
2. Automate contributions. Set it and forget it. Treat savings like rent: non-negotiable.
3. Balance ambition and caution. A portfolio that mixes high-growth assets with stable income vehicles grows smoother and faster.
4. Understand what you own. Never invest in anything you cannot explain to a 12-year-old.
5. Think about tax strategy first, not last. Structure determines survival.

Part 4: The Long March Toward Your Financial Freedom

If you are a FLYer in your 20s, you should focus on positioning, not perfection. Your first house may not be your dream home, but it serves as a useful launch pad. Real estate compounds wealth not just through appreciation but also through depreciation, leverage, and cash flow. It is a business, a hedge against inflation, and a pathway to independence.

Avoid high-fee products and anyone promising "guaranteed" returns. When something sounds too good to be true, it usually is. Always remember that ethical, long-term investment is not about excitement, but rather consistency and persistence.

Researchers have observed a downward trend in real estate ownership among young people. According to a 2025 survey by the National Association of REALTORS®, the share of first-time homebuyers has fallen to a historic low of 21%, while the median age of first-time buyers has risen to 40. Multiple factors have contributed to delayed homeownership in the U.S., including:

1. high student debt;
2. high rents that erode savings for a down payment;
3. career displacement or replacement driven by AI; and
4. delayed marriage and household formation—or choosing not to marry or raise children at all.

These are key drivers behind our FLY book's effort to help reverse this worrisome demographic trend.

Final Reflection

Financial Literacy for Youth is not about getting rich fast, but rather about *never becoming poor again.* The FLY Vision Board gives you control over your financial destiny before you turn 25.

- Real estate gives you leverage and tax shelter.
- Stocks give you growth.
- Insurance gives you protection and liquidity.
- Crypto gives you innovation and optionality.

When all four work together, you create not just wealth but financial independence that compounds across generations.

Real estate is not just about owning property: it is about owning your time and choices.
When you combine real estate with disciplined investing across all four pillars, you create the foundation of true financial freedom before age 25.

Chapter 2

Real Estate A to Z

"*Real estate is the alphabet of freedom. Learn one letter, and you'll start spelling wealth.*" – Mike Nie, CPA

Buying a rental in your 20s isn't just about bricks and cash flow, but about designing freedom. Real estate becomes the physical textbook of financial literacy: every mortgage payment teaches leverage, every lease teaches negotiation, and every repair teaches resilience. The 26 items below decode that journey from *A* to *Z*.

A – Appreciating Assets

Most possessions depreciate—phones, cars, and laptops lose value. Real estate belongs to the rare class of appreciating assets that usually rise in value because land is finite, population grows, and inflation quietly pushes replacement costs higher.

Economic logic: Limited supply + steady demand = price pressure upward.

- Practical lesson: Every mortgage payment moves you from consumer to capital owner.
- FLY takeaway: Buy one appreciating asset early and let compounding do the heavy lifting; a 4% annual price growth doubles value about every 18 years.

B – Be Your Own Bank

Young investors often feel "bankless." When you own property, the equity you build becomes a private savings bank you can borrow from later—through HELOCs, cash-out refinancing, or collateral loans—instead of begging a lender for approval.

- Each rent check deposits into your personal bank of equity.
- That equity can later finance a business, education, or the next property.
- Lesson: *Owning one asset that pays you* beats keeping ten that drains you.

C – Control Your Costs

Knowledge trims costs. Earning a real-estate license can save you 3% commission each time you buy or sell. Learning basic maintenance avoids overpaying contractors. Think of your property like Costco for wealth: buy quality in bulk, track every expense, and price-match everything. Cost discipline compounds the same way returns do.

D – Depreciation and Deduction

Congress allows landlords to recover building costs over 27.5 years (residential) or 39 years (commercial)—a *paper expense* that shelters real cash flow. Example: a $275K structure yields a $10K annual deduction. Advanced investors layer on bonus or cost-segregation depreciation, pulling forward deductions to offset other income. It's like taking a tax deduction for natural wear and tear.

E – Exceptional Returns through Leverage

Real estate power is OPM—Other People's Money. Invest $100K down on a $500K home; if the value rises 7%, you earn $35K on $100K, which leads to an ROI of 35%. When rent and tax savings are added, total returns can approach 25–30% annually during good markets. No stock margin account gives you a 30-year fixed leverage with government insurance backing.

F – Financing Freedom

The United States is a financing paradise: FHA, VA, USDA, and conventional loans, adjustable or fixed, 15 or 30 years—and no refinance penalties. Mastery of terms equals mastery of destiny. Rate-shop, refinance, and redeploy equity whenever it benefits you. Debt here is not a danger—it's a design.

G – Government Support and Subsidy

Housing policy rewards initiative. First-time buyers can put 3% down and deduct mortgage interest. Because homeownership stabilizes neighborhoods and employment, public incentives exist for *you* to participate. Each dollar of government credit is fuel for generational growth.

H – Homeownership as Identity

Owning a home builds agency. Today, 30% of adults under 30 live with parents—a lost opportunity for independence. The first property you buy, even a small condo, teaches budgeting, maintenance, and leadership. Communities thrive when young people plant roots; so do their futures.

I – Inflation as Your Ally

A 30-year fixed loan is a secret weapon. When inflation runs 3% and your rate is 5%, each payment is made with cheaper dollars. Meanwhile, rent usually rises with inflation. You pay yesterday's mortgage with tomorrow's inflated income. Owning fixed debt is like owning stock in inflation itself.

J – Just-in-Time Strategy

Timing magnifies returns. Follow employment trends: new data centers, hospitals, or transit lines create *micro-booms*. Buy before the ribbon cutting. Real estate rewards those who study *when* as much as *what*.

K – Knowledge and Network

Information is currency. Read zoning codes, attend investor meetups, and find mentors at church, community, or campus groups. Local insight beats Wall Street forecasts. Knowledge converts fear into focus; every hour of learning earns compound confidence.

L – Location, Location, Location

The five golden geographies: near universities, hospitals, military bases, major retailers, and tech hubs. These anchors guarantee year-round tenants. Within each city, zoom into school quality, transit, and future zoning. Buy where people must live, not just where they want to.

M – Mindset Shift

Mindset separates workers from wealth builders. As Robert Kiyosaki famously said in his book *Rich Dad Poor Dad*, employees trade time for taxed income; owners trade vision for assets. In your 20s, embrace risk as tuition. Real learning happens when the rent check bounces and you fix it. Every failure is a paid internship in wealth.

N – New Builds and Next-Gen Design

Modern properties bring energy efficiency, smart-home tech, and lower maintenance. Builders often offer seller credits or buy-down incentives, letting first-timers start with minimal cash. A new roof equals fewer surprises; a new design attracts better tenants. New saves you from a lot of headaches.

O – Options and Opportunity

Real estate's menu is endless: long-term lease, Airbnb, house-hack, 1031 exchange, cost seg, or ADU conversion. Unlike stocks, property lets you *engineer* returns—by remodeling, refinancing, or re-tenanting. Flexibility is the ultimate ROI.

P – Protection and Planning

Structure equals safety. Hold assets in LLCs, maintain liability insurance, and use trusts to avoid probate. Keep high-equity properties separate from new purchases. Asset protection isn't paranoia; it's professionalism.

Q – Qualified Business Income (QBI) deduction

A real estate agent operating as a sole proprietor or an LLC may qualify for the QBI deduction, allowing up to 20% of net business income to be deducted, subject to income thresholds and wage or property limitations.

R – Retirement Ready Real Estate

Rental income is the heartbeat of FIRE – Financial Independence, Retire Early. Each property adds a predictable stream that inflation cannot erode. Combine depreciation losses with passive-income limits ($25K deductible under $100K AGI) to reduce taxes now while compounding future freedom. Through 1031 exchanges and the step-up basis, families can transfer millions tax-free.

S – Snowball and Swap

Reinvest appreciation through refinancing or 1031 exchange instead of selling. One duplex funds the next four-plex; rents service debt; equity snowballs. Patience + discipline = geometric growth.

T – Tenants, Timing & Trash

Tenants are partners in your business. Screen well, respond fast, and treat property management like hospitality. Time your purchases around local job cycles; sell only when opportunity cost outweighs cash flow. And yes, trash day happens; but twenty-something should roll the bins anyway.

U – Umbrella Insurance

For $200–$400 per year, a $1–2 million policy guards against lawsuits. It's the cheapest sleep-aid you'll ever buy. Peace of mind is part of total return.

V – Variety and Verticals

Mix property types—single-family, multi-unit, student housing, or short-term rentals. Diversify geography to buffer hurricanes, wildfires, or local layoffs. Variety is resilience.

W – Wealth Waves

Every decade brings disruption—dotcoms, AI, pandemics. Through all of them, shelter remains non-optional. When panic hits, equity holders refinance and acquire; renters retreat. Ride each wave; don't drown in it.

X – Cross-Generational Building

Turn your rentals into a family enterprise. Hire children for property maintenance or bookkeeping under a family LLC. Pay them reasonable wages, teach real skills, and convert allowance into earned income. The next generation learns stewardship instead of spending.

Y – Young and Early

Start early, even small. A $15,000 down payment on a starter condo at age 25 can become $300K in equity by 40. Youth is your unfair advantage: time multiplies returns faster than any market timing.

Z – Zero Taxes, Zero Excuses

With depreciation, 1031 exchanges, and step-up basis, investors legally erase most capital gain taxes. Estate thresholds near $30 million per couple mean most families can pass assets tax-free at the federal level. Zero is the hero—and procrastination is the only tax you truly pay.

Final Reflections

Owning rental property in your 20s transforms financial theory into tangible skill. It teaches delayed gratification, systems thinking, and community impact. Each letter from A to Z is more than a concept—it's a lifelong cycle of buying, borrowing, building, and blessing. Real estate is the alphabet of freedom. Learn one letter, and you'll start spelling wealth.

Chapter 3

20 Benefits of Young Professionals Owning Real Estate

"*A ship is safe in the harbor, but it is not what the ships are built for.*" – John A. Shedd

Few can deny that owning real estate at a young age is one of the best ways to learn responsibility, strategy, and financial independence early in life. Below are ten real-world benefits synthesized by Chris, Kevin, and me that young professionals can experience when they take their first step into real estate ownership.

1. Real Estate Offers Valuable Tax Benefits

The tax code provides powerful incentives for property owners, especially younger investors. If your Adjusted Gross Income (AGI) is under $100,000, you can deduct up to $25,000 in rental losses to offset W-2 income. If your straight-line depreciation cannot produce enough losses, try bonus depreciation under cost segregation.

FLY Tip: Normally a landlord has two ways to depreciate the rental property and recoup the cost: straight-line depreciation and bonus depreciation:

- Straight-line depreciation: think of this as the slow and steady method, and you divide the cost evenly across the asset's useful life. For real estate, the life expectancy is 27.5 years.
- Cost depreciation: Instead of waiting 27.5 years, you can segregate the property into various components (structure, appliances, floor, roof, etc.). Some short-lived assets (5-, 7- or 15-year assets) can have a full (100%) depreciation of the cost in year one.

Even if your income exceeds $100,000, you can still benefit. By contributing to retirement accounts (such as Traditional 401(k), Traditional IRA and HSA), you can reduce your AGI below the threshold, reclaiming eligibility for the deduction. The result can be thousands of dollars in federal and state tax savings every year.

2. Low Down Payments and High Leverage

Young buyers often qualify for FHA loans with as little as 3% down, sometimes even less with seller credits. This means a motivated young investor can purchase property with almost no out-of-pocket cash.

FLY Tip: FHA loan (FHA stands for Federal Housing Administration). An FHA loan is a government-backed loan that helps first-time homebuyers (such as a FLYer) to afford a house. The loan underwriting criteria is somewhat less rigid: your credit score is not amazing (580 or higher works), you have got a small down payment (as low as 3.5%), and you have student loans or some debt. If you can find a co-borrower, such as your parent(s) with stable W-2 income, your low- or no-income barriers can be solved too.

Leverage is the key and the king. Using "Other People's Money" (OPM) allows you to control an asset with minimal capital. When home values rise, even by 3–5% annually, your return on investment can exceed 100% on paper, especially in high-demand college towns or urban centers.

3. Rental Income Covers Living Costs

Owning a property with multiple rooms can offset personal living expenses. You can live in one bedroom and rent out the others: turning your home into a hybrid personal and business property.

Expenses such as car mileage (picking up tenants or going to the Home Depot), cell phone use, internet service, and even occasional tenant meals (50%) or events (e.g., Superbowl party) can qualify as business expenses on your Schedule E. This creates legitimate tax deductions while generating income that helps cover your rent or mortgage.

4. College 529 Plans Can Cover Room and Board Expenses

Few families realize that a 529 plan can pay for rent. Under IRS Publication 970, qualified tuition programs (QTPs) such as 529s can fund room and board expenses for students enrolled at least part-time. In other words, if a FLYer rents spare rooms to his/ her friends or classmates, they can use the 529 money to pay for rent.

FLY Tax Term: Qualified tuition program (QTP, or 529 plan) are well described in the IRS Publication 970 Tax Benefits for Education. Chapter 7 defines qualified higher education expenses to include expenses for room and board if (1) students are enrolled at least half-time; (2) such expenses may not be more than the greater of the following two amounts: (a) the allowance for room and board, as determined by the school; and (b) the actual amount charged if the student is residing in housing owned or operated by the school.

The IRS also published 529 Q&As further list the main advantage of a typical 529 plan that "earnings are not subject to federal tax and generally not subject to state tax when used for the qualified education expenses of the designated beneficiary, such as tuition, fees, books, as well as room and board at an eligible education institution."

Each university publishes its Cost of Attendance (COA), a figure that sets the maximum amount eligible for 529 reimbursement. By purchasing property near campus and renting rooms to classmates, parents can use 529 withdrawals (tax-free) to cover mortgage and utility costs up to the COA limit. The student landlord gains practical experience as a landlord, and the family enjoys tax-free income for an essential living expense—a win-win strategy that merges education and entrepreneurship.

Below is a table of cost of attendance of ten sampled universities in the U.S. (2025)

University	Tuition ($)	Fees ($)	Room & Board ($)	Total Cost of Attendance ($)
Harvard	59,320	8,000*	22,130	$86,926
Stanford	$60,000	$2,000	$19,000	$81,000
UPenn	63,200	8,000	19,200	$90,400
MIT	64,310	420	21,264	$89,340
Yale	69,900	175	20,650	$90,725
U of Michigan	16,736	Included*	13,170	$30,000*
UVA	17,784	Included*	13,000	$30,000*
UC Berkeley	16,832	Included*	$13,000	$30,000*
Florida State University	$5,656	Minimal	$13,474	$25,400*
Georgia Institute of Technology	$10,512	$1,696	$14,548	$26,756*

Note: * in-state tuition. Source: college websites.

It is estimated that five-year growth rates for total cost of attendance in the Ivies have exceeded 20%. Distribution from a 529 plan may be eligible to cover room and board (at least half-time student), providing a tax-saving opportunity for FLYers to own a campus apartment that rents extra rooms to their friends or classmates who have a 529 plan.

5. Mastering OPM—Other People's Money

Leverage is the cornerstone of wealth. By using Other People's Money, young investors can buy, borrow, and build—known as the so-called "BBB" strategy. Parental co-signer fits well in the OPM principle as well.

Start with a small property, gain appreciation, then use either a home equity line of credit (HELOC), a securities backed line of credit (SBLOC), or a life insurance backed line of credit (IBLOC) loans to acquire additional rentals. Instead of selling and paying capital gain taxes, the owner borrows against equity, keeping ownership while expanding their portfolio. OPM teaches young professionals how to multiply assets strategically, a fundamental skill of every successful investor.

FLY Tip: The Buy, borrow, and build (BBB) strategy is the top secret of wealthy people in accessing cash without paying taxes or without missing future asset growth opportunities. Yes, you can have your cake and eat it too!

FLYers can start this wealth building habit through HELOCs, SBLOCs, and IBLOCs—three ways to turn your assets into tax-free liquidity.

- Home Equity Line of Credit (HELOC): Think of a HELOC as a credit card that uses your house (either primary residence or rental property) as the limit. If your home's worth $500K and your mortgage is $300K, you've got $200K in equity—meaning you could open a HELOC and borrow against that equity.
- Securities Backed Line of Credit (SBLOC): An SBLOC is the Wall Street version of HELOC. Instead of using your house, you use your stocks, ETFs, or mutual funds as collateral. Example: You've got $200K in a brokerage account. You open an SBLOC with Schwab or Fidelity and borrow, say, $100K—without selling a single share.
- Insurance Backed Line of Credit (IBLOC): Now for the ultimate money-ninja move—the IBLOC. This one uses your life insurance cash value. We prefer a whole-life insurance as collateral over indexed universal life insurance. This subject will be in our future FLY book series. No credit check or repayment schedule (much more flexible than HELOC borrowing)—you can even let it roll till death. Death benefit pays off the loan and leaves the rest to your family.

6. First-Time Homebuyer Incentives

Both federal and state governments provide closing cost credits or down payment assistance for first-time buyers. For example, Maryland offers programs providing up to $15,000 in closing cost relief. These incentives significantly reduce the financial barrier to entry, making property ownership accessible for motivated young professionals.

This table lists some states (with high median house prices) that offer incentives to first time homebuyers, many of whom are FLYers. You can research your residence state for similar benefits.

State	Median Home Price (2025)	Agency Program	Key Incentives	Eligibility Criteria
Hawaii	$975,500	Hawaii Housing Finance & Development Corp, Homeownership Center	Mortgage Credit Certificate; down-payment assistance; low down payment loans	First-time homebuyer; principal residence in HI; income/property limits
California	$866,100	CalHFA – MyHome Assistance, Dream for All	Down-payment & closing-cost help; shared appreciation loan up to $150K	First-time home buyer or qualifier; buy in CA; income limits
District of Columbia	$920,000	DC Housing Finance Agency – Open Doors, HPAP	Up to $202,000 as interest-free loan, down payment & closing cost assistance	First-time buyer; income/asset limits; principal residence
Massachusetts	$749,900	MassHousing – Down Payment Assistance, Operation Welcome Home	Up to $50,000 assistance, lower rates, veterans grant	First-time/eligible buyers, income/property/county limits
Washington	$658,700	WA State Housing Finance Commission – Home Advantage, House Key	Down payment assistance (4% of loan), 0% second mortgage, low rates	First-time buyer; primary residence in WA; income limits; education
Colorado	$640,000	CO Housing and Finance Authority (CHFA) – CHFA Advantage	3% down payment grant or 4% second loan, mortgage tax credit	First-time or qualified buyers; income and price limits; education

State	Median Home Price (2025)	Agency Program	Key Incentives	Eligibility Criteria
New York	$576,100	NYS Div. of Housing & Community Renewal, NYC HomeFirst	Up to $40,000 down payment assistance, mortgage credit	First-time buyer; NY/NYC region; income/price limits
New Jersey	$526,500	NJ Housing and Mortgage Finance Agency – First-Time Buyer, Smart Start	$10,000 down-payment/closing help; below-market mortgage rates	First-time buyer; NJ purchase; income/price limits
Utah	$588,500	Utah Housing Corporation – FirstHome, HomeAgain	Up to 6% down payment/closing loans	First-time buyer/income limits/purchase price/credit minimum
Oregon	$521,500	Oregon Housing & Community Services – DPA Program	Up to $60,000 or 20% of price for eligible buyers	First-time/first-gen buyer; below 100% AMI; education
Montana	$528,000	Montana Board of Housing – Bond/Score Advantage	3.5% down payment, closing cost grant	First-time; or no ownership 3 yrs; income/property limits; education
Rhode Island	$484,800	Rhode Island Housing – FirstHomes, Extra Assistance	$17,500 zero-interest forgivable loan, closing cost help	First-time; residence; income limits; education certificate
New Hampshire	$502,300	NH Housing Finance Authority – Home Flex Plus	4% DP assistance, cash grant, mortgage tax credit	First-time; income/purchase limits; principal residence

State	Median Home Price (2025)	Agency Program	Key Incentives	Eligibility Criteria
Nevada	$496,000	Nevada Housing Division – Home is Possible, HIP Plus	Up to 4% of loan as grant (forgivable)	First-time; income limits; 640+ credit; education
Connecticut	$466,000	CT Housing Finance Authority – Homebuyer Mortgages, DPA, MCC	$20,000+ in loan/grant, mortgage credit	First-time; principal residence; income and education

Note: states may change their benefit offering from time to time. Visit your state agency's website for the information update.

7. Maximized Deductions and Family Collaboration

Every cost associated with rental can become a deductible business expense—from repairs and maintenance to professional fees. For instance, I prepared my son's tax returns as his CPA. That service is a legitimate business deduction for him. When I travel to his property to review records or inspect the premises, it counts as a business visit—deductible hotel lodging, mileage and meals included. Real estate allows families to collaborate, teach financial literacy, and build intergenerational wealth in a transparent, tax-efficient way.

8. Appreciation Multiplies Returns

A 3% annual increase in property value may not sound like much, but when you have only invested 3% down, that appreciation represents an enormous return on equity. In sprawling college towns, appreciation tends to be steady and reliable, backed by continuous demand for housing. Over a few years, a modest home can produce tens of thousands of dollars in unrealized gain, often outpacing stock investments.

When Kevin's $14,000 down payment enabled him to own a house, any price appreciation (yes, $45,000 in three months) yields a 300%+ return on investment without Kevin's sweaty effort or heart-wrenching risk-taking!

9. Parent Co-Signers Provide Stability

Most student rentals operate smoothly because parents co-sign leases. This reduces the risk of missed payments or eviction. It also gives young landlords predictable income and strong tenant relationships. For parents, co-signing is a form of financial mentorship and sponsorship and a way to support independence without direct subsidy.

10. Strengthening Relationships Through Shared Ownership

Real estate can even build partnerships. Young couples can buy a property individually using low down-payment programs (3–5%) and parental co-signers. By hiring each other in rental (e.g., one partner handling cleaning, décor, and photography, the other managing repairs, or logistics) they learn teamwork, budgeting, and mutual accountability.

The IRS does not allow deduction of personal labor, but you can pay each other legitimately for work performed (such as cleaning, photography, or marketing) creating real business transactions within the partnership. In the process, relationships deepen through shared goals and responsibility.

11. Learning OPT—Other People's Time

Beyond money, smart investors learn to use Other People's Time. College rentals can be semi-automated by hiring friends or peers to help with cleaning, check-ins, or transportation services during busy campus weekends.

For example, during football games or parent weekends, students can rent out rooms short-term and offer airport pickups, earning additional income while delegating tasks. Managing others' time, both responsibly and fairly, is an early lesson in leadership and entrepreneurship.

12. A Launchpad for Future Real Estate Projects

Owning one property successfully gives confidence and credibility to buy the next. With two or more properties, a young investor can qualify as a Real Estate Professional (REP) for tax purposes, unlocking advanced deductions and cost-segregation benefits.

FLY Tip: Real Estate Professional (REP) is an IRS term for people who live and breathe real estate. If you qualify (spent over 750 hours in managing your rental and more than other job duty time commitment), you can use rental losses to offset your other income, like a part-time W-2 or 1099 NEC money, and reduce taxes. Most income earners cannot claim REP status because of their full time W-2 job.

This launchpad effect transforms a simple college rental into a long-term wealth engine. Over time, cash flow from one home can fund another, creating a compounding cycle of growth that supports future businesses or philanthropic projects.

13. Privacy and Stability in Personal Life

Owning a home at a young age also brings a unique personal advantage: stability. Instead of relying on crowded college dorms or costly hotels, young owners have a private, reliable space of their own. It is not only financially smarter—it supports mental health, privacy, and balanced relationships.

14. Minimal Effect on Financial Aid Eligibility

Many parents fear that owning property will hurt a student's financial aid eligibility. However, under FAFSA and CSS Profile rules, only *liquid assets* are heavily weighted. A property with a 3%–5% down payment and 95% loan value shows minimal net equity.

That means the student's homeownership does not significantly reduce financial aid, while the long-term benefits (credit history, appreciation, and rental income) remain substantial.

15. Hosting Events and Short-Term Rentals Tax-Free

College towns attract crowds for football games, graduation, and homecoming events—and hotel rooms sell out fast. Homeowners can use the IRS "Augusta Rule," which allows you to rent your primary residence for up to 14 days per year tax-free.

FLY Tip: The Augusta Rule is a tax loophole for homeowners: it lets you rent out your home to your own business (or your college body staying overnight) for up to 14 days per year and collect that rent 100% tax-free.

Renting a home for even 14 weekend nights (such as an NCAA game, graduation ceremony, or parent week) at $1,000 per night can bring in $14,000 in completely tax-exempt income—often enough to cover the half-year mortgage. It is one of the most overlooked benefits of homeownership for young people in vibrant college communities.

16. Turning Your Home into a Business Hub

Young professionals often dream of launching side hustles: graphic design, tutoring, or tech startups. Owning a home makes that easier.

By designating a room as a home office, they can deduct a portion of utilities, insurance, depreciation, and internet costs under IRS Form 8829. This also establishes the property as a legitimate business location, allowing mileage deductions for trips to suppliers, clients, or conferences. A home can be both a living space and a launchpad for innovation.

FLY Tip: For home office related tax saving strategies, refer Chapter 12 of the SMART Family Tax Guide, my book published in 2025.

17. Multiple Exit Strategies After Graduation

A campus rental does not have to end when college does. Upon graduation, young owners can choose from three smart exit paths:

1. Continue renting to faculty members or Ph.D. students, many of whom often prefer quiet, stable housing near campus and tend to stay longer.
2. Sell the property and use Section 121 capital gain exclusion (up to $250,000 tax-free for individuals, $500,000 for married couples). The pro-rata rule may apply for half-living in and half-rental property.
3. Defer taxes entirely through a 1031 exchange, rolling the profits into a new rental closer to work or family.

Each route builds financial flexibility, allowing young investors to adapt their real estate journey as life evolves.

18. Ownership Builds Maturity and Responsibility

When a young person owns a home, whether near a college campus or in their first job city, something changes. Ownership creates accountability. It encourages financial discipline and pride of care. For college students, renting out rooms to friends or classmates not only builds income, but also teaches management skills that schools do not teach: handling rent payments, managing maintenance, and resolving conflicts fairly.

Many parents co-sign student leases, making rent payments reliable. This turns the property into a practical business, often supported indirectly by 529 plan funds (which can be used for student housing). The result is steady cash flow, and a confidence boost that comes from running a real operation.

19. Real Estate Develops Social and Leadership Skills

Schools teach academics (such as math, literature, and computer science) but not much on social intelligence. Real estate does. Owning property forces young people to interact with real tenants, contractors, and even local authorities.

I remember my son, Chris, organized a beach rental to celebrate high school graduation in Hilton Head, SC. A noise complaint brought the police to the door, but he handled it calmly with maturity and tact. That single event taught him how to deal with high-pressure situations, a real-world skill far more valuable than just reading PowerPoint in a classroom.

20. Real Estate Builds Business Acumen

Finally, owning real estate develops entrepreneurial intelligence. From marketing vacancies to negotiating repairs, filing taxes, and managing tenants, young investors gain firsthand experience running a small business. These skills—negotiation, accounting, budgeting, communication, and decision-making—prepare them for leadership roles in any career.

Owning property is not just about money. It is about mindset: learning to think like an investor, not a consumer. It teaches qualities such as patience, foresight, and responsibility, which compound over time just like wealth itself.

Conclusion: Teaching the Next Generation to Build, Not Just Consume

When young professionals own property, they are not just collecting rent: they are collecting lessons. Real estate is the perfect training ground for adulthood. It combines financial management, social growth, and the thrill of building something real.

As the old Chinese proverb goes, *"Give a man a fish and you feed him for a day; teach a man to fish and you feed him for a lifetime."* Real estate is that fishing pole: one that can help a young person sustain their life, secure their freedom, and achieve their dreams long before retirement age.

Chapter 4

Real Estate Mindset

"Do not wait to buy real estate. Buy real estate and wait."—Will Rogers

Embarking on real estate investment as a young professional offers a strategic pathway to wealth and independence. This chapter delivers actionable steps and frameworks to help you cultivate the mindset and habits of a successful real estate investor. You will learn practical strategies, centered on university campus rentals and alternative entry points, which leverage financial skills, manage risk, and maximize tax and income opportunities from the start.

Step 1: Start Early

I began with a simple but powerful question: "Why do young people need to own a house as early as possible?"

Chris was the first to respond. "It is important to develop a sense of ownership early on," he said. "Owning something gives you maturity. It forces you to think differently about responsibility and value."

Mike nodded. "Exactly. Ownership is part of the maturity process. But what if young people are not mature yet? How can they grow into it?"

Chris replied thoughtfully, "There must be a transition. You start with your parents' guidance, but as you gain confidence and experience, they slowly step back. You start taking full responsibility."

Kevin added, "Yes, when you sign that first contract, it is serious. Getting the keys changes you. You feel like you have entered adult life. It is not just property. It is identity."

Mike smiled. "That is ownership, maturity, and control. Those are the foundations. When you own a house, you have control. You decide who rents it, how to manage it, and how much you charge the rent. That is freedom most people never get when they depend on the government, parents, or employers."

Kevin chimed in, "And it is real. Stocks and crypto can vanish, but real estate is *real*: you can see it, touch it, and live in it."

The conversation evolved into the four pillars of early real estate ownership:

1. Ownership – cultivating responsibility.
2. Maturity – learning to manage life's realities.

3. Control – taking charge of decisions.
4. Preservation – protecting wealth in something tangible.

Chris added a fifth: Personal development. "You learn people skills. You learn to evaluate others: tenants, contractors, partners. You cannot get that from school." Kevin agreed. "You read people by how they speak, how they carry themselves, even their car or handshake. It teaches judgment."

Step 2: Start Smartly

The second half of the conversation turned from *why* to *how*. Mike asked, "So, Kevin, how did you start?"

Kevin replied, "I found a house I liked and just went for it. I visited, researched the area, and bought it. I knew Manassas was growing, so timing mattered. With my parents' co-sign, I bought it for around $480,000, and a few months later, it was appraised at $520,000. That is $40,000 in growth, just by acting early."

Mike turned to Chris. "How about your first one? That first step is always the hardest." Chris said, "We did not overthink it. You cannot analyze every detail forever. Most people miss opportunities because they overanalyze."

Mike laughed. "Exactly! Life rewards those who act. The best time to plant a tree was 20 years ago; the second-best time is now. Whether it is buying a house, starting a job, or even dating someone, stop overthinking and take action."

Kevin added, "Action builds confidence. You will never be 'ready.' You just learn along the way."

Step 3: Analyze the Pros and Cons of Campus Rentals

Pros	**Cons**
Ideal rental rate for large colleges	Not all colleges have strong rental markets
Develop people skills and business acumen. Be street smart	Tenant management headaches (the "three Ts": Tenants, Trash, and Toilets)
Up to $25,000 in rental loss can offset W-2 income	Need fee-based tax pro advice
Low down payment, high leverage	Maintenance and repair workload for a full-time college student
Access to first-time buyer credits	Must stay organized to avoid pitfalls

Pros	Cons
Rental income may cover living costs	State, county and HOA rules and regulation complexity
Tax deduction for many expenses	Vacancies affect cash flow (e.g., summer break)
Potential for property appreciation	Some risk of property damage (e.g., college student party)
Parental co-signing can improve credit	Building business systems is critical and time consuming

Step 4: Financing and Proactivity

Mike emphasized the practical side. "To buy young, you do not need to be rich. Start small—get your first credit card, build credit, file your taxes, save some income. You can even use a parent as a co-signer."

He continued, "Be responsive to lenders. When they ask for documents, do not delay. Responsiveness shows seriousness. It builds trust."

Chris nodded. "That is true in everything. Even when you make mistakes, taking the initiative helps you recover faster."

Mike concluded the point: "Proactivity is a universal principle. It is in the *Seven Habits of Highly Effective People*. Be proactive: whether it is sending a thank-you note, following up with a recruiter, or managing a loan. Initiative separates achievers from delayers."

Step 5: Research and Select Prime Locations

- Study rental trends, vacancy rates, and neighborhood amenities.
- Target areas near large colleges, urban cores, and high-demand student housing zones.
- Utilize online platforms and consult local real estate professionals.

Step 6: Build Your Financing Toolkit

- Credit Awareness: Manage credit use, pay bills promptly, and avoid unnecessary debt.
- Down Payment Assistance: Tap first-time homebuyer programs in your state or city.
- Creative Leveraging: Explore low-money-down solutions like FHA loans (as low as 3%) as the first-time home buyer benefit.

Step 7: Secure Quality Tenants and Guarantee Payment

- Require cosigners (e.g., parents) for student rentals.

- Apply clear, objective tenant screening criteria.
- Use written leases and regular inspections for risk management.

Step 8: Maximize Tax Benefits and Deductions

Leverage a combined approach using a small business LLC (Schedule C) alongside your rental entity (Schedule E), allowing you to split and maximize deductions up to 80% on major expenses.

Expense	LLC Deduction (Schedule C)	Rental Deduction (Schedule E)	Non-Deductible (Personal)
Mortgage	15%	65%	20%
Tax	15%	65%	20%
Auto/Meals (50%)/Cell	30%-50%	20%-30%	NA
Internet	15%	65%	20%
Supplies	40%	40%	20%
Repairs	15%	65%	20%

Note: Deductions are maximized when items are truly used for business or rental purposes. Precise recordkeeping is required. Refer to Case Study 3 and 4 for sample tax returns for tax deduction tips. Percentages in the table are for illustration only. Consult a tax pro for your specific situation.

Schedule C vs. Schedule E: Both are IRS forms that go with your Form 1040 (your main tax return). They are used to report income you earn on your own, not from a W-2 job. But they are used for different kinds of money:

(1) Schedule C: "I Work for Mondy" on side hustle income; and

(2) Schedule E: "My Money Works for Me" from rental or passive income

See Chris and Kevin's real-life examples:

Category	Chris's Flight Instruction LLC	Chris's Rental Property
Business Type	Flight training & instruction (single-member LLC)	Residential rental property in FL
IRS Form Used	Schedule C	Schedule E
Income Type	Active earned business income	Passive rental income
Ownership Split	100% Chris	100% Chris
Typical Deductions	Fuel, headset, insurance, licensing, travel, marketing, training	Mortgage interest, taxes, repairs, depreciation, auto, HOA
Tax Type	Income tax + Self-Employment tax	Income tax only (no SE tax), if profitable
How Income Is Earned	Chris teaches and flies with students	Tenants pay rent
Effort Level	High (active work)	Low (passive once rented)
Retirement Planning	Solo 401(k) and Roth IRA	NA
Key Tax Concept	You work for your money	Your money works for you

Category	Kevin's Junk Removal LLC	Kevin's Rental Property
Business Type	Home junk removal & moving (single-member LLC)	Residential rental property in VA
IRS Form Used	Schedule C	Schedule E
Income Type	Active earned business income	Passive rental income
Ownership Split	100% Kevin	100% Kevin
Typical Deductions	Truck fuel, dump fees, tools, uniforms, insurance	Mortgage interest, taxes, repairs, depreciation, HOA
Tax Type	Income tax + Self-Employment tax	Income tax only (no SE tax)
How Income Is Earned	Kevin performs hauling/moving services	Tenants pay rent
Effort Level	High (physical labor)	Low (passive once rented)
Retirement Planning	Solo 401(k) and Roth IRA	NA
Key Tax Concept	You work for your money	Your money works for you

Step 9: Prepare for Common Challenges and Pitfalls

- Understand local landlord–tenant laws to ensure compliance.

- Set aside emergency funds for repairs, vacancies, and operational hiccups.
- Prepare for vacancy using short-term rental strategies when needed.
- Seek professional advice (CPA, property manager, agent) to avoid legal and tax traps.

Step 10: Scale Your Investment for Long-Term Wealth

- Target properties that promise both appreciation and cash flow.
- Reinvest early profits to expand into new properties or diversify (e.g., commercial real estate).
- Maintain an ongoing commitment to learning by joining workshops, networking with other investors, and following real estate trends.

Step 11: Build Your Professional Network

Find a Real Estate Mentor

- Seek out experienced investors or agents willing to share practical knowledge and honest feedback.
- Look for mentors through professional groups, local brokerages, alumni associations, or trusted online forums.
- Establish clear expectations with your mentor. Commit to regular meetings, ask strategic questions, and be receptive to constructive criticism.

Attend Local Real Estate Meetups

- Join real estate investment clubs, association gatherings, or meetup groups in your area.
- Participate in networking events to connect with lenders, property managers, brokers, and fellow investors.
- Use these opportunities to gain experience market trends, discover deals, and collaborate on joint ventures.

Step 12: Take Action. Your Next Steps as a Young Investor

- Identify your preferred entry point based on your goals and resources.
- Build your financing and support network early.
- Track all income and expenses diligently to maximize legal tax savings.
- Approach investing as a business and a learning journey.

Closing Thoughts: Help Others with a Clear Message: Impossible vs. I-am-possible.

Finally, the trio reflected on a bigger question: how to share this opportunity with others.

Mike asked, "So how can we help more young people start this journey?" Chris answered, "People are curious. When I tell friends I own a house, they ask how. One of my friends in Gainesville Florida just started the same process by touring homes near major state colleges."

Kevin added, "The best way to help is proof: showing it is possible. Once people see someone their age doing it, it breaks the mental barrier."

Mike agreed. "Exactly. Spread the information, the mindset, and the action steps. It is not about luck; it is about learning the process."

He leaned forward with a smile. "And that is why we're writing this book with a message that achieving your financial freedom at 18 is not just a dream, but a plan."

As Chris summarized best, "It is proof that it is possible. Once you see the results, you want others to experience it too. That is how we build not just wealth, but a legacy."

PART 2: House Ownership Road Map

Chapter 5

Location, Location, Location

- *By Mike and Kevin Nie*

"The three most important things in real estate: location, location, location." – Ancient Proverb

Every successful investor knows that real estate is not just about timing—it is about *location.* The right property in the right place can generate steady income, loyal tenants, and long-term appreciation. For young professionals beginning their real estate journey, understanding *where* to invest is just as important as *how.*

Two main strategies dominate real estate investment: long-term rentals and short-term rentals. Each works best in specific geographic settings and comes with its own set of financial advantages, tax opportunities, and lifestyle considerations.

Long-Term Rentals: The Power of Stability

A long-term rental typically means a lease lasting more than 180 days or more. This approach provides predictable cash flow, fewer turnovers, and minimal maintenance interruptions. It is ideal for busy young professionals, college students, or those building careers who do not have time to handle constant check-ins and cleaning between guests.

There are five prime locations that make long-term rentals both profitable and low-risk.

1. College Towns

Properties near major universities are some of the most reliable investments in the country. Colleges such as Penn State, Ohio State, the University of Michigan, the University of Virginia, and the University of Florida attract tens of thousands of students each year. These "mega campuses" come with built-in demand: undergraduates, graduate students, visiting professors, and sports fans all need housing.

Universities with strong athletic programs or large graduate populations create year-round activity—from football weekends to conferences, from homecoming to graduation. Renting to graduates or Ph.D. students also offers more stable tenants who stay multiple years and respect the property. Smaller liberal arts schools, especially in remote areas, may not provide the same consistency in traffic or income.

2. Hospitals and Medical Centers

Properties near major hospitals can be gold mines for steady, responsible tenants. Medical residents, nurses, and travel doctors often rent nearby for two to four years while completing rotations.

For example, I have a condo near a large medical facility (Inova Fairfax Hospital in Northern Virginia). It can stay fully occupied year-round. These tenants are typically hard-working, financially reliable, and quiet medical professionals. Being close to a hospital also attracts patients' families who need temporary housing during extended treatments.

3. Military Bases

Another excellent long-term strategy is investing near military installations. Bases create constant demand from enlisted personnel and civilian contractors. Payments are stable because military housing allowances are backed by the U.S. government. In areas near the Pentagon, Norfolk Naval Base, or Fort Belvoir, for instance, landlords rarely experience late rent or long vacancies.

4. Costco Stores or Sam's Clubs

Here are several reasons why rentals located near a Costco or Sam's Club can be a good deal, drawn from insights in the market and reflected in commentary like in The Wall Street Journal article "*Is Living on Top of a Costco the Answer to the Affordable-Housing Crisis?*"

The Entrepreneur magazine has a similar report in 2025 titled "*Thrive Living Hopes to Build 'Thousands of Apartments' a Year Starting With One Complex on Top of the Warehouse Chain.*"

A University of British Columbia study in 2024 showed that Costco openings caused a 7.9% increase in property values within 5 miles in counties with above-average population density. See a table below listing the number of Costco clubs vs. Sam's clubs ranked by states.

- Built-in demand and tenant convenience: A key advantage: being near a major retailer like Costco helps drive constant foot-traffic, support services, and convenience for residents. House developers noted that having a Costco on the ground floor or adjacent means the residential tenant base benefits from the accessibility of shopping, bulk goods, membership services and so forth.
- For a rental property investor or for residents, this tends to translate into:
  - Higher desirability (people like the one-stop shopping and strong amenity base)
  - Potential for somewhat more stable occupancy (because the anchor retail helps fuel the area)
  - Ancillary benefits: easier parking, services, infrastructure that support both the retail and residential side
  - Lower risk via co-location with a strong tenant

Table: Costco vs Sam's Club Locations by State (Combined Ranking from High to Low)

Rank	State	Costco Locations	Sam's Club Locations
1	California	144	29
2	Texas	44	82
3	Florida	35	46
4	Washington	35	16
5	Illinois	24	13
6	New Jersey	21	8
7	Arizona	20	13
8	New York	19	12
9	Michigan	19	15
10	Georgia	17	15
11	Virginia	17	15
12	Colorado	16	12
13	Minnesota	14	12
14	Utah	14	8
15	Oregon	13	0
16	North Carolina	10	12
17	Indiana	9	10
18	Tennessee	9	12
19	Nevada	8	7
20	Connecticut	8	1
21	Hawaii	8	2
22	Maryland	11	10
23	Alabama	5	8
24	Alaska	6	0
25	Idaho	7	1
26	Montana	5	2
27	Arkansas	1	9
28	Massachusetts	7	0
29	Delaware	1	0
30	Vermont	1	0

Source: company disclosures.

One of the strategic moves in the mixed-use development was that the retail space leased by Costco provides a credit-worthy anchor tenant that makes the overall project less risky.

- Potential for value-added or growth upside: A SMART real estate investor believes the Costco-anchored development will reduce dependence on heavy subsidies and enable more "affordable housing" units by leveraging the synergy. From the rental economics viewpoint:
    - If the site is under-utilized today (for example older buildings or retail/residential mix is not maximized), there may be opportunities to increase rent or improve the property because of the retail draw
    - As the area around Costco grows (or is redeveloped), rental demand may increase faster than in locations without such anchors
    - For longer-term hold, being near or part of a mixed-use retail/residential project may offer more resilience in uncertain markets

5. AI Data Center

With the explosive growth of the AI industry, SMART real estate investors note three key reasons why rentals near AI data centers are likely to be a strong investment.

- Surge in high-paying job creation. For example, a Nvidia or Meta's AI Factory Research Center and the AI chip factory will create demand for engineers, data-center technicians, software developers, and skilled traders. These are high-income professionals who typically seek quality housing close to work. The resulting influx of tech workers will increase rental demand in Manassas, VA; Seattle, WA; and Austin, TX. The rentals adjacent to the data centers have historically produced above-average rent appreciation.
- Infrastructure expansion and urban revitalization. The AI data center projects trigger major upgrades to local infrastructure, including roads, utilities, and broadband expansion, to support gigawatt-scale AI operations. Infrastructure spending tends to raise surrounding property values and improve livability, attracting additional tenants. For example, in Manassas VA, Kevin read about Dominion Energy and federal agencies partnering to modernize Virginia's power systems, reliable energy and connectivity, making the region even more desirable for both residents and employers.
- Regional economic transformation and tech hub momentum. For example, Manassas, VA is evolving from an industrial suburb into an AI innovation hub at the center of Northern Virginia's "Data Center Alley." Nvidia's move cements the area's status as the epicenter of America's AI future, joining Microsoft, Amazon, and Google. Kevin is pleased with his early footprint in this area. This transformation attracts supporting industries (energy tech, logistics, professional services) that will further fuel population and housing growth. Rental investors benefit from sustained appreciation and low vacancy in markets anchored by long-term tech infrastructure investments.

Here is a table listing top ten AI data centers in the U.S., sorted by the mean housing price.

AI Data Center or AI Chip Factory	City	State	Size / Scale	Typical Home Value
Edged Energy – Council Bluffs AI Campus	Council Bluffs	IA	200 MW	$219K
Google – Council Bluffs Campus	Council Bluffs	IA	>100 MW / $6.8B	$219K
Meta – DeKalb Data Center	DeKalb	IL	2.3M sq ft / $1B+	$250K
Microsoft Fairwater AI DC (Mount Pleasant)	Mount Pleasant	WI	315 acres / ~1.2M sq ft	$330K
Google – The Dalles	The Dalles	OR	Large campus / high footprint	$390K
Microsoft – Columbia DC (Quincy)	Quincy	WA	800k sq ft / 30–50 MW	$426K
Meta – Prineville Data Center	Prineville	OR	3.2M sq ft	$427K
Meta – Mesa Data Center	Mesa	AZ	2.5M sq ft	$432K
Google – Henderson (Las Vegas area)	Henderson	NV	750k sq ft / 115 MW	$487K
NVIDIA Aurora AI Factory	Manassas	VA	96 MW	$547K

Note: MW = megawatt in electricity output. Home value source: Zillow as of October 2025.

Short-Term Rentals: The Power of Flexibility

The second strategy is short-term rentals, properties leased for no longer than seven days, often through platforms like Airbnb or VRBO. This approach involves more active management: cleaning between guests, updating listings, and handling frequent turnovers. However, it also opens unique tax advantages and higher earning potential.

According to IRS guidelines, short-term rentals can sometimes qualify as active income businesses, allowing owners to deduct depreciation, cleaning costs, and repairs *against regular W-2 income.* For example, a high-earning professional (e.g., an investment analyst making $250,000) could operate a short-term rental in Delaware or Virginia Beach and use rental losses to offset active income, significantly reducing taxes.

Beyond the numbers, short-term rentals work best in three types of locations:

1. Beach Destinations

Beach towns have built-in seasonal traffic. Think Daytona Beach, Virginia Beach, Ocean City, Hilton Head, or the Jersey Shore. These areas attract tourists during summer, spring break, and special events such as NASCAR races or music festivals. Properties in beach zones can earn high weekly rates, especially if well-furnished and located within walking distance of the water.

2. Airports and Transit Hubs

Condos near large airports (such as Dallas-Fort Worth (DFW), Atlanta Hartsfield-Jackson, or Washington Dulles (IAD)) are ideal for airline crews and business travelers. Pilots, flight attendants, and traveling professionals often seek short stays between flights or conferences. A property near an airport or convention center ensures constant rotation of short-term guests and strong occupancy rates.

3. Major Medical Facilities

Short-term housing near major hospitals is another underappreciated niche. Families visiting loved ones for surgeries or cancer treatments often need comfortable, nearby accommodation for just a few days or weeks. A quiet condo within walking distance of a major hospital offers convenience and compassion, while generating premium rent.

The Tax Advantage of Travel

Another overlooked perk: when you personally visit your short-term rental for inspection or maintenance, your trip qualifies as a business expense. A weekend at your beach house or airport condo, when combined with property upkeep or marketing tasks, becomes deductible travel. The IRS recognizes such trips as legitimate business activity, lowering your taxable income while allowing you to enjoy your business visit to your rental responsibly.

Choosing the Right Path

Both long-term and short-term strategies work beautifully, but for young professionals, the right choice depends on time, temperament, and location.

- If you want stability, minimal management, and reliable tenants, look for nearby colleges, hospitals, or military bases.
- If you prefer flexibility, higher returns, and active engagement, focus on beach towns, airport hubs, or medical centers.

In real estate, *location* determines not only your rent, but your rhythm of life. A well-chosen property becomes both a financial asset and a classroom, teaching young investors how to balance cash flow, taxes, and time management.

Conclusion: Invest Where Life Happens

"Location, location, location" is not just a cliché; it is the foundation of real estate success. A property near the right type of activity will almost always outperform one in a quiet corner of nowhere.

For young professionals, the goal is not just to own real estate. It is to have opportunity. Choose locations where life happens: campuses filled with energy, hospitals filled with purpose, airports filled with movement, and beaches filled with dreams.

Because in the end, the right location does not just build wealth; it builds wisdom.

Chapter 6

How to Raise Down Payment for Your First Home Purchase

"*It is not about having resources. It is about being resourceful.*"—Tony Robbins

When most 18-year-olds are saving for a car or a college trip, my sons Chris and Kevin were already planning how to buy their first homes. They knew that the biggest challenge was not getting a mortgage but raising the down payment.

As a father, CPA, and coach of financial literacy, I wanted to show them that wealth building begins early, and that owning property young is one of the most powerful steps toward freedom. Together, we explored ten practical ways to raise the down payment for a first house before age 20.

1. Personal Savings

Chris worked part-time at a café and occasionally helped in our family business. Kevin waited for tables at a restaurant. Every paycheck, no matter how small, taught them the value of consistency. By saving just $300–$500 per month, a young person can build $5,000–$6,000 in a single year. Two-year savings are enough to form the foundation of a home down payment. Discipline, not income, is the secret here.

2. Roth IRA Early Withdrawals

Both Chris and Kevin began contributing to Roth IRAs when they were just children through our family business. They earned legitimate pay by washing cars, cleaning our home office, scanning receipts, and even performing music at business events: all qualified as real work.

By age 18, each had nearly $60,000 in their Roth IRA accounts, invested in Fidelity S&P 500 index fund. Under IRS rules (IRC §408A(d)(5)), a first-time homebuyer can withdraw up to $10,000 principal from an IRA without 10% early withdrawal penalty for a down payment. Roth distribution is tax free too. That single rule became a cornerstone of their plan.

FLY Tip: IRA early draw safe harbor: normally, if you pull money out of your Roth IRA before age 59½, the IRS will require a 10% early-withdrawal penalty. But FLYers can take advantage of an exception called the first-time homebuyer safe harbor. Here's how it works: You can withdraw up to $10,000 from your Roth IRA penalty-free to buy your first home.

FLYers should include Form 5329—Additional Taxes on Qualified Plans (Including IRAs) in his or her 1040 tax return:

(1) receiving Form 1099-R from the IRA custodian showing $10,000 as a gross distribution with distribution code (often code 1 = early distribution, no known exception);

(2) filling out Form 5329, Part I: Line 1 – Enter early IRA distributions $10,000; and

(3) enter Exception Code "09" on Line 2. Code 09 = First-time homebuyer.

3. UTMA, the Gift that Keeps on Giving

Through the Uniform Transfers to Minors Act (UTMA), we gifted each child $15,000–$19,000 annually, within the IRS's annual gift exclusion. We invested those gifts into long-term holdings like Berkshire Hathaway. Compounded over 18 years, those accounts grew close to $800,000.

When they turned 18, Chris and Kevin became the legal owners of their UTMA accounts.

- Between 18 and 24, if you are (1) a full-time college student, and (2) do not earn more than half of your living expenses, you should not liquidate UTMA stocks due to kiddie tax provision (i.e., in most cases your capital gain will be subject to ordinary income tax at your parents' tax bracket). Instead, use the securities backed line of credit to draw a loan to use as house down payment; and
- After age 24, kiddie tax is aged out. If a FLYer's taxable income was low, they could sell a small portion for a down payment and pay zero capital gains tax (thanks to the 0% long-term capital gains rate for taxable incomes under about $49K). Considering the standard deduction of $15K, you can realize capital gain about $64K tax-free, assuming no other earned income.

FLY Tip: Uniform Transfers to Minors Act (UTMA) is your "starter investment account" before you're a real adult. Parents gift you up to an annual exclusion amount ($19K in 2026, and inflation indexed in future years). Each parent can gift this amount, doubling the total if both parents have sufficient cash. Given the penalizing kiddie tax issue, parents elect to invest the UTMA money into long-running, broad-based, and zero-dividend stocks.

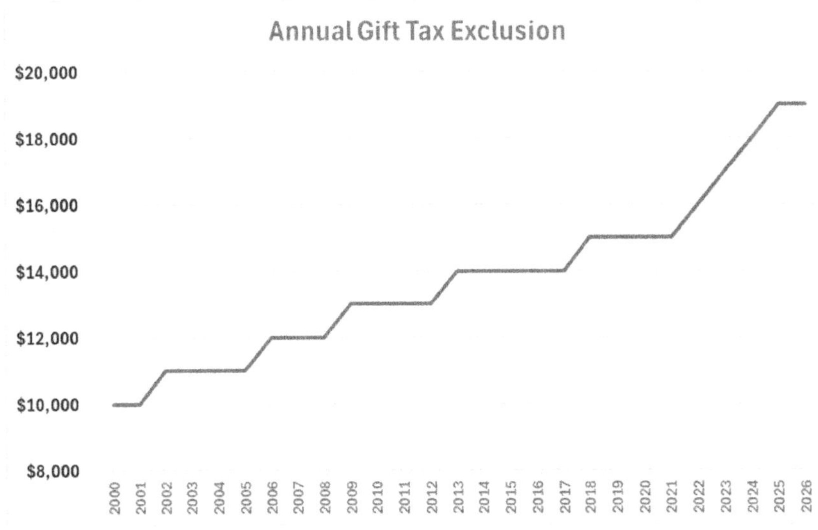

Source: IRS. Chart created by author

The table below shows the earliest FLYer can take over the UTMA account.

State	Age of Takeover	Notes
California	18	One of the few where you can take over at 18
New York	21	Must wait until 21
Florida	21 (can be extended to 25)	You can't take it at 18 unless account says so
Texas	21	
Virginia	18, 21, or 25	Could be early if parent approves the ownership change at 18
Washington Illinois Massachusetts	21	Standard age

Note: State law changes frequently. A FLYer should check their state regulation.

4. The UTMA "BBB Strategy": Borrow, Buy, and Build

Instead of selling stocks, I showed them how to use their portfolios as collateral for a Securities-Backed Line of Credit (SBLOC) with Schwab or Fidelity. This allowed them to borrow the $15,000 needed for the down payment, while the investments continued compounding.

The interest paid on this loan could even be tax-deductible if used to purchase the property. It is a strategy that lets young investors "borrow, buy, and build" without interrupting long-term compounding.

5. Borrow from a a Solo 401(k)

For families running small businesses, hiring your children with 1099 NEC allows them to contribute to a Solo 401(k). This is funded after they fully funded their Roth IRA accounts. Chris and Kevin started contributing as teenagers, and by 18, they had more than $70,000 each invested.

IRS rules permit borrowing up to 50% of the vested balance (max $50,000) from 401(k) (per IRC §72(p)). The best part? The interest you pay goes back into your own account, effectively paying yourself back while using the funds for your home. You have up to five years to pay back the loan.

6. Family Gifting and Relative-funding

When Kevin graduated from high school, we asked family and friends to contribute toward his "First Home Fund" instead of typical gifts. Twenty relatives each gave $500 or more. That single celebration raised $10,000, a creative, tax-free, and community-driven way to launch a dream.

7. Smart Use of Student Loans

Sometimes, student loans can provide flexibility. If a student borrows slightly more than tuition costs or transfers unused 529 funds after graduation, that surplus can be used for housing near campus, often qualifying as an owner-occupied rental.

8. Cash Value Life Insurance

A whole life insurance policy can accumulate cash value over time. I established policies for both Chris and Kevin when they were young. When they reached 18, the policies had enough value to borrow $10,000–$15,000 tax-free, with the loan repaid over time. It is another way to leverage family planning for early asset building.

9. Home Equity Line of Credit (HELOC)

Finally, as parents, we can borrow from our own home equity to help fund their first down payment. This approach uses the growth in our home's value, the "sleeping equity," to empower the next generation to start their own real estate journey.

10. Trump Account

Trump Accounts are a new type of custodial-style traditional IRA for minors, designed to help families begin saving and investing early. The child owns the assets, while an adult (most likely a parent) acts on the child's behalf until age 18. The annual funding limit is $5,000. Investment are limited to low-cost index mutual funds or ETFs, subject to a 0.10% expense cap. A Fidelity S&P 500 index fund may satisfy this requirement. Withdrawals after 18 and before age 59½ typically incur a 10% early-withdrawal penalty, with exceptions such as a first-time homebuyer down payment (up to $10,000).

A Father's Reflection

Watching Chris close on his first home in Florida with a 5% down conventional loan, and Kevin secure his house in Virginia with a 3% down FHA loan, was one of my proudest moments. They learned that down payments are not about luck. They are about planning, discipline, and creativity. Every dollar, whether saved, invested, borrowed wisely, or gifted, becomes a building block of financial independence.

Lesson: "Do not wait for the perfect time to buy your first home. Create it. Wealth favors the prepared and the patient."

Chapter 7

Ten Steps to Be Homebuyer Ready

"By failing to prepare, you are preparing to fail."—Benjamin Franklin

Buying your first home is one of life's greatest milestones. It is never too early to start preparing. In our family, I have always believed that financial readiness is as important as mental readiness. Chris and Kevin began their journey toward homeownership in their teens. What they learned can serve as a blueprint for every young person who dreams of owning a home before age 25.

Here are the ten steps we follow to get ready, financially, mentally, and strategically, to buy that first home.

Step 1: Build Credit Early

Credit is the foundation of homeownership. Before my boys turned 18, I added them as authorized users on both our personal and business credit cards. Each month, I used my boys' cards for grocery shopping, gas station, and family expenses—paying every balance in full and on time. This created a strong credit history tied to their names.

By the time Chris and Kevin reached 18, they each had a FICO score above 750, years before most young adults even opened their first account.

Tip: Parents can "turbocharge" their children's credit by adding them as authorized users on accounts with long histories and perfect payment records. Parents use children's cards frequently to build up activities.

Step 2: Establish Independent Credit at 18

As soon as your child turns 18, help them apply for their own credit cards. Starter cards like the American Express Blue Cash or Capital One card are ideal. Even with a modest $300–$500 limit, the goal is to build independent credit history.

At the same time, encourage them to apply for a business credit card under their LLC (more on that below). Business credit opens doors to higher credit limits, reward programs, and future access to financing opportunities. Capital One Venture X for business or Chase Ink is a good option.

Step 3: Form an LLC

Both Chris and Kevin established single-member LLCs:

- Chris, as a flight instructor, created his aviation consulting LLC for liability protection and professional legitimacy.
- Kevin launched his house junk removal and moving services business under his own LLC (gym-operator.com).

Each child filed a W-9 using their business EIN instead of their Social Security Number, an early lesson in protecting privacy and separating personal and business finances.

Why it matters: Lenders love seeing business ownership and independent income on mortgage applications.

Step 4: Open Bank Accounts (Personal and Business)

Once the LLCs were formed, we visited the bank to open two accounts for each child:

1. Personal Checking Account for daily life and personal spending.
2. Business Checking Account tied to the LLC's EIN for all business deposits and expenses.

This clear separation helps when filing taxes, tracking business deductions, and proving legitimate income for mortgage purposes.

Step 5: Get a W-2 Job Early

Both boys started part-time jobs as teenagers: Kevin at a local pizzeria, and Chris at the flight school. Even small paychecks mattered. Lenders look for W-2 income as a sign of steady employment.

Refer to case studies 3 and 4 of the book to see how Kevin optimizes his W-4 deduction and avoids unnecessary withholding. Many young workers lose hundreds in over-withheld taxes (10-20% of gross pay) simply because they do not adjust their W-4. Filing accurately means keeping more cash flow savings and for the down payment.

Step 6: File a Tax Return Independently

Once they had both W-2 and 1099 income, I guided them through filing their own Form 1040. Doing this early has three powerful benefits:

1. Health Savings Account (HSA):
   Both boys opened HSAs through Fidelity, since they were covered under my high-deductible family health plan. In 2025, each was able to contribute $8,550 tax-free. HSAs grow tax-free and can be used later for medical or housing-related expenses—a hidden wealth-building tool. Parents can gift this amount to adult children, who file their own tax return to deduct from their earned income.
2. American Opportunity Tax Credit (AOTC):
   Paying college tuition with their own credit cards qualified them for a $1,000 refundable education credit each year. Filing independently allowed them to claim this directly, doubling the benefit compared to being dependent. FLYers must carefully document that they earn more than half of their own living expenses to meet the independence requirement.
3. For example, FLYers sum up W-2 wages, 1099 income, and other earned income to prove their funding is more than half of the living expenses (tuition and fees, rent or housing costs,

utilities, food, transportation, and personal expenses). That's why an in-state college student is more likely than an Ivy League college student to be eligible for the AOTC.

4. Business Deductions:
   Filing Schedule C let them deduct cell phone bills, mileage, and meals: all legitimate expenses for their side businesses.

These tax returns later served as vital proof of income when applying for their first home loans.

Step 7: Understand How Loans Work

To get approved for a mortgage, banks look at the three Cs: Credit, Capacity, and Collateral.

- Credit: Already built through years of responsible card use.
- Capacity: Demonstrated through consistent W-2 or 1099 NEC income.
- Collateral: Comes from the property being purchased.

By age 18, both boys had 700+ credit scores, verifiable income, Roth IRA (up to $10,000 penalty free for first home purchase) and savings—well enough to qualify for 3%–5% down payment programs.

Step 8: Learn from Rental Property Experience

Real learning happens through experience. As a parent and landlord, I often brought Chris and Kevin to help manage my rental properties, take rent checks, scan receipts, and talk with tenants.

They soon learned how to maintain and manage assets. Every time they worked for the rentals, they earned income, reinforcing the link between effort, ownership, and reward.

Step 9: Practice Financial Independence

Once your child has income, encourage budgeting and saving discipline. Chris and Kevin divided every dollar into three categories:

- 50% essentials: rent, groceries, gas
- 30% investing/saving: Roth IRA, brokerage, HSA
- 20% fun/spending: travel, hobbies, entertainment

The sooner young adults develop these habits, the easier it becomes to handle a mortgage later.

Step 10: Build a Mindset of Ownership

Financial readiness is important, but mindset seals the deal. I have often told Chris and Kevin: "You work for money; but more importantly, let money work for you."

Owning a home teaches responsibility, discipline, and pride. Whether through managing credit, saving strategically, or investing early, every step builds confidence.

Chris and Kevin each bought their first homes before 20: one in Florida and one in Virginia. These feats were not through luck, but through preparation and guidance.

Final Thought

The path to homeownership lies more in readiness than wealth. Parents can start this process long before a child turns 18: build credit, file taxes, open accounts, form an LLC, and practice financial independence. By combining practical steps with patient mentoring, you will give your children the greatest gift of all: a foundation for lifelong financial freedom.

Chapter 8

A Tale of Two Mortgages

"The roads may be different, but the destination is the same: freedom through ownership."—*Kevin Nie*

Buying a home as a teenager is an achievement. But doing it twice in one family tells a powerful story about timing, discipline, and smart financial leverage. The Nie family's two journeys (Chris's Florida townhouse and Kevin's Virginia condominium) illustrate how different paths can both lead to successful mortgage approval.

Aspect	Chris's Story (Florida)	Kevin's Story (Virginia)
Age at Purchase	19 years old	19 years old
Property Type	Brand-new townhouse in Daytona Beach, FL	Brand-new two-level condo in Manassas, VA
Purchase Price	$320,000	$483,000
Loan Type	Conventional loan	FHA loan
Down Payment	5% ($16,000)	3% ($15,000)
Interest Rate at Approval	5.5% (2023 market rate)	6.5% (2025 market rate)
Credit Score	720	715
Key Approval Documents	Admission letter to college, W-2 from local pizzeria, 1040 tax return, parents' returns	W-2 and 1040 for Kevin, parents' returns, business financials, six-month pro forma
Special Challenge	Young age and limited credit history	High Debt-to-Income (DTI) ratio of parents due to existing loans borrowed by parents
Loan Participants	Chris + parents as co-signers	Kevin + parents as co-signers
Solution Used	Proved financial independence via 12-month bank statements showing	College enrollment letter + co-signers with strong credit

Aspect	Chris's Story (Florida)	Kevin's Story (Virginia)
	Chris handled his own mortgage payments	
Builder Incentives	Not available	$25,000 seller + lender credit package
Closing Logistics	Power of Attorney used while family traveled abroad; signed through mobile notary service	Longer approval timeline due to FHA verification and federal processing delays
Timeline from Offer to Keys	2–3 months (smooth)	3–4 months (rigorous due diligence due to FHA loan underwriting)
Location Advantages	Close to Embry-Riddle University: ideal for student housing	Near Manassas Airport, George Mason University Science Campus, and AI data-center projects: strong future rental demand
Post-Purchase Gain	Stable home and credit foundation for Chris	Appreciated from $480K to $520K within three months (+$40K paper gain)
Lesson Learned	Early planning and documentation make youth no barrier to homeownership	Timing and decisiveness create immediate returns; do not over-analyze a good deal
Next step after graduation	Obtain FL state resident. No state income tax. Continue house rental	Rent at market rate to mother, who works nearby

Analysis

Chris's path was a model of simplicity and preparation. He leveraged academic proof, family support, and clear intent to secure a conventional loan with minimal friction. His story shows that lenders respond positively to a structured and credible plan.

Kevin's path, on the other hand, required strategic problem-solving. The family's existing debt could have derailed approval, but showing Chris's independent financial management allowed the lender to disregard that liability on parents' names. The FHA route meant more paperwork but far greater leverage, with a lower down payment and immediate appreciation.

Key Takeaways

1. Documentation beats age. Even a 19-year-old can get a mortgage with proof of income, tax return and purpose.
2. Show independence. Lenders want evidence of self-sustained payments, not parental subsidies.
3. Builder incentives matter. Kevin's $25,000 credit package was equivalent to over eight months' worth of payments.

4. Timing is profitable. Quick action during early construction phases led to Kevin's triple-digit return within three months.
5. Each story complements the other. Chris's discipline built credibility; Kevin's decisiveness turned that credibility into wealth.

The table below is Chris's closing document (with information revised for illustration purpose).

DDD Title of Florida, Inc.

Orlando, FL 32888

File No./Escrow No.:	110-333333
Print Date & Time:	July 20, 2023 11:56 am
Officer/Escrow Officer:	Alex Doe
Settlement Location:	100 Freedom Road, Suite 100 Orlando, FL 32888
Property Address:	888 Regal Drive Daytona Beach, FL 32999
Borrower:	Chris Nie Mike Nie Yuqin Ding

Seller		Description	Borrower	
Debit	**Credit**		**Debit**	**Credit**
		Financial		
	325,990.00	Sale Price of Property	325,990.00	
		Deposit		12,000.00
		Loan Amount		309,691.00
4,513.00		Seller Credit		4,513.00
12,000.00		Excess Deposit		
		Prorations/Adjustments		
	0.00	Buyer Reimburse Seller Survey	0.00	
1,705.00		Seller credit to otp		1,705.00
2,282.00		Seller credit to deed		2,282.00
132.20		County Taxes 01/01/23-07/26/23		132.20
		Loan Charges to DHI Mortgage Company Ltd.		
250.00		Origination Fee		

The table below is Kevin's closing document.

	Property	6666 Michael Jackson Avenue Manassas, VA 20999	Settlement Date Disbursement Date	08/18/2025 08/18/2025
	Buyer	Kevin Nie Fairfax, VA 22000		
Suite 350 Fairfax, VA, 22030	Seller	SMART Homes, LLC Reston, VA 20190		
	Lender	First Mortgage, LLC Fairfax, VA 22000		

Description	Buyer	
	Debit	Credit
Financial		
Sale Price of Property	$483,970.00	
Loan Amount		$475,204.00
Seller Credit		$23,811.99
Lender Credit		$1,188.01
Prorations/Adjustments		
County Taxes 07/01/2025 to 08/18/2025		$251.04
Est Suppl Taxes 07/01/2025 to 08/18/2025		$455.52
Parent Tract Taxes 08/18/2025 to 01/01/2026	$62.56	
Loan Charges		
1.50% of Loan Amount (Points)	$7,128.06	
Commitment Fee to First Mortgage, LLC	$250.00	
Processing Fee to First Mortgage, LLC	$845.00	
Underwri ng Fee to First Mortgage, LLC	$845.00	
Appraisal Fee to Appraisers Inc. ($585.00 POC by Borrower)		
Condo Cert of Insurance to EOI Directs	$47.95	
Credit Report Fee to Excel LLC	$260.00	
Flood Cer fica on Fee	$14.00	
Mortgage Insurance Premiyum to Dept of HUD	$8,173.04	
Prepaid Interest ($79.74 per day from 08/18/2025 to 09/01/2025)	$1,116.36	
Impounds		
Homeowner's insurance $42.42 per month for 3 mo.	$127.26	
Property taxes $315.39 per month for 5 mo.	$1,576.95	
Aggregate adjustment		$169.68
Government Recording and Transfer Charges		
Recording Fees	$107.00	
---Deed: $47.00		

Chapter 9

My Room, My Rules, My Rental

"Financial independence does not wait for age; it waits for awareness." – Chris

Chapters 5 to 8 cover our advice of house searching, downpayment readiness, and mortgage application. The following chapters are a collection of father-son interviews that provide real life experiences of Chris and Kevin. Enjoy.

"It Makes Sense."

Mike: Chris, let's start with something positive. You bought your first property at 18. That is a huge milestone for anyone, let alone a college student. What was it like stepping into homeownership so young?

Chris: Honestly, it felt amazing. I did not have to stay in a dorm, which was important for me. Having my own place meant freedom—my room, my rules, my space. I could cook when I wanted, study in peace, and not worry about quiet hours or dorm restrictions.

Mike: That is true. A lot of students would envy that independence. I remember how proud we felt by showing your college admission letter to prove you were committed to staying for four years. It helped justify buying instead of renting.

Chris: Exactly. It showed the lenders I was serious. It is funny: people always ask, "Why buy a house in Florida when you are from Virginia?" But once they saw I was enrolled at Embry-Riddle and that I changed my state residence from VA to FL, it made more sense.

The Benefits of Early Ownership

Mike: Let us talk about the good parts first. What benefits have you enjoyed as a young homeowner?

Chris: Well, aside from freedom, it has been a great learning experience. Managing a property taught me responsibility: budgeting, cleaning, maintenance, even tenant relations. My tenants know I keep things tidy, so they try to do the same. That is a nice example to set.

Mike: That is a hidden benefit: you are not just a landlord; you are a role model. I have noticed your tenants respect the place because you set that tone.

Chris: Yes, and it was fun hosting friends too. They are always impressed. Some even say, "I wish I would have thought of this in college." It is a cool feeling to have a real home when everyone else is living in cramped dorms.

Mike: And you have even had spring-break visitors from other schools: UVA, Virginia Tech, for instance. I remember you giving them a tour and them being shocked a college student owned the place.

Chris: Yes, they couldn't believe it. It opened a lot of their eyes to what is possible.

Cash Flow and Management

Mike: You have decided not to sell after graduation, right?

Chris: No way. I plan to keep it. It's already producing a steady stream of cash. I just need to find someone trustworthy to manage it when I move.

Mike: Smart move. Property management can easily be outsourced, usually around 7-10% of rent. And remember, you were even approached by someone on Airbnb asking you to manage *their* property.

Chris: Yes! That was wild. Someone was unhappy with their current manager and thought I would do better. It made me realize how valuable being responsive and responsible can be. You can build a business around that.

Mike: Exactly. A property manager has a fascinating role: low risk, steady income. You can even deduct business expenses like travel, meals, and your car when it is tied to property visits. It is the perfect setup for young entrepreneurs.

Financing the Dream

Mike: A lot of people probably wonder how you afforded it in the first place.

Chris: All the time. I tell them it is not as impossible as it looks. We used the 3% or 5% down payment rule: around $15,000 on a $300,000 house. Most families could save that with some discipline.

Mike: And for first-time buyers, remember, you can withdraw up to $10,000 from Roth IRA without penalty to buy your first home. That is a great tool for young investors.

Chris: That is good to know! I did not realize that at the time.

Mike: Of course, there is always risk: if you cannot find tenants early on, cash flow becomes a challenge. That is why location matters. You are in a perfect location: near Embry-Riddle, Daytona Beach, Daytona 500, Ladies Professional Golf Association (LPGA), and all the other exciting events.

Chris: Yes, it is basically a college town. Plus, the racecar events bring in seasonal renters. And the area is growing with more people moving in from northern states because it is affordable.

Marketing, Marketing, Marketing

Mike: When it came to finding tenants, how did you market it?

Chris: Mostly Zillow and Facebook Marketplace. Marketplace worked best with fewer scams, and better real people. I got tons of messages asking about pets, full-house rentals, all kinds of things.

Mike: You handled it like a pro: polite, professional, detail-oriented. That is how you build a reputation.

Chris: Thanks! I learned quickly that professionalism pays off. It is not just about renting a room; it is about managing relationships.

Mike: Exactly. Real estate is a people business.

Challenges and Growth

Mike: Let us be honest: not everything is smooth sailing. What challenges have you faced?

Chris: Turnover was tough at first. Having new tenants every six months was stressful. The first night with a new person in the house always felt weird. But over time, I found stable long-term renters, like Tiger and Jack.

Mike: Jack? The SpaceX guy, right?

Chris: Yes! He is amazing. A Navy guy with no college degree, but brilliant. He is 24 and making around $250,000 a year at Elon Musk's SpaceX. That is inspiring. Shows how far skills can take you.

Mike: Absolutely. That is the spirit of entrepreneurship, proving your worth through capability, not credentials. I would love to interview him sometime.

Chris: He would have a great story to tell.

Final Reflections

Mike: Looking back, what advice would you give other young people thinking about buying their first property?

Chris: Start early, learn as you go, and do not be afraid of responsibility. You will make mistakes, but owning property builds confidence. It forces you to think long-term.

Mike: That is wisdom beyond your years. Real estate is not just an investment—it is an education in discipline, strategy, and independence.

Final reflection: Chris's journey shows that financial maturity is not tied to age but to mindset. Homeownership at 18 might sound ambitious, but with family guidance, careful planning, and a willingness to learn, it is entirely possible. The lesson is clear: do not wait for opportunity—create it, live in it, and rent out the extra rooms.

Chapter 10

Tenant, Trash, and Toilet

"*Do not overuse the excuses.*" – Chris

1. The Reality Behind the "Three T's"

Mike: So, Chris, you have had your share of what I call the "Three T's": tenants, trash, and toilets. Tell me the truth: what is it really like being an 18-year-old landlord?

Chris: (laughs) Well, it is not that different from having roommates in college. You get the same problems: people with different cleanliness standards, noise late at night, random friends showing up. It is just that when you are the landlord, you are also the one responsible for fixing things when they go wrong.

2. Leadership Through Responsibility

Mike: Yes, I remember when I was your age. I snored so loud that my roommates threw spoons and shoes at me! But you are right: when you own the place, the dynamics change. The tenants are your *customers*.

Chris: Exactly. I try to keep everyone happy, even when issues come up. Once, two of my tenants got into an argument, almost a fistfight. I had to step in and mediate the situation. It was stressful, but I learned that being *fair, transparent, and impartial* solves a lot. It taught me conflict management, a skill I will need anywhere, either in a cockpit or in a cocktail party.

Mike: That is leadership. On an airplane, the captain has authority. But in a shared house, there is no "captain," right?

Chris: Right. Everyone feels equal, so you cannot just give orders. You must communicate and set expectations clearly. That is a challenge for someone young like me managing older tenants.

3. Cleanliness and Communication

Mike: I have seen that at work too. People resent unfairness: who gets which shifts, who works late. Life is not fair, but clarity helps. Now, tell me—cleanliness. How big of a deal is it?

Chris: Huge. I am clean, maybe too clean. My biggest frustration is dishes left out or messy counters. But I have learned that getting angry does not solve anything. If it is minor, I just clean it. If it is ongoing, I will say, "Hey, can you take care of this, please?" Communication is key.

Mike: Good. Lead by example. You clean your stuff first, and others will follow. Most young people are not trained in tidiness: you and Kevin were well trained because Mom insisted on it.

Chris: I do not think it is about age. It is about habits. Good personal habits make everything easier, from hygiene to handling money.

4. **Lessons from the Toilet Incident**

Mike: Speaking of habits…What about the toilet incident? (laughs)

Chris: (groans) Yes, that one. I was away in Switzerland when my roommate called—the toilet was clogged. His fault, obviously. I told him, "Get it fixed, send me the receipt."The cost was about $500. I was annoyed, but I reimbursed him. He learned his lesson. Sometimes paying for a mistake once teaches more than a lecture.

Mike: That is how you build trust. One mistake is fine; but three strikes and you are out. You gave him a chance and kept the relationship. That is long-term thinking.

Chris: Exactly. A loyal, responsible tenant is worth far more than replacing people every few months. Vacancies are expensive: a month or two without rent really adds up painfully.

Mike: Right. Cash flow is king; leverage is queen. (smiles)

5. **Tenant Management and Timing**

Mike: What about finding tenants? Easy or hard?

Chris: Harder than I thought. Timing matters: summer is busy, winter is slow. Sometimes it is just luck. People are not always ready to move mid-year. Managing remotely is another challenge, but I check in often. They are adults, not kids, so I treat them with respect.

Mike: Good mindset. Respect brings responsibility. Just be careful with bad habits. I can smell trouble from 500 yards away (laughs).

Chris: (laughs) Yes, no issues so far. Everyone has been fine: I screen carefully.

Mike: You also involve me: you share email drafts before sending to tenants. I like that. Shows you are learning from experience and asking for feedback.

Chris: Yes, I value your input. Even though I manage the place, it is reassuring to know I am not alone. Dad, you are right behind me.

Mike: Always.

6. **Real Estate Appreciation and Long-Term Growth**

Mike: Now, what about appreciation? Have you checked the property's value lately?

Chris: Last I looked, it went from around $305K to $330K in three years, about a 6% gain. Considering my down payment is only $15K. My return on investment is 166%, not bad.

Mike: Not bad at all. That is $25,000 up, and you have already earned back your down payment. It is proof that real estate builds wealth even while you sleep. Kevin's property went up too—from $470K to much higher in just a few months.

Chris: Yes, the market's slow sometimes, but overall, it is solid. It is rewarding to see real growth from something I own.

7. The Bigger Picture: Building Character Through Ownership

Mike: You are learning business, responsibility, and people skills before most of your peers even start. You have handled tenants, repairs, cash flow, and conflict. That is worth more than any textbook.

Chris: Definitely. I wish more young people would try it. It is not as hard as it looks to be, just takes patience and discipline.

Mike: That is true. Someday, maybe you will manage more properties or even get your property manager's license. Every state has its own rules, but the principles are universal: be fair, keep good records, and treat people with respect.

Chris: Yes, maybe I will. It has been a learning experience. It is not always easy, but worth it.

Mike: Then that is our chapter right there. The real lesson from your first rental: Success is not just in cash flow; it is in character flow.

Key Takeaways

- Conflict management builds leadership. Learn to be fair and calm under pressure.
- Cleanliness and communication reflect professionalism and self-discipline.
- Trust and long-term thinking matter more than quick profit.
- Cash flow is king; and leverage is queen.
- Early real estate ownership teaches independence, problem-solving, and respect for responsibility.

Chapter 11

My Condo; My Cash Flow; My Cash Cow

"Time is key. The earlier you act, the more control you gain over your future."—*Kevin Nie*

1. A Dream Realized Early

My name is Kevin Nie, son of Mike. I just turned 19, but one of my proudest milestones happened a year earlier. When I was only 18, in the summer after high school, I became a first-time homeowner.

I bought a brand-new condominium in Manassas, Virginia, a city on the rise. Data centers are expanding everywhere, the Innovation Center is being built, and new shops and restaurants are arriving each month. It is not just a good neighborhood: it is a growth hub for the next decade. I did not just buy a home; I invested in the future.

Owning that home at 18 was surreal. Signing the papers, walking through my own place—it felt like stepping into adulthood. It was not only about owning property; it was about earning independence, maturity, and confidence.

2. Learning Responsibility Through Real Estate

Being a landlord at 18 taught me more about business, communication, and responsibility than any classroom could. I began managing the property myself, meeting potential renters, scheduling tours, and learning how to screen tenants. Most people were shocked to find out the landlord giving them a tour was a teenager. But once we talked, respect grew in both ways.

These experiences built my confidence. I realized that ownership is not about age; it is about mindset. Managing a property requires communication, patience, and problem-solving. I learned how to keep track of payments, handle maintenance calls, and treat it like a small business.

Every day of managing that condo helped me mature faster than I expected.

3. Why Starting Early Matters

Many people do not think about buying property until their 30s or 40s, but time is the greatest multiplier of wealth. When I bought my condo for around $480,000, the value rose to over $520,000 in just three months. That appreciation showed me the power of timing and action.

As my dad often says, *"Every year you wait is a year of compounding lost."* Real estate is one of the few assets that grows while you sleep—and if you start young, your growth window is much longer.

Cities like Manassas, VA, or Daytona Beach, FL (where my brother bought his first home), are perfect examples. They are fueled by technology, aerospace, and education industries—all magnets for long-term value. Investing in such areas early means catching the wave before it crests.

4. Beyond the 9-to-5: Building Multiple Income Streams

My dad likes to remind young people: "You cannot rely on one paycheck forever." Automation, AI, and corporate downsizing are changing everything. Even the biggest names, such as Amazon, Meta, Boeing, Oracle, and Intel, go through massive layoffs. That is why financial independence comes from having multiple income streams, not just one job.

Real estate is one of the best starting points for young professionals because it provides:

- Monthly rental income that covers the mortgage
- Equity growth as property values appreciate
- Tax benefits through depreciation and deductions
- Leverage through low-interest borrowing

The goal is simple: let your assets, not your working hours, compound.

5. The Four-Prong Investment Framework

To build stability, my dad introduced what we call the Four-Prong Strategy, a balance between growth, liquidity, and protection.

Category	Example Assets	Why It Matters
Real Estate	Rentals, Airbnb, VRBO	Leverage, appreciation, tax benefits
Life Insurance (Cash Value)	Whole Life, IUL	Tax-free loans, wealth protection
Brokerage Accounts	Stocks, index funds	Liquidity and passive growth; loan feature
Retirement Accounts	401(k), Roth IRA, HSA	Long-term, tax-free compounding

Diversification means you allocate roughly 25% to each bucket. That balance helps young investors grow wealth without overexposing themselves to one market.

6. The Buy–Borrow–Build (BBB) Mindset

This family wealth strategy, Buy, Borrow, and Build, is how we teach sustainable wealth creation.

1. Buy: acquire appreciating assets (real estate, index funds, or crypto).
2. Borrow: use those assets as collateral for low-interest credit lines.
3. Build: reinvest borrowed capital into income-producing and profit-generating opportunities. Interest may be deductible if you structure the loan correctly (the IRS interest tracing rule).

It is a cycle that allows you to grow without selling your best assets or triggering taxes.
For instance:

- Borrow from a HELOC or Securities-Backed Line of Credit to buy another property.
- Use a life insurance policy loan to fund a down payment instead of dipping into savings.
- Channel rental profits into a Roth IRA, HSA, or family foundation.

Lesson: Do not liquidate. Do leverage.

7. Lessons in Accountability and Legacy

My dad often says: no matter how much wealth we build, if our children do not learn responsibility, they won't appreciate it.

Starting young builds not only financial independence but character. It teaches discipline, accountability, and confidence: the foundation of generational wealth.

For me, this journey was not just about buying a condo. It was about learning how to build, manage, and protect something real. That one decision at 18 has shaped the way I think about adulthood, money, and freedom.

8. Final Reflection

Owning a property at 18 changed everything. It gave me a head start in both mindset and money management. If there is one message I would share with other young people, it is this: "Do not wait to 'feel ready.' You will grow *because* you act. Buy early, learn fast, and let your money work while you build your life."

Chapter 12

The Art of the Deal: Sign a Lease Contract Like a Pro

- By Mike and Kevin

"The best tenants are not found; they are earned through communication, compassion, and common sense."—*Mike*

Below is an interview between father and son. Readers will see how Mike uses the rental business to mentor Kevin in building wealth smartly.

Part I: How to Find the Right Tenant

Mike: Kevin, now that you have had a few months of managing the Manassas condo, what has been your biggest challenge so far?

Kevin: Finding the right tenant, hands down. You can list a property on Zillow or Apartments.com and get ten calls in the first week, but that does not mean ten qualified tenants. I have realized that finding a great tenant is 70% psychology and 30% paperwork.

Mike: That is a good way to put it. What is the first thing you look for when someone reaches out?

Kevin: Responsiveness. If someone takes three days to reply to a message or keeps canceling showings, that is a red flag. The best tenants are organized and polite from the first text. It is a preview of how they will pay rent and communicate later.

Mike: So, their communication style is your first screening tool.

Kevin: Exactly. I have met all kinds of applicants: families, single professionals, Ph.D. students, people relocating for work. The first impression matters. A young nurse who moved in to work at Inova Hospital had every document ready in a folder: credit report, pay stubs, references. She was so prepared that I approved her application before she even finished asking. Compare that with another applicant who arrived late and complained about the rent before seeing the property—that is a clear sign of future problems.

Mike: What about judging based on profession?

Kevin: That is where patterns emerge. In Manassas, most applicants work in data centers, construction, or healthcare. Those fields are stable, and the people are used to structure. They are usually reliable. I once rented it to a data-center engineer who had perfect credit but worked night shifts. So, I made sure the condo had blackout curtains. Anticipating lifestyle needs helps retain tenants.

Mike: That is smart. Small accommodation can turn a one-year tenant into a five-year one.

Kevin: Right. I also learned to stay emotionally neutral. Some applicants seem perfect: they say all the right things; but until that lease is signed and the deposit clears up, nothing is guaranteed. I once waited on a family who promised to move in "next week." They ghosted after a week of silence. Now, I keep two or three prospects active until the deal is final.

Mike: Always keep your pipeline full. That is what seasoned landlords learn. What about competition? The neighbor's house was listed around the same time.

Kevin: I focused on differentiation. I cleaned the place until it sparkled, added a scent diffuser, professional photos, and offered a small move-in bonus: a $100 Lowe's gift card for new tenants. It made a great impression—cost little, gained a lot.

Mike: That is great marketing. And showing empathy matters too. Once, we rented to a family who had just moved from overseas. They did not know U.S. credit systems, so we accepted a larger deposit instead of a high credit score. It built trust, and they turned out to be one of our best long-term tenants.

Kevin: That is true. Flexibility helps, especially when the person's situation makes sense. For example, one applicant had just graduated but had a co-signer with excellent credit. We took a chance, and she paid timely every month for two years.

Mike: It is about reading the *story* behind the numbers. A credit score of 650 does not always mean trouble; it might mean they just started their monthly payment habit with a few late credit card payments.

Kevin: And let us not forget patience. The market slows down sometimes. It is better to wait one more month for a great tenant than to rush and regret it. A bad tenant can cost thousands in damages or unpaid rent.

Mike: Exactly. Remember Sally, the tenant who has been with us for ten years? One reliable tenant like that can be worth $100,000 in saved headaches.

Kevin: Totally agree. I would rather have one stable renter than five fast turnovers.

Part II: How to Make the Right Lease Contract

Mike: Once you find the right tenant, the real test begins with the lease. A lease is not just a document; it is the constitution of your property. It defines expectations and prevents misunderstandings.

Kevin: I learned that every clause exists because some landlord, somewhere, got burned. Every late fee, every rule, every deposit requirement was written after a lesson.

1. The Application and Screening Process

Mike: Let us start at the beginning. What do you collect from applicants?

Kevin: A standard packet:

- Two most recent pay stubs

- Photo ID
- Credit report (preferably 700+)
- Contact for previous landlord
- Employment verification

I also include a rental questionnaire that asks lifestyle questions: pets, smoking, parking needs, number of occupants. It helps spot potential mismatches early.

Mike: That is thorough. You also started doing background checks, right?

Kevin: Yes, through TransUnion's Smart Move. It is inexpensive and gives credit, eviction, and criminal history. I once avoided a major headache when a background check revealed an applicant had two prior cases in another county.

Mike: Good save. And we both learned, always call prior landlords. Ask three simple questions:

1. Did they pay rent on time?
2. Did they maintain the property well?
3. Would you rent them again?

The third question is the truth test.

2. Deposits and Documentation

Mike: Deposits are both financial and psychological. They show commitment. In Virginia, leases longer than one year must accrue interest, which few landlords remember. And taking dated, timestamped photos of the property before move-in is essential.

Kevin: We also have tenants sign a "Condition Checklist." It lists every appliance and room condition before they move in. One photo can save a thousand arguments.

3. Pet Policy—Clarity Over Emotion

Kevin: Pets are emotional. Tenants love them; landlords worry about them. Our rule:

- Pet Fee (Non-Refundable): $150/month
- Pet Deposit (Refundable): $400, half returned if there is no damage

Mike: And do not mix pet deposits with the main security deposit. It causes confusion in accounting and refunds. Clarity is kindness.

4. Rent Payment and Late Fees

Kevin: We require rent through Zelle or PayPal. No checks, no cash. Digital payments create records and privacy.

Mike: And we charge $200 per overdue week. That might sound tough, but it creates accountability. Late rent becomes the exception, not the norm.

Kevin: One tenant once called to say they would be three days late. Because they communicated early, we waived the fee. Strict rules, but human flexibility—that is balance.

5. Renewal and Rent Adjustment

Mike: Our lease allows up to a 7% annual increase, but we rarely use it. A dependable tenant is worth more than inflation.

Kevin: I had a tenant whose rent stayed the same for three years, but she referred two new families to us. That is free marketing.

6. Repairs and Responsibility

Mike: Maintenance calls can drain a landlord. We added a "small repair co-pay" clause—if the fix costs under $50, the tenant handles it. It encourages independence.

Kevin: It works. Tenants stop calling for loose doorknobs or dead lightbulbs. They feel responsible and capable.

7. Move-In, Move-Out, and Mid-Term Inspections

Mike: We also do a walk-through inspection every three months. It is preventive maintenance, not surveillance. I once found a leaking sink early and saved hundreds in future damage.

Kevin: Tenants appreciate it too. It shows we care about the property's condition.

Real-Life Example: The Power of a Clear Lease

We once rented to a traveling nurse on a six-month term. She asked to leave early due to reassignment. Our contract included a "60-day early termination clause" — if she gave notice and paid a one-month termination fee, we would release her. Because the rule was written clearly, there were no disputes, and she even referred her replacement tenant to us.

Lesson: A clear lease turns conflict into cooperation.

Part 3: Key Takeaways

Finding the Right Tenant

- First impressions and communication matter as much as credit scores.
- Verify everything: employment, background, and references.
- Stay patient; never rush to fill a vacancy.
- Adapt to markets; offer incentives, maintain curb appeal, and stay professional.
- Treat good tenants as long-term partners, not short-term profits.

Making the Right Lease

- Screen carefully and keep written records.
- Separate all fees—security, pet, cleaning—to avoid confusion.
- Use electronic payments for security and documentation.
- Review laws in your state (e.g., deposit interest rules).

- Add repair co-pays and inspection schedules for accountability.
- Be firm on rules but fair in practice—human relationships come first.

Closing Reflection

Kevin: I used to think being a landlord was just about collecting rent. Now I see it is about building relationships and managing trust.

Mike: Exactly. The lease is the *blueprint of that trust.* Finding the right tenant and crafting the right contract are two sides of one coin: stability.

Kevin: And every time we refine the process, the property becomes not just an investment, but a classroom.

Mike: That is right. Real estate teaches life: patience, negotiation, empathy, and foresight. The rent is just the reward for mastering those lessons.

PART 3: FLY Beyond Real Estate

Chapter 13

FLY with Parents – How Parents Build Legacies Through College Rentals

- By Mike Nie

"*Do not just pay for your child's education; invest in it.*"—Mike Nie

Not every young person is ready or able to buy their own property while in college. Some lack credit history, income, or simply the interest in managing tenants and repairs. Yet parents can still play a major role in turning college housing into a long-term wealth and tax strategy. This chapter explores how parents can purchase campus rentals, lease them to their children and their children's friends, and use legitimate IRS-approved tools to build wealth tax-efficiently.

Working-class families are increasingly frustrated by the rising cost of college education (see chart below). The rapid disappearance of entry-level jobs due to the advent of AI has further intensified these concerns. Nevertheless, many families remain committed to using every available source of funding to ensure their children complete their education and successfully enter the job market.

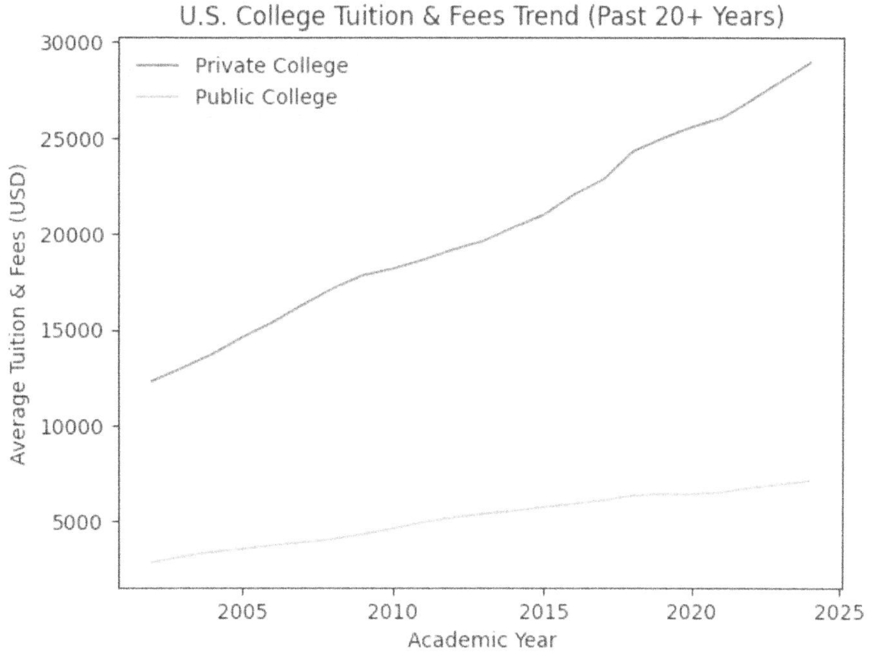

Source: National Center for Education Statistics (NCES), U.S. Department of Education. Chart created by author

Part I: Enter the campus rental market

When do parents step in? The central idea of this strategy is simple: parents buy the property, and the student rents from them. The arrangement becomes even more effective when the student's roommates pay rent too. This setup can transform college housing from a sunk cost into an appreciating asset.

There are several reasons parents might take this route instead of helping their child buy directly:

1. Credit or income limitations: The student or family might not qualify for a co-signed mortgage.
2. Lack of interest or time: Some students prefer to focus on academics and avoid landlord responsibilities.
3. Market constraints: The local market might be too expensive or competitive for a first-time buyer.

When any of these apply, parents can still achieve the same outcome by purchasing and managing the property themselves.

Strategy 1: Parent-Owned Campus Property

Parents can buy the property in their own name as an investment rental near their child's university, such as Princeton, Duke, Rice, Penn State, Ohio State, Michigan State, University of Maryland, Virginia Tech, or the University of Virginia.

FLY Term: "Kiddie House" is a nickname for a real-estate investment in which parents buy property near their child's college or university, not just as housing, but as a long-term wealth and tax strategy. Instead of paying dorm rent to the school, parents redirect that money into a property they own.

They can then rent to:

- Their child (at a fair market rent)
- The child's classmates or friends
- Parents who visit their children occasionally

This transforms what would normally be dorm or apartment rent into income-producing property, often with substantial tax advantages.

Strategy 2: Using a 1031 Exchange

For parents who already own investment in real estate, this is where the plan shines. A §1031 exchange allows them to sell an existing property and reinvest the proceeds into a new, like-kind property near the child's college, without paying capital gains or depreciation recapture taxes immediately.

For example: Mike owns a rental home in Vienna, Virginia that has appreciated significantly since COVID. He sells it, and within 180 days, closes on a townhouse near Virginia Tech, where his son attends college.

By reinvesting the full proceeds and keeping or increasing the loan amount, Mike defers taxes and gains a new property (or two) with rental potential during and after his child's college years.

If parents have two children at different colleges, they can even split the proceeds into two separate properties, if the combined purchase price and loan amount exceed the proceeds of the property sold.

Strategy 3: Leveraging the 529 Plan for Rent Payments

This is where financial planning and tax law meet creativity.

Under IRS Publication 970, funds from a 529 plan can be withdrawn tax-free for "qualified higher education expenses," including room and board for students enrolled at least half-time.

Most universities list room and board costs in the Cost of Attendance section of their websites, typically around $10,000–$12,000 for housing and $5,000–$6,000 for meals per year.

That means parents (and the parents of roommates) can:

- Withdraw 529 funds tax-free for room and board.
- Use those funds to pay rent to the parent-owned property.

This creates a legitimate, tax-free cash flow loop:

- Parents receive rent income.
- Children use qualified 529 funds to make payments.
- The family benefits from state tax deductions on 529 contributions and tax-free withdrawals.

To stay compliant, ensure:

- A written lease agreement is in place.
- The rental amount matches market rates.
- Payments are documented with a clear audit trail (e.g., rent paid monthly from child's bank account to parent's rental bank account).

Strategy 4: Hiring a Child as a Property Manager

Parents can also employ their child to manage the property: a real job that includes handling tenant communication, repairs, and inspections.

- The child earns a reasonable management fee, which parents can deduct on Schedule E as a rental expense.
- The parents effectively shift income from their tax bracket (32% or higher at the federal level) to their children, with a much lower tax bracket.
- The child files his or her own tax return, and reports the 1099 NEC income on Schedule C, allowing them to deduct expenses such as:
    - Cell phone use
    - Mileage for errands

    - Small home office expenses
    - Meals during management duties

If the parent qualifies as a real estate professional, the management costs may directly offset active income. If not, the losses can be deferred until the property is sold, still creating long-term benefit.

Strategy 5: Deducting Business Travel

Because the property is an active rental, travel to visit and inspect it can also be tax-deductible. Trips to see the student become legitimate business expenses, covering:

- Airfare or mileage
- Lodging during visits
- Meals while managing or maintaining property

These deductions reduce taxable income while also making family visits financially efficient.

The Full Circle of Smart Planning

When done right, this model turns an ordinary family expense into a multi-layered financial engine:

1. Investment appreciation in a university-area property.
2. Tax-deferred gains via 1031 exchanges.
3. Tax-free rent payments through 529 plans.
4. Deductible expenses for management and travel.
5. Income shifting to children through reasonable pay.
6. Bonus depreciation (100%) and cost segregation available under OBBB.

In essence, money flows from one pocket to another—but in a fully IRS-compliant and tax-optimized way.

The strategy blends education, real estate, and family finance into a single, powerful framework for intergenerational wealth.

Part II: Exit the campus rental market

The second part of this chapter explores how parents can purchase campus rentals, lease them to their children and their children's friends, and use legitimate IRS-approved tools to build wealth tax-efficiently—and eventually, how to exit these investments strategically after graduation.

Strategy of the Exit Plan: Transitioning After Graduation

Eventually, the time will come when your child graduates and moves on to a new city. What happens next?

1. Continue Renting the Property

If the college remains strong with steady enrollment and funding, simply hire a local property manager and continue renting to Ph.D. students or faculty. After four or more years, the property will likely have strong cash flow and appreciation, turning into a long-term passive income source.

2. 1031 Exchange to Follow Your Child

Parents can also execute another 1031 exchange, sell the campus property, and purchase a new rental near the child's job location: Chicago, Austin, or Miami. This move defers taxes again while bringing the assets closer to family and potential grandchildren. Over time, one property can become two, then four, multiplying wealth while continually deferring taxes.

3. Sell After Retirement for a Low-Tax Exit

If you prefer to simplify, selling after retirement can be surprisingly efficient. In retirement, your tax bracket is likely lower, so capital gains and depreciation recapture taxes are minimized (e.g., 24%). By timing the sale strategically, you can enjoy the appreciation and pay less tax, closing the loop on a powerful, multi-year tax-efficient investment.

From a family perspective, this is more than a property. It is a financial classroom. It teaches children how wealth is created, managed, and eventually transferred. Do not just pay for your child's education; invest in it.

Chapter 14

The Exit Plan

"*It is not how much money you make, but how much money you keep, how hard it works for you, and how many generations you keep it for.*"—Robert Kiyosaki, author of *Rich Dad Poor Dad*

When you are 18 and just beginning college, buying your first property feels like the ultimate victory. You live in one room, rent out the others, and suddenly you are earning income while your classmates pay rent elsewhere. But every investment eventually comes to a crossroads: what happens *after* graduation?

This chapter explores the exit strategies young investors can use once they have finished school and are ready to move on to the next phase of life.

The Case of Chris in Daytona Beach, Florida

Take Chris, for example, a college student in Daytona Beach, Florida. At 18, he purchased a brand-new townhouse near campus. By renting out the extra rooms to classmates, he covered the mortgage, earned cash flow, and built equity while living for free.

Now, four years later, Chris is graduating. His question: "What should I do with my property now?"

Like many young real estate investors, he faces three possible paths.

Option 1: Keep Renting It Out

Chris's first thought was simple: keep the property. He could hire a local property manager to handle tenants and maintenance while he moves to another city for work. This approach allows him to:

- Continue generating passive rental income
- Deduct travel expenses when returning to Florida for property visits (yes, even when visiting his college pals too!)
- Retain ownership of a high-potential asset in a desirable state

As Chris put it, "Who can say no to Florida?"

Holding the property means staying in the game—the mortgage continues to be paid down by tenants, and the property may appreciate over time. For college-area homes, there is always a steady stream of potential renters: students, faculty, and university staff.

Chris lists ten reasons for keeping his rental:

#	Reason to Keep the House	Explanation / Investor Advantage
1	World-Famous Beaches	More than 23 miles of drivable white-sand beaches attract millions of tourists annually, ensuring strong rental occupancy.
2	Daytona 500 & Year-Round Events	Major events like the Daytona 500, Rolex 24, and Bike Week drive recurring rental surges and premium pricing.
3	No State Income Tax	Florida's zero state income tax boosts net yields and after-tax profits for property owners.
4	Low Cost of Ownership	Property taxes and insurance are generally lower than in other coastal cities, improving ROI.
5	Proximity to Embry-Riddle Aeronautical University (ERAU)	ERAU, Bethune-Cookman, and Daytona State College supply steady student rental demand near Clyde Morris Blvd and LPGA Blvd.
6	LPGA International & Golf Tourism	LPGA International community and golf tourism attract affluent short-term renters beyond motorsports season.
7	Growing Infrastructure & Accessibility	Expanding Daytona Beach International Airport, I-95/I-4 connectivity, and Brightline rail boost tenant and visitor access.
8	Redevelopment & Economic Growth	Downtown and beachfront revitalization projects like Riverfront Esplanade and Tanger Outlets increase property value.
9	Year-Round Climate	Mild winters and warm summers ensure strong year-round rental demand and lower vacancy risk.
10	Diversified Rental Demand	Multiple tenant bases—students, retirees, professionals, and tourists—stabilize income and reduce market risk. One hour to Disneyworld, Orlando.

Option 2: Sell the Property

The second option is to sell the house and capture the gains. But selling an investment property brings tax considerations.

Because Chris lived in one room while renting out others, he qualifies for a partial §121 exclusion, up to a portion of $250,000 in capital gains for the portion used as his primary residence. The remainder of the property, the rented rooms, triggers depreciation recapture at the lower of marginal tax bracket and 25%.

However, because Chris's income in his first job will likely be modest, the capital gains rate may still be low. Selling can provide liquidity to pay down student loans or fund a down payment on his next home.

Option 3: Execute a 1031 Exchange

The third path is the §1031 exchange, i.e., selling the property and rolling the proceeds into another investment property without paying capital gains tax immediately.

For example, Chris could sell his Florida home and buy another rental property closer to his job in Chicago or Austin, deferring taxes while upgrading to a property that aligns with his new career and lifestyle. This move allows compounding wealth through *tax deferral*, rather than paying Uncle Sam early.

Other Creative Exits

Location matters. Properties near universities like Penn State, Virginia Tech, or Embry-Riddle are ideal for flexible rental strategies. After graduation, a young owner might:

- Rent long-term to faculty or staff
- Transition to short-term rentals during special events: NCAA game weekends, parent visits, or graduation
- Use cost segregation to accelerate depreciation and shelter income

Platforms like Airbnb and VRBO also make property management easier. Hosts are protected by built-in liability coverage, and there is less worry about long-term eviction issues.

The Smart Exit Mindset

Whether you sell, hold, or exchange, the goal is not just to "exit"; it is to evolve. Real estate ownership in college is more than a financial win; it is a foundation for lifelong wealth-building habits.

The best investors do not view graduation as the finish line. They see it as a pivot point — from active student-landlord to strategic investor.

Chris's story shows that a smart exit plan can be just as powerful as the first down payment.

The Case of Kevin in Manassas, Virginia

Kevin bought his first rental home in Manassas, Virginia when he was 19, drawn by the region's steady job market, proximity to Washington D.C., and access to the Northern Virginia data-center corridor. What began as a small family duplex now sits less than five miles from NVIDIA's new AI Factory Research Center, a project transforming Prince William County into one of America's fastest-growing tech economies.

As Kevin's professional career expands, he faces the same decision Chris once did: keep, sell, or exchange?

Option 1: Keep Renting It Out

Kevin's first instinct is to *hold*. Northern Virginia's tech expansion means growing demand for housing, from engineers, contractors, and supporting industries. Keeping the property allows him to:

- Benefit from rising rents as AI-related employment surges.

- Depreciate the property annually to offset W-2 or business income.
- Enjoy proximity to D.C. without the high property taxes of Fairfax or Arlington.

Top 10 Reasons to Keep the Manassas Rental

Holding means **leveraging Northern Virginia's economic boom** while tenants pay down the mortgage.

#	Reason to Keep the House	Investor Advantage
1	NVIDIA AI Factory Research Center	Creates hundreds of high-paying jobs; rental demand and appreciation.
2	Data Center Alley Expansion	Amazon, Microsoft, Google operate nearby; steady tenant pipeline of tech workers.
3	Close to Washington D.C.	Commute-friendly location (walking to Virginia Railway Express (VRE) station) draws federal and contractor tenants.
4	Energy and Infrastructure Investments	Dominion Energy and Emerald AI projects modernize the grid, boosting property values.
5	Strong School Districts and Safety	Attractive for families and long-term leases.
6	Historic and Cultural Appeal	Civil War heritage + growing arts facilities such as Jiffy Lube Live enhance tourism and Airbnb potential.
7	Low Inventory, High Demand	Limited new housing supply keeps vacancy rates below 4%.
8	Transportation Growth Hub	VRE commuter rail, I-66 expansion, and Manassas Airport upgrades support mobility.
9	Virginia's Business-Friendly Policies	The pro-growth environment encourages tech and real-estate investment.
10	Diversified Tenant Base	Engineers, government staff, college students, and families stabilize income.

Option 2: Sell and Reallocate

Kevin could also sell to lock in appreciation. Property values in Manassas have climbed sharply since NVIDIA's announcement. Selling might allow him to:

- Capture equity to reinvest in higher-cash-flow markets (e.g., Florida or Texas).
- Pay minimal long-term capital-gains taxes if offset by prior depreciation or loss carryforwards.
- Free capital for diversification into stocks, start-ups, or new construction.

However, selling triggers recapture tax on depreciation and possible capital-gains liability. A carefully timed sale, possibly split over two tax years, can minimize the impact.

Option 3: Use a §1031 Exchange

Kevin can execute a §1031 exchange, swapping his Manassas property for a higher-yield rental elsewhere while deferring taxes. He could:

- Exchange into a multi-unit property in his future job city.
- Partner with family through a family LLC or trust for generational wealth transfer.
- Continue building equity and cash flow without losing momentum to taxes.

Other Creative Exits

- Convert to corporate short-term housing for tech-contractors.
- Lease to federal agencies or defense contractors (GSA leases offer stability).
- Use cost segregation + bonus depreciation to offset active income.
- Create a joint venture with family, reinvesting gains into new developments.

The Smart Exit Mindset

For Kevin, an exit is not just about cashing out—it is about positioning for the next decade. Manassas is no longer only a suburb; it is part of America's AI innovation corridor.

Whether he keeps, sells, or exchanges, Kevin's plan will reflect the same principle that guided Chris in Florida: "Use every property as a springboard, not an endpoint, in the journey to financial freedom."

Chapter 15

Leave Your Real Property to Your Loved Ones

- By Mike and Kevin

"Trust is a Must." – Ryan Avery, the 2012 Toastmasters World Champion of Public Speaking

"*Love ended in tears, but the checkbook dried them.*" – Margaret of Valois, French Princess

Why Trust Planning Matters

Now that both Kevin and Chris own their first homes, along with brokerage accounts, retirement plans, and business interests, one essential question remains: How do you protect and pass on what you have built?

The answer lies in five words: Build a living trust early.

A living trust does not just decide *who* receives your property after death; it defines *how* your values, purpose, and discipline continue. Without one, your assets can be tied up in probate courts for months or even fall into the wrong hands.

In our family, we view trust not as a legal document, but as a love letter wrapped in structure. It protects your spouse, your children, and your mission, while keeping your affairs private and efficient.

The Family Conversation: "Dad, do i really need a trust?"

Kevin: Dad, I am only 19. I just bought my condo and started investing. Do I really need a trust already?

Mike: That is exactly when you need one most. Trust is not just for the wealthy; it is for anyone who wants control. Life moves fast: you will have tenants, a business, maybe a wife or kids one day. You cannot predict the future, but you can prepare for it.

Kevin: So, what happens if someone does not have a trust?

Mike: The court steps in. That means lawyers, public hearings, and delays. A revocable living trust lets you *skip probate* entirely. The moment something happens, your designated trustee—usually a parent, spouse, or sibling, who can manage the assets smoothly, privately, and immediately.

Kevin: Okay, so it is like a "backup pilot" for your financial life.

Mike: Exactly. You are still captain while you are alive. But if something happens, the co-pilot already knows the flight plan.

Trusts, Marriage, and Prenuptial Wisdom

Trust planning becomes even more vital when marriage enters the picture. When two people marry, they merge not only their hearts but also their liabilities and inheritances.

A well-designed trust and a prenuptial agreement are not signs of distrust; they are acts of clarity and mutual respect. They protect both partners' pre-marital assets and define how property will be managed or inherited if life takes an unexpected turn.

For example:

- If Kevin marries Helen, who brings her own savings and a small business, a trust allows them to separate business assets from joint property, avoiding confusion later.
- If Chris has children someday, his trust can stipulate that his property passes to them directly, or into a "family education fund" to pay for college.
- If one spouse remarries, a properly structured trust can prevent children from the first marriage from being unintentionally disinherited.

Mike: A prenuptial agreement and a living trust are like seatbelts. You hope you never need them, but they protect everyone in case of turbulence.

Kevin: So, it is not about lack of trust; it is about keeping peace and clarity.

Mike: Exactly. Love builds relationships; documents protect it.

Kevin, using publicly available information, found and listed successful and unsuccessful stories about ending marriage and prenuptial arrangements.

Smart and rich business people often make costly mistakes

1. Jeff Bezos & MacKenzie Scott

- People magazine (2019) reported that they had no prenuptial agreement. When Jeff Bezos, Amazon's founder, married MacKenzie Scott, he was not yet a billionaire. By the time of their divorce in 2019, Amazon was worth hundreds of billions.
- Outcome: The couple settled amicably, but without a prenup, MacKenzie received a sizable portion of Jeff's Amazon holdings, one of the largest divorce settlements in history.
- Lesson: Early marriages before major success should still be planned. A fair prenup protects both spouses from unintentional windfalls and resentment.

Source: https://people.com/movies/jeff-bezos-wife-mackenzie-dont-have-prenup/

2. Elon Musk & Justine Musk

- *Forbes* (2025) reported that they did not sign a prenup but signed a post-nuptial agreement. When Elon married his first wife, Justine, he was a rising tech entrepreneur but not yet the Tesla-SpaceX icon. They had multiple children together and no prenuptial agreement.

- Outcome: Their 2008 divorce resulted in a large financial settlement (reportedly millions in cash, alimony, and child support). The emotional strain was severe; Justine later wrote candidly about the turmoil and lack of clarity over finances.
- Lesson: Even brilliant innovators can overlook legal structure. A prenup does not limit love—it clarifies expectations before success changes everything.

Source: https://www.forbes.com/sites/kerryadolan/2025/04/18/what-elon-musks-first-wife-isnt-even-close-to-being-a-billionaire/

3. Bill Gates & Melinda French Gates

- They married in 1994. Public reporting suggests they did not have a prenuptial agreement.
- Their divorce announced in 2021 involved tens of billions of dollars in shared assets, often cited as one of the largest divorces because of the absence of a prenup.
- Lesson in the context: even for mega-wealth couples, skipping the prenup can lead to high complexity and large payouts.

Source: https://www.wilmingtontrust.com/library/article/reprint--lessons-learned-from-the-bill-and-melinda-gates-divorce

Smart planning ensures a stronger marriage.

1. Rupert Murdoch & Wendi Deng

- Based on a *Guardian* report (2013), when media mogul Rupert Murdoch (then 68) married Wendi Deng (then 30) in 1999, he was already one of the richest men in the world.
- Prenup Strategy: Murdoch had an exceptionally detailed prenuptial and postnuptial agreement. It clearly separated his vast holdings in News Corp and Fox, ensuring that Deng would not gain controlling interests or voting power in his media empire.
- Outcome: When the couple divorced in 2013, the split was swift, civil, and private—with no disruption to Murdoch's companies or heirs. Deng received luxury properties and personal assets but no ownership stake in the Murdoch media businesses.

Lesson: A strong prenup safeguards both love and legacy. Murdoch's was a masterclass in protecting corporate control while ensuring personal fairness.Source: https://www.theguardian.com/media/2013/jun/14/rupert-murdoch-divorce-money-wendi-deng

2. Michael Douglas & Catherine Zeta-Jones

- Background based on a family law firm post (Frost & Beck, P.C.):When they married in 2000, Douglas was a Hollywood veteran worth tens of millions; Zeta-Jones was a successful actor in her own right.
- Prenup Strategy: Their agreement was mutually beneficial and precise—Catherine reportedly receives $2.8 million per year of marriage if they divorce, plus a $5 million fidelity clause in her favor if Douglas is ever unfaithful.
- Outcome: Despite temporary separation in 2013, the marriage endured. The prenup's fairness and transparency are credited with reducing tension during their break.
- Lesson: A well-balanced prenup can protect both spouses while encouraging accountability, not mistrust.

Source: https://www.frostbecklaw.com/blog/2013/june/lifestyle-clauses-becoming-a-common-part-of-pren/

3. Beyoncé & Jay-Z

- Background based on ABA Journal run by American Bar Association: Both were already wealthy stars when they married in 2008. Their combined net worth now exceeds multi-billion dollars.
- Prenup Strategy: Their reported agreement includes carefully structured financial clauses tied to years of marriage and family milestones:
  - $5 million to Beyoncé for each child born.
  - A share of Jay-Z's estate after a set number of marriage years.
  - Individual ownership of pre-marital intellectual property (songs, royalties, trademarks).
- Outcome: The arrangement encouraged mutual respect for their independent brands while aligning family goals. It is a model of how two high-achievers can protect their art, assets, and privacy.
- Lesson: A smart prenup is not about division—it is about clarity, creativity, and long-term peace between equals.

Source: https://www.businessinsider.com/surprising-prenups-americas-richest-couples-2017-11

Disclaimer: Dollar amounts and details of these marriages (or divorces) were obtained from public sources. Please visit these sites (and corresponding sources) if you want to do more research in this subject.

How a Trust Works

Creating trust is like opening a company for your personal life. You (the Grantor) place your assets inside a legal entity called a Living Trust. You remain the Trustee, in full control, but you also name Successor Trustees who take over if you become incapacitated or pass away.

When you die, your property transfers automatically to your chosen beneficiaries—without going through court or probate.

Common assets placed into a trust include:

- Your home and property
- Brokerage, Roth IRA, or 401(k) accounts
- Checking or business accounts
- LLC ownership shares
- Life insurance or crypto holdings

It may cost us $1,500 - $2,500 to design a set of documents via an estate attorney. If the assets are plain vanilla and ownership structure is simple, it may be economical and efficient to use a DIY approach.

Provider	Website	Key Pricing/Packages
Trust & Will	trustandwill.com	Will: $199 individual / $299 couple. Trust: $499 individual / $599 couple + $39/year updates.

Provider	Website	Key Pricing/Packages
LegalZoom	legalzoom.com	Will from $149; Trust packages $399+ (varies by state and features).
GoodTrust	goodtrust.com	Estate-plan bundle $149 one-time; annual updates $39/year.
Rocket Lawyer	rocketlawyer.com	Free will template option; subscription $39.99/month for full access.
FreeWill	freewill.com	Free will online (basic coverage).
LawDepot	lawdepot.com	1-Year Pro subscription: $199/year unlimited docs.

If you have complicated assets and are involved in a blended family, a state-registered estate attorney may be a better option than the DIY model.

Below is estate planning done by Kevin, and with father's help. I use Kevin as an example to demonstrate how his assets will be distributed if, in a one out of a million chance, he passes away before me.

The Kevin Nie Revocable Living Trust

I, Kevin Ding Nie, presently of Fairfax, Virginia, (the "Grantor") declare and make this revocable living trust (the "Living Trust"). This Living Trust will be known as The Kevin Ding Nie Revocable Living Trust.

Trust Purpose

1. This Living Trust is created for the benefit of the Beneficiaries to ensure they are well provided for after the death of the Grantor; however, during the lifetime of the Grantor, the interests of the Grantor will be considered primary and superior to the interests of the Beneficiaries. With this purpose, the primary asset management goal for this Living Trust will be the protection of the value of the Property. The secondary asset management goal for this Living Trust is to generate income and growth at a reasonable risk.

Trustee

2. During the lifetime of the Grantor, and while the Grantor is not Incapacitated, the Grantor will serve as the primary trustee (the "Primary Trustee") and the Acting Trustee of this Living Trust.

3. Upon the death of or during the Incapacity of the Grantor, then Mike Nie, CPA will serve as the Acting Trustee of this Living Trust.

If the Grantor should recover such that they are no longer considered Incapacitated then the Grantor will resume their control of the management of this Living Trust.

Beneficiaries

4. Upon the death of the Grantor, the following individual(s) will comprise the beneficiaries (the "Beneficiaries") of this Living Trust:

a. The residuary beneficiary, **SMART Life Family Foundation** of Vienna, Virginia; and

b. Any heir or issue of those beneficiaries that is entitled to a benefit under this Living Trust in the place of any then deceased beneficiary.

Ownership of Property

5. The Grantor presently owns property (the "Property") as described in Schedule A.

Schedule A (As of 2025 and Updated Annually Thereafter)

The Grantor (Kevin NIE) assigns, conveys and delivers to this Living Trust all the rights, title and interest, tangible, or intangible, to the following properties, real or personal:

1. Capital One Checking Account (3615888888)
2. Vanguard Roth IRA (8810 888888)
3. Charles Schwab Brokerage account (1888888)
4. Charles Schwab Coverdell ESA (888888)
5. Gym and Home Operator LLC
6. 401(k) plan maintained under employer, Smart Life Family Foundation (Plan number 888888)
7. Wells Fargo Gym Operator LLC business banking account: Routing 051488888 Checking 9019888888
8. Health Savings Account at Fidelity Account (257888888)
9. Crypto account at Fidelity Account Brokerage (323888888)
10. Primary residence: 6666 Michael Jackson Avenue, Manassas VA 22222

SIGNED AND DECLARED by Kevin Nie on the ________ day of ________________,

________ to be the Testator's Last Will, in our presence, at ____________________________, Virginia, who at the Testator's request and in the presence of the Testator and of each other, all being present at the same time, have signed our names as witnesses.

Witness #1 Signature __________________________	Witness #2 Signature __________________________
Witness #1 Name (Please Print) __________________________	Witness #2 Name (Please Print) __________________________
Witness #1 Street Address __________________________	Witness #2 Street Address __________________________
Witness #1 City, State __________________________	Witness #2 City, State __________________________

PART 4: Expert Interviews

Chapter 16

A Mother Teaching Her Sons about Love and Independence: Interview With Yuqin Ding

"*Be your kids' role model, not their nanny.*" – Yuqin Ding

About Yuqin Ding, Chris' and Kevin's mother:

Yuqin Ding is an accomplished professional with deep roots in both higher education and life science industries. After earning her undergraduate and master's degrees in China, she moved to the United States to pursue her second master's degree in information systems prior to building a career spanning software development and business management.

Yuqin combines meticulous financial discipline with compassionate leadership — qualities that enabled her to prepare her two sons, Chris and Kevin, for early financial independence and homeownership well before their 20th birthday.

She believes that parenting is less about protecting and telling, and more about guiding and modeling. Yuqin brings this philosophy into every facet of her life: at work, in her community, and at home.

1. Leading by Example

Mike: Yuqin, you've raised two incredible young men—Chris and Kevin—both under the age of 25, and both financially independent homeowners. What do you think made the biggest difference in their upbringing?

Yuqin: The most important thing is to *show them*, not just *tell them*. Children watch everything. If they see me working hard, keeping things clean, exercising, and managing money carefully, they learn that naturally.

When they were young, I didn't give long lectures. I just lived the way I wanted them to live. I kept a routine: I'd go to work, cook, do laundry, and be available for exercise. They saw consistency, learning to be steady rather than perfect. They learned that success is never sudden, but built from small, repeated healthy habits.

Sometimes parents think their kids don't notice, but they do. If you stay up late scrolling on your phone, they think that's normal. If you're responsible and organized, that becomes their normal. I always tell parents: don't just *say* discipline, *be* disciplined. Be your kids' role model, not their nanny.

Parental Insight: Children mirror consistency more than words. Live the habits you wish to see—order, discipline, health, gratitude. *Your routine is your child's silent teacher.*

2. Building a Financial Mindset

Mike: How did you help Chris and Kevin understand money so young?

Yuqin: I tried to make financial discussions part of our everyday life. When we went shopping, I didn't just buy. I compared. I explained sales, discounts, and quality. I never said, "We can't afford it." I said, "Let's decide if it's worth it." That simple change builds reasoning instead of fear.

From middle school, I gave them small allowances but didn't monitor every cent. I let them make choices, sometimes even bad ones. If they spent too fast, they learned the consequences themselves. I didn't bail them out. I wanted them to *feel* the result of poor decisions while it was still relatively minor.

By high school, they were saving. When they wanted something expensive, they learned to wait. They understood delayed gratification. The best rewards take time.

Parental Insight:
Financial literacy starts early, and emotionally. Replace "no" with "let's evaluate." Teach them to measure value, not price. *A child who learns to wait will one day afford anything.*

3. Chris Buys His First Home at 18

Mike: Chris bought his first house at 18 while attending Embry-Riddle University. That's almost unheard of. Were you nervous about letting him take that on?

Yuqin: Of course I was nervous! At 18, he was still in college, and buying a home sounded like too much. I worried it would distract him or become a burden. But when he explained his plan—how he'd manage tenants, handle maintenance, and live responsibly—I realized he wasn't just buying property. He was building a future.

When I visited his home, I was stunned. It was so clean and organized. When I left a paper towel on the counter, he would pick it up immediately. He had routines, checklists, and rental documents. That's when I knew this was a maturity lesson more than an investment.

He wasn't just learning about mortgages; he was learning about accountability. Every repair, every rent payment, every phone call with a tenant molded him into a disciplined adult.

Parental Insight: Big responsibilities accelerate growth. Trust your child's initiative if they've earned it. The journey itself is education. *When you hand a child responsibility, you hand them confidence.*

4. Kevin's Journey to Independence

Mike: Way to go, Chris! Now let's shift gears to Kevin, the younger one. When Kevin decided to buy his townhouse in Manassas, VA, did you feel different than Chris?

Yuqin: Yes, by then, I was calmer. Chris had proven that it could work, so I felt more confident letting Kevin try. But Kevin is different—he's gentler, more easygoing. I wondered if he'd manage tenants well. To my surprise, he grew up overnight. He stepped out of the shadow of his elder brother.

He learned how to talk with renters politely but firmly, how to fix small issues, and how to present himself as a young professional. I watched his confidence grow over months, to the point where he even told me, "Mom, I'm not buying Lululemon anymore." That line made me laugh, but it showed his priorities had shifted. Before owning it, he liked comfort and brand names. But now, he valued stability. He learned that every dollar had a purpose.

Parental Insight: Responsibility changes perspective. True financial maturity happens when *wants* turn into *goals. A mortgage teaches discipline faster than a lecture ever can.*

5. Teaching Independence Through Trust

Mike: A lot of parents hesitate to give their kids so much responsibility. What's your philosophy on that?

Yuqin: parents love their children too much sometimes. They want to protect their children from failure, but that protection can make them weak and risk averse. I believe in *guided independence.* Let them try things, even if they make mistakes. They're stronger than we think.

If something goes wrong, I'm there to advise—not to fix. That's how they learn to solve problems. When Chris had tenant issues or Kevin had maintenance headaches, I didn't rush to rescue them. I asked questions, helped them think, and let them handle them.

Sometimes the best help is confidence—letting your children know you believe they can do it.

Parental Insight: Don't mistake love for rescue. Confidence grows from trial, not comfort. *If you never let them fall, they'll never learn how to land.*

6. Planning Beyond Parenthood

Mike: You've spoken about planning, such as living trusts, living will, and medical power of attorney. Why is that important to you?

Yuqin: Because life is unpredictable. If something happens to me, I want my children and my loved ones to know exactly what to do. Not every family member is financially or legally savvy.

So, I always recommend having a living trust with a clear successor trustee**.** Choose someone you deeply trust, someone younger and financially capable. The goal is not just to protect money, but to protect peace.

I've seen families disintegrate due to distrust and disagreement over asset distribution. That's why structure matters—clear records, titles, instructions. You don't want chaos. You want continuity.

Parental Insight: Estate planning is part of parenting. It ensures the lessons you taught live beyond you. *A well-written plan is the quietest form of love.*

7. Raising with Balance and Purpose

Mike: Beyond money and success, what core values did you want to pass down?

Yuqin: Balance, kindness, gratitude. You can be successful and still be unhappy if you lose those three. I always told Chris and Kevin that kindness costs nothing. When you're blessed, share. When you rise, lift someone else.

Every person has a calling bigger than money. Even if you're busy or tired, find something meaningful: help the poor, support education, or protect animals. That's what gives life value.

Parental Insight: Teach your children that wealth is only worthwhile when it benefits others. Gratitude and giving protect success from arrogance. *A rich heart makes money humble.*

8. The Legacy Mindset

Mike: If you could summarize your parenting philosophy in one sentence, what would it be?

Yuqin: Live the life you want your children to admire—because they're always watching. You can't expect them to be disciplined if you aren't. You can't ask them to be generous if you're selfish. Kids copy who you are, not what you say.

If parents live with purpose and balance, their children will do the same. That's the best legacy we can give—not money, but mindset.

Parental Insight: Your example becomes your children's compass. Lead with purpose and they'll never lose direction. *The best inheritance isn't a house. It's a heart of discipline and gratitude.*

Final Thoughts

Listening to Yuqin reminded me that true teaching happens long before any formal lesson. She didn't lecture; she lived. Her sons watched, absorbed, and followed. Through every chore, every budget, every healthy meal, she was quietly building the habits that now shape Chris and Kevin's adult lives.

In the end, Yuqin Ding didn't just raise homeowners. She raised visionaries with humility, purpose, and self-control. Her parenting wasn't about producing success stories. It was about producing good men: grounded, grateful, and ready to give.

Chapter 17

The Power of Starting Young: Interview with Dr. Maxwell Adekoje

"Most people die at 25 but are not buried until 85. Do not die early. Stay alive inside. Keep growing, dreaming, and building."—Dr. Maxwell Adekoje, Author of *Just Eat the Worm*

About the expert: Maxwell's life is a story of hard work, endurance, and inspiration. A great adventure underwritten by perpetual self-belief, and readiness to always improve alongside working with others in a team to achieve shared goals. He is a successful real estate agent with Goldmine Realty Group, LLC based in Virginia.

Born in Nigeria, Max first traveled to the USA as a young man with $20 seeking the American dream. Like so many who began their working life and career in a new land, the first ventures in Max's career in the United States were not particularly successful. Ultimately, he suffered a few failures, but each one served to grow his ambition and sense of belief in the promise of the United States. He soon gleaned all that his adopted country could offer to him as a businessperson and professional. The American Dream became his reality.

He authored a book, *Just Eat The Worm: Six Great Strategies That Will Help You Earn More And Never Waste A Crisis*, available on Amazon.com.

Mike: Dr. Maxwell, thank you so much for joining me today. Before we get into the details, can you briefly introduce yourself? I know you have built a successful real estate agent mentorship business and own several properties. From your experience, why is owning real estate early in life so important for young people?

Dr. Maxwell: The greatest point is investing in your future, *early*. Most people wait until they are older to start, and by then it is often too late. I remember meeting a 68-year-old flight attendant who could not retire because she still had a mortgage to pay off. That moment changed how I thought about money and property. Starting young gives you time for your investments to grow and eventually work for you.

If I decided not to work today, my rental income would cover all my bills. One of my first condos cost $70,000, it is worth $300,000 now and still generates rent. That is why I tell young people: plant the seeds early, and your future self will thank you.

Mike: That is powerful. There is a popular saying I love: *"The best time to start was yesterday. The second-best time is today."*

Dr. Maxwell: Exactly! When people ask, "When should I buy a house?" my answer is always—*today*. Timing is everything.

Mike: I saw this with Kevin. We bought a property for $470,000, and the same model is now selling for $520,000. We did not even lift a finger—timing really does matter.

Dr. Maxwell: It does. And when interest rates drop, more people can afford homes, which pushes prices even higher. So, the earlier you start, the better positioned you are.

1. Book Smart vs. Street Smart

Mike: I tell my students, "School teaches book smarts, but success demands street smarts." Would you agree?

Dr. Maxwell: Absolutely. Book knowledge is good, but street smart is essential. You cannot learn negotiation, cultural awareness, or emotional intelligence from a textbook. I even learned bits of other languages to connect better with clients. When people trust you, they want to work with you. Relationships are everything in real estate.

Mike: I love that. When you speak English, you speak to their ears; when you speak their language, you speak to their heart.

Dr. Maxwell: Exactly! That is how you build connection and trust, the foundation of every great deal.

2. Building Strong Families and Strong Futures

Mike: Parents cannot outsource everything to schools. They must lead from the front. Broken families often lead to broken discipline. That is one reason I am authoring this book: to help young people find purpose and build wealth.

Dr. Maxwell: You are right. Wealth is not just money; it is mindset. We must train our children to think differently, to move from poverty thinking to wealth creation. Real estate can be their bridge toward their financial dreamland.

3. Success Traits for Young Investors

Mike: You have mentored many young people. What three traits do you see in those who become successful?

Dr. Maxwell: First, *consistency*. Many say they'll take action, but never follow through.
Second, *independence from school structure*. School teaches us to get a job, get paid, and get a mortgage. That is fine, but you also need to build additional income streams. And third, *focus*. In real estate,

there is no glass ceiling. Your income depends on your effort. I tell my students, "It only works when you work." Real estate is not just buying and selling—there are so many avenues: short-term rentals, buy, rehab, rent, refinance, and repeat (BRRR), or property management. It is a lifelong wealth builder.

Mike: That is true. I often tell my students that AI may replace many jobs, but not real estate. People will always need a place to live.

Dr. Maxwell: Exactly. AI can replace knowledge jobs, but it cannot replace property ownership. Real estate is real, tangible, and lasting. You cannot outsource it to a machine.

4. Mindset and Motivation

Mike: You mentioned motivation. I have noticed many people hate their jobs. How does that mindset affect success?

Dr. Maxwell: My mentor Les Brown said something profound—most heart attacks happen on Monday mornings. People wake up dreading the week because they hate their jobs. That is not living a meaningful life.

In real estate, I get joy from helping families buy their first home. The excitement on their faces — that is self-actualization. You are not just earning; you are impacting lives.

5. Lessons from "Just Eat The Worm"

Mike: You authored a book *Just Eat The Worm*, a great read. Do those principles apply to real estate investment?

Dr. Maxwell: Absolutely. Real estate, like life, is not always smooth. There will be challenges, but each one teaches you strategy and resilience. I once let go of my commission so a cash-strapped client could close on her dream home. That one act of generosity brought me countless referrals later. Sometimes short-term sacrifice brings long-term reward.

Mike: Do you think your book *Just Eat The Worm* provides life changing advice to the FLYers, especially when Gen Zs grow up in a well-protected, well-designed environment and many young people are not aware of the challenges they will face when they enter adulthood, so called the "jungle world"?

Dr. Maxwell: I believe *Just Eat the Worm* offers life-changing guidance for FLYers and for Gen Zs growing up in a world that is carefully designed to protect them. Many young people have been raised in environments where systems are optimized, safety nets are present, and guidance and guardrail are always within reach. Yet adulthood does not operate by the same rules. I was born and raised in Nigeria, a country where children constantly face poverty and uncertainty.

Outside of Africa, I use my book to teach young people who are to step into what I call the "jungle world," they often encounter resistance, disappointment, and uncertainty for the first time. This book exists to prepare them for that moment — not with fear, but with truth. I want them to understand that challenges are not signs of failure; they are signals that growth has begun.

What I aim to change in young people's lives is their internal dialogue. I want them to stop waiting for permission, rescue, or perfect conditions, and start recognizing the power they already carry within themselves. When I say "eat the worm," I am teaching discipline, responsibility, and courage — the habits that separate those who drift from those who lead.

For FLYers especially, this mindset becomes a foundation for adulthood. It helps them face failure without quitting, uncertainty without panic, and pressure without losing direction. My hope is that this book doesn't just motivate young readers — it equips them to step confidently into adulthood, ready to create opportunity rather than wait for it.

6. The Value of a Real Estate License

Mike: You teach real estate licensing classes. Why is that license so valuable for young people?

Dr. Maxwell: It is a significant change. But do not underestimate it: the real estate exam is tough. Even doctors and professors fail it the first time if they do not study. Passing requires discipline. But once you do, it opens endless income opportunities. There is *no limit* to what you can earn. You are your own ceiling.

7. Discipline, Tenacity, and Grit

Mike: I constantly hear young people say: "I want to be a doctor. I want to create a unicorn business. I want to be a professional trader in options or in prediction markets." I admire their ambitions, but I doubt their career prospects without seeing their vision and tenacity. What do you think?

Dr. Maxwell: I agree. Talk is just empty words when they lack consistency and discipline. Motivation fades fast. Discipline keeps you going. I tell my students, "Motivation without consistency makes you a motivated fool."

Discipline is cultivated through consistent daily habits, not sudden bursts of motivation. As Angela Duckworth shows in her bestselling book G*rit*, true discipline develops when children learn to sustain effort long after enthusiasm fades. Parents build discipline by setting routines, enforcing boundaries, and modeling self-control, while schools reinforce it by rewarding persistence rather than raw talent and by holding students accountable for their actions.

Coaches, mentors, and communities further strengthen discipline through repetition, feedback, and lessons in delayed gratification. Our generation needs discipline, and it must be taught early — because it takes a village to raise disciplined children. Without this collective effort, children too often grow into undisciplined adults, struggling in work, in money, and in life.

Mike: I agree with your point here. My wife, Olga, is a private piano teacher, and piano practice is a clear example of how discipline and endurance are developed over time. Students learn that progress comes from daily, focused practice, even on days when motivation is low. Repeating scales, correcting mistakes, and refining technique trains patience and mental stamina. Over months and years, this process builds not only musical skill, but also the discipline to persist through frustration and the endurance to pursue long-term goals in life beyond the piano.

8. One More Message to Young Dreamers

Mike: Dr. Maxwell, this was incredibly inspiring. To close: if you could leave young readers with one quote, what would it be?

Dr. Maxwell: I will borrow one from my mentor: "Most people die at 25 but are not buried until 85." Do not die early. Stay alive inside. Keep growing, dreaming, and building. The richest place on earth is the graveyard—full of unused dreams and untold books. Do not take your gift to the grave. Use it. Build. Invest. Live fully.

Mike: Beautiful. Thank you, Dr. Maxwell. This message will change many lives, forever.

Dr. Maxwell: Thank you, Mike. What you are doing—giving young people knowledge and direction—is powerful. Information transforms lives. Together, we can help this generation grow into wise investors and leaders.

Final Thoughts

After talking with Dr. Maxwell, I found myself in deep thought: Dr. Maxwell uses his own grown-up success story to teach us a simple but often overlooked truth: success is rarely accidental. It is shaped by timing, discipline, and the willingness to act before certainty arrives.

The example of a single real estate purchase appreciating without effort underscores a powerful lesson for young people — starting early matters. Markets move, opportunities compound, and those who position themselves ahead of the curve benefit not because they are lucky, but because they show up on time, well prepared.

Chapter 18

Hand Up, Not Handout: Interview with Dr. Thomas Forbang

"Do not give your children a handout—give them a hand up. Comfort creates weakness; challenge creates warriors."—Dr. Thomas Forbang

About the expert: Armed with a Ph.D. in computer science, Dr. Forbang is a polyglot: an IT consulting firm owner, high end real estate developer, and 2018 World Yoga Champion. His journey from Cameroon to the United States inspires millions of FLYers:

(1) he runs a successful IT consulting firm serving federal government agencies;

(2) he managed dozens of rental properties near a main state university, selling them at a high price and trading up to high-end villas in Florida;

(3) he raises five children as a proud father and a great husband; and

(4) he is a seasoned yogi, acclaimed in the world championship of yoga sport.

Mike: Dr. Forbang, great to see you again! I hear you have been busy building homes in Florida.

Dr. Forbang: Yes, every other month I am down here checking on the builders and designs, making sure everything runs smoothly. These are high-end villas now.

Mike: From college rentals to luxury villas. What a journey!

Dr. Forbang: (Laughs) It has been a great journey. To make it happen, you have got to keep the body, mind, and soul together. It is about survival and progress: staying active in every sense.

Mike: I am thrilled to include your story in this book. You are one of the most versatile and successful people I know—Ph.D. in computer science, fluent in three languages—French, Russian, and English—and you even own an IT consulting firm serving federal agencies. There is one more thing: how did you find time to raise five great children? How did you find time to teach and practice yoga, and become the world champion of yoga competition in Beijing in 2018?

Dr. Forbang: (Laughs) Thank you. I also speak a few local dialects from Cameroon and Pidgin English. So yes, technically five languages — but we will settle for three!

Mike: No wonder your brain is wired differently! You have built a solid real estate portfolio—from campus housing to luxury homes. Let's start with my first question.

1. Passing Down Wealth Without Weakness

Mike: How do you preserve wealth for your children without spoiling them?

Dr. Forbang: Education is the foundation. School education lands you a job that affords food on the table, a roof over your head, and clothes on your back. But it does not make you rich. To survive in society, go to school. To thrive, you must be street-smart. Look at Elon Musk, Jeff Bezos, and Tony Robbins: they succeeded by far more than formal education can offer, driven instead by their ability to think independently, take calculated risks, and operate beyond the status quo stated in textbooks.

My favorite movie, *The Godfather*, reminds us that real power and success come from understanding human behavior, incentives, and negotiation — not just credentials or technical skill. Those who master discipline, judgment, and real-world awareness move beyond survival and learn how to operate effectively in life, money, and business.

There is a Russian proverb: *"If you do not take risks, you cannot drink champagne."* You have got to take risks, go through pain, and earn it. I tell my kids, "I will give you a hand up — not a handout."

Mike: That is powerful — a hand up, not handout.

Dr. Forbang: Send them to school, help them stand on their own feet, but never let them live in your basement. Comfort kills growth. Nothing grows in a comfort zone.

2. Discipline, Challenge, and Mindset

Mike: You have also been a world champion in yoga—how do you find balance between work, family, and yoga competition?

Dr. Forbang: (Smiles) Discipline. I get up around 5 A.M., completing my morning meditation. After a healthy breakfast, I log in my company computer to make important business assignments and decisions. I kiss my daughter and say "have a good day at school" in front of the school bus. I drive to my client office to attend executive meetings. Twice a week, I teach Bikram yoga classes at a local hot yoga studio. I call my college boys a few times a week to get an update of their school and life.

Wealth building? You cannot wait for the right time—you make time by investing at an early age. Challenge yourself constantly. As parents who have made it, we risk overprotecting our children. I remember a quote, "Children of affluent parents often turn out useless." It is harsh, but there is truth there.

My children have heard my childhood story hundreds of times. It is worthwhile to let your FLY readers know how lucky and fortunate they are! I was born and raised in Cameroon, where education was not just encouraged — it was seen as the clearest, maybe the only path to opportunity. Frustrated by the poverty and political corruption, I decided to leave Cameroon as a student and pursue higher education abroad. After a few years of rigorous study, I eventually moved to the United States.

Looking back to where I was from, and where I landed, I can tell you that our kids will not build strength unless they face their own storms.

Mike: So true. Parents need to stop hovering. Like lion cubs, they must hunt their own game.

Dr. Forbang: Do not give them fish; teach them to fish. If you give a fish, they will eat it once. If you teach them to fish, they will feed their families for generations.

Mike: That is why we teach youth to manage tenants, toilets, and trash — the three Ts of real estate management.

Dr. Forbang: (Laughs) Absolutely. Real skills build real character.

3. The First Step Toward Ownership

Dr. Forbang: Buying your first home (or your tenth) comes down to three key factors every lender looks at.

1. Credit Score. Start there. Aim for 720 or higher. A score of 750 puts you in a strong position, and 800+ gets you the best rate.
2. Loan-to-Value (Down Payment). Essentially, how much "skin" you have in the game. For first-time buyers, programs like FHA may only require 3% down. Forget the "no money down" myths; you need to save that 3%, plus about 1% more for closing costs.
3. Income Ratio. The most challenging piece. You need to show a steady income that supports repayment.

Mike: That is simple and powerful. For young people today, it is even easier to lean on parents for co-signs or down payments.

Dr. Forbang: True, but they are also spoiled. My grandfather walked ten miles to work; my father walked five. I drive a Cadillac, my son drives a Mercedes, and my grandson might drive a Ferrari — but his son will walk again.

Mike: The wealth cycle.

Dr. Forbang: Exactly. Hard times create strong people. Strong people create easy times. Easy times create weak people. Weak people create hard times. It is a cycle. We must raise our children as warriors, not comfort-dwellers.

Final Thoughts

Dr. Forbang's insights are invaluable. His self-made success from career to real estate, from family to sport inspires thousands of young readers. Dr. Forbang tells us that life does not hand you anything. Do not sugarcoat success. It is earned through struggle, discipline, and faith. Parents should raise warriors, not dependents. My kids know that they are not staying in my basement. I gave them education, opportunity, and love. Now, it is their turn to face the world.

Chapter 19

Faith, Flight, and Foundations: Interview with Brett Korade

"*Faith, focus, and financial stewardship form the wings that let young people soar.*"—Brett Korade, Co-Founder, LAB Realty Group

About the expert: Mr. Brett Korade is a Christ follower, mentor, real estate investor, business owner of LAB Realty Group in Northern Virginia. LAB Realty Group was ranked top 100 real estate firms in the Washington DC metro area in 2025. You can find more of Brett's 25+ years of quality service at https://www.labrealtygroup.com/team/brett-korade.

Brett is a church leader at McLean Bible Church, mentoring hundreds of young people to follow Jesus, and live a godly life. In 2014, Brett coached me and my boys in the creation of the Coat of Arms of NIE Manhood (see picture below), which hangs on my living room wall.

Isaiah 40:31 (NIV)

"But those who hope in the Lord

will renew their strength.

They will soar on wings like eagles;

they will run and not grow weary,

they will walk and not be faint."

Opening Prayer

Mike: Let us begin with prayer. Heavenly Father, thank you for this wonderful opportunity to interview my Christian brother, Brett Korade. As Ezekiel 17:3 says, "A great eagle with powerful wings and long feathers… took hold of the top of the cedar." Lord, we are building the wings for ourselves and nurturing our children to build strong wings so they can fly high and glorify You. Bless Brett and his family, his wife Lisa, and their business, LAB Realty Group. Bless Chris and Kevin on their journey of faith and financial growth. In Jesus' name, Amen.

Brett: Amen!

---

1. Grounding the Conversation in Faith

Mike: Now that we are settled with the prayer, let's start this interview about helping youth build a financial foundation.

Brett: Absolutely—start at the foot of the Cross.

2. Mission to Help Young People

Brett: Yes. It is Lisa and Brett—and "labs," because we have always had Labradors and used to train service animals.

Mike: You have built something special. My current mission is helping young people and entrepreneurs build wealth through smart, tax-efficient planning. You are one of D.C.'s top realtors—congrats!

Brett: Thank you. It is a blessing to see that recognition year after year.

3. Building Wealth Through Real Estate: A Rich Dad Mindset

Mike: You have been in real estate for 27 years. Why is real estate property so important for young people seeking financial success?

Brett: Real estate teaches strategic thinking—something missing in our culture today. Too many people live within poverty or middle-class mindset, rationalizing where they are instead of striving for growth.

God calls us to move, to build, to pursue. Real estate aligns with that—it lets young people leverage other people's money to generate outsized returns. Buy a $500,000 property with $25,000 down; if it appreciates 10%, that is $50,000 in equity within two years, or 200% return on investment (ROI). You cannot replicate that anywhere else.

Mike: So true. My son Kevin bought a condo in Manassas for $480,000. Now, within months, similar models are selling for $520,000. Banks lend most of the money, but we gain the equity.

Brett: Exactly. That is leverage in action.

"By wisdom a house is built, and by understanding it is established; by knowledge the rooms are filled with all precious and pleasant riches." – Proverbs 24:3–4

4. Financial Discipline and Delayed Gratification

Mike: Yet many Americans live paycheck to paycheck.

Brett: The savings rate is shockingly low. Social media and instant gratification undermine discipline—if we do not get something now, we feel we have failed. When I led a financial literacy class in a church youth group, I used Bible verses to stress the importance of financial patience and fiscal discipline.

Mike: Credit cards and "buy now, pay later" offers play into that.

Brett: Completely. Credit cards are *not* smart leverage: they charge 25% interest. Strategic debt builds wealth, not consumerism.

Mike: Our youth need to learn delayed gratification: letting money compound instead of being consumed by credit card debt.

Brett: Exactly. Compound growth requires patience and purpose, principles missing from mainstream culture.

"Wealth gained hastily will dwindle, but whoever gathers little by little will increase it." – Proverbs 13:11.

5. Heart-Driven Success and the Role of Mentorship

Mike: You mentor young agents. What traits lead to success today, especially in an AI-driven world?

Brett: AI cannot feel someone's heart. A great agent listens to dreams, values, and goals, guiding clients through both business and emotion. The early years are tough; returns are minimal, but that is where you build character. Success comes to those who serve with purpose, not greed.

Mike: It is called the "hockey stick" curve: long grind, then sudden growth.

Brett: Exactly. You need patience and calling. Money alone will not sustain you.

"But if we hope for what we do not see, we wait for it with patience." – Romans 8:25

6. Mentorship and Fatherhood

Mike: What advice do you have for teens and young adults starting out?

Brett: Find a mentor. It could be your dad, uncle, or church member. If not, ask someone to grab coffee every other week. You will find many people eager to provide their own insights.

Mike: I do that with my sons' friends at Chick-fil-A, sharing my life lessons and telling them my stories. I truly enjoy this mentorship.

Brett: Perfect example. Intentional mentorship transforms lives.

Mike: I tell my son, "No money, no honey." Earn before you spend.

Brett: (Laughs) Exactly. And remember—it is okay if your wife earns more, if you lead, protect, and provide. That is godly adulthood.

"Whoever walks with the wise becomes wise, but the companion of fools will suffer harm." – Proverbs 13:20

7. Embracing Responsibility and Growth

Mike: Too many young men avoid hardship. They fear responsibility and family duty.

Brett: Right. God calls us to grow and lead. Growth means facing challenges, not fleeing them. Balance is key: we must run toward meaningful adversity, not reckless chaos. The Bible offers clear examples. Moses did not grow while living comfortably in Pharaoh's palace; his growth began when he accepted the burden of leading difficult, resistant and complaining people through the wilderness. Likewise, King David was shaped not by ease, but by adversity — first as a shepherd facing danger, then as a warrior, and later as a king navigating moral failure and responsibility. In both cases, growth came from confronting hardship with purpose and discipline, not from avoiding struggle or chasing disorder.

Mike: Well said! Choosing the right battles, like Don Quixote!

Brett: Exactly. Wisdom is knowing which "windmills" are worth charging at.

"Be watchful, stand firm in the faith, act like men, be strong." – 1 Corinthians 16:13 (ESV)

8. Local Knowledge, Learning, and Intentionality

Mike: Real estate is hyper-local: every area's rules and taxes differ. How do you manage that?

Brett: Join a local real estate meet-up group. Find a mentor who is kind, knowledgeable and keen to help out. Learn risk versus opportunity. Once you have built discernment, expand confidently. Lisa and I even interviewed other agents for local government rental rule change and zoning code change. We make sure they share our integrity.

Mike: That is intentional leadership. Laws change constantly, like tax codes.

Brett: Exactly. Nothing is written in ink. Stay humble and ready to learn.

"Give instruction to a wise man, and he will be still wiser; teach a righteous man, and he will increase in learning." – Proverbs 9:9

9. Overcoming Fear and Taking the First Step

Mike: Many teens think buying property at 18 is impossible.

Brett: It is not. It is just intimidating. We fear what we do not understand. Break it down into steps, seek help, and start. Fear is the only real obstacle, whether fear of failure or even fear of success.

10. Street Smarts and Emotional Intelligence

Mike: My son Kevin's rental property taught him so much: meeting tenants, managing expectations, and negotiating lease terms.

Brett: That is priceless. Real estate develops emotional intelligence. You learn to read people, interpret unspoken cues, and build trust. Those skills are the foundation of leadership.

"*The prudent see danger and take refuge, but the simple keep going and pay the penalty.*" Proverbs 22:3

11. The Long Game: Building Legacy Wealth

Brett: Real estate is a get-rich-slow path. It rewards patience, discipline, and community.

It is not just appreciation: the tax code favors real estate. Deferring capital gain tax through like-kind rental property exchanges, cost segregation, and step-up basis allow legal wealth transfer across generations with minimal tax. That is how families build a legacy, purposefully and lawfully.

Mike: Yes, always consult your accountant before selling any property.

Brett: Exactly. If your realtor never asks whether you have talked to your CPA, they have failed you.

"A good person leaves an inheritance for their children's children." – Proverbs 13:22

12. Fear of Failure and the 80% Rule

Mike: "Analysis paralysis" stops so many people. They tend to overthink, overanalyze, and over worry. Great deals go away fast.

Brett: Aim for 70-80% certainty. If you wait for perfect certainty, you will miss the window of opportunity. This truth is captured in a leadership lesson often attributed to Colin Powell during the Gulf War: you never have 100% of the information. Powell taught that leaders should act when they have between 40% and 70% of the available information. Less than 40% is reckless; more than 70% often means the decision has come too late. In military operations in the desert, waiting for flawless intelligence would have led to paralysis and failure. Effective leadership, therefore, requires action with sufficient clarity—not perfect clarity.

The same principle applies to investing and life. Every successful investor learned by acting before perfect certainty arrived. Even crossing the street involves risk — yet we move forward by assessing, not eliminating, uncertainty. Progress belongs to those who accept risk, exercise judgment, and act decisively when the moment calls.

"*Whoever watches the wind will not plant; whoever looks at the clouds will not reap.*" – Ecclesiastes 11:4

13. Investing in Family and Education

Mike: You mentioned college housing as a startup idea.

Brett: Fantastic model—buy near a university, rent to students, and let peers pay the mortgage. That is how many small investors start.

Mike: My daughter's campus in Lexington has limited lodging: graduation season brings record rents.

Brett: Exactly. Seasonal demand creates amazing yields. You are teaching both business and stewardship.

"*Train up a child in the way he should go; even when he is old he will not depart from it.*" – Proverbs 22:6

14. Faith, Legacy, and Leadership

Mike: This has been wonderful: a talk about courage, timing, and faith. Sometimes I wish I had started 20 years ago!

Brett: One of my favorite sayings is: "The best time to plant a tree was 20 years ago. The second-best time is today."

Mike: Yes, ultimately, that is true even though we keep wishing otherwise.

Brett: It will always feel like a big leap. But the only wrong move is standing still.

Mike: Thank you again. I would love to have you at my FLY summer camp program (Financial Literacy for Young People).

Brett: I would love that. It would fill my heart. And one last thing is to remove the word "cannot" from your vocabulary. As soon as you declare you cannot, your brain stops seeking solutions. Faith begins with possibility.

Mike: Amen to that. Mindset is everything.

Brett: Indeed. Thank you, brother; it has been a blessing.

"*Faith by itself, if it is not accompanied by action, is dead.*" – James 2:17

Final Thoughts

Our conversation ends as it began, in gratitude. Brett reminds us that investing is not just financial: it is spiritual training. When young people build homes and habits on faith, they do not just gain equity: they gain character. Through discipline, prayer, and stewardship, we build wings strong enough to FLY.

Chapter 20

Building Financially Independent Youth: Interview with Yuyan Zhou

"Financial literacy is not about money; it is about mindset. Learn early, think boldly, and give back. The sooner you act, the sooner you own not just a house, but your future."—Yuyan Zhou, President of CAPA NoVA

About the expert: Yuyan Zhou currently serves as President of Chinese American Parents Association of Northern Virginia (CAPA NoVA). Under her leadership, CAPA NoVA was incorporated in Virginia in 2020 as a 501(c)(3) nonprofit. She has taken a visible community-engagement role.

Yuyan Zhou earned a Bachelor of Science in Architecture degree from Beijing University of Technology, and a Master of Science in Architecture degree from Iowa State University. She currently serves as Senior Project Manager at a federal government agency.

Mission Behind CAPA NoVA

Mike: Yuyan, can you start by sharing what CAPA NoVA is all about and the mission behind your work?

Yuyan: CAPA NoVA stands for Chinese American Parents Association – Northern Virginia. It is an IRS-approved 501(c)(3) public charity. Its mission grew from the idea that schools do not teach many of the essential life skills our youth need, especially financial literacy. Even top high schools like Thomas Jefferson focus heavily on STEM but neglect personal finance. We use education to build stronger communities, teaching what families and schools often overlook: how to manage money, plan wisely, and serve others.

Rethinking Education in the Age of AI

Mike: You and I both believe schools are too narrow in academic focus. How do you see AI changing the educational model?

Yuyan: The old formula (i.e., study hard, get a degree, and get a job) no longer guarantees success. AI makes knowledge-learning cheap but jobs harder to keep. To thrive, students must learn adaptability and financial independence. We should be teaching them how to think and how to manage financial decisions, not just how to memorize formulas.

Why Financial Literacy Matters

Mike: Why is financial literacy such a critical life skill today?

Yuyan: Because it is a survival skill. Everyone will face financial challenges: job loss, business downturns, or unexpected emergencies. Financial literacy gives you control and freedom. It is lifelong knowledge: saving, investing, building, sustaining, and passing on wealth responsibly.

Teaching Entrepreneurship Early

Mike: CAPA NoVA recently launched a youth entrepreneurship initiative. What inspired this program?

Yuyan: We created the Entrepreneur Club, a hands-on learning experience. Students form teams, learn basic business principles, and design their own startup ideas. Then CAPA NoVA gives each student seed money to execute their projects. They learn teamwork, budgeting, taxes, and problem-solving in the real world.

The Courage to Take Risks

Mike: Risk-taking seems central to your message. Why are young people becoming more risk-averse?

Yuyan: Schools condition children to fear failure. We glorify perfect grades but rarely teach persistence and resilience. Yet, history shows every great innovator failed repeatedly before succeeding. Parents must foster courage: try new things, accept setbacks, and show that failure builds character.

The Decline of Early Homeownership

Mike: You mentioned that buying homes later in life is becoming an alarming trend. Why do you think that is?

Yuyan: The average first-time homebuyer used to be 30; now, it is much older (see chart below). Wages have stagnated while home prices rise. But mindset plays a role too. Many youths delay learning about credit or saving. Your sons are great examples of what is possible — they purchased homes at 18 because they understood financial planning and risk. Those early moves create significant lifelong wealth growth.

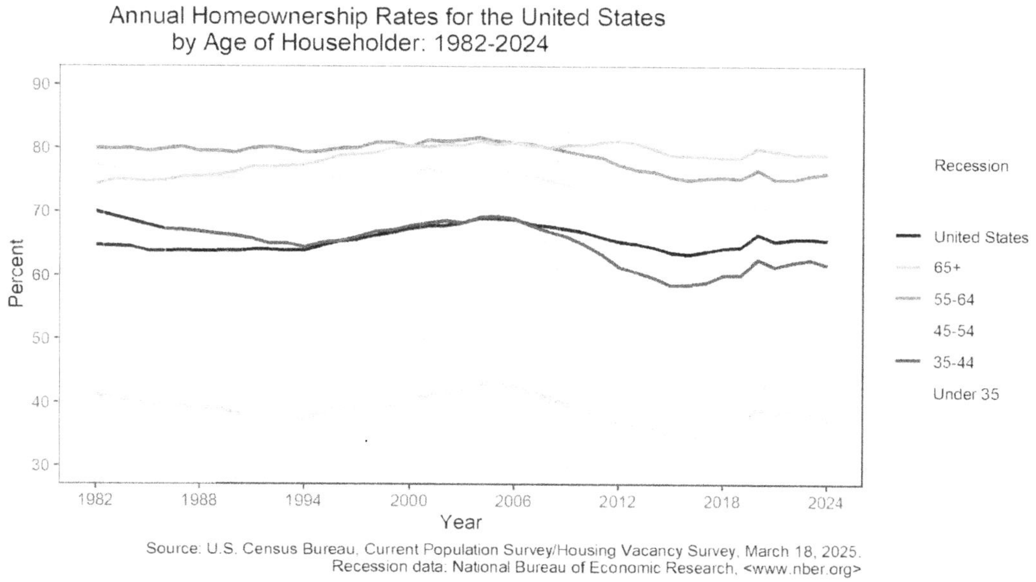

On the opposite side, more young people live with parents through their thirties, and young men are more likely than young women to live at home with their parents. We as parents are concerned with young men losing accountability and appetite for risk. The chart shows this worrisome pattern:

- About 20% of young men (25-34) live with parents in recent years' survey (2020 to present);
- About 13% of young women live with parents during the same time period; and
- Both lines have trended up since 2000, and peaked in 2020 (Covid 19 pandemic).

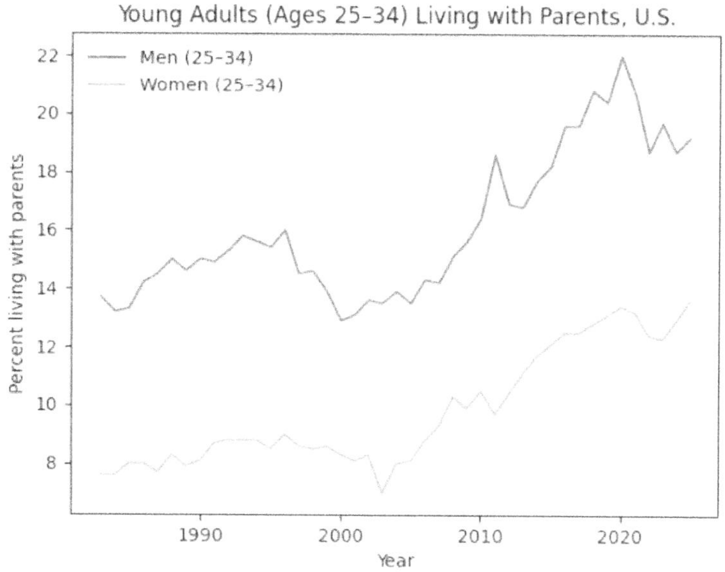

Source: U.S. Census Bureau, Historical Living Arrangements of Adults (selected years). Chart created by author

Preparing for a Changing Future

Mike: How can young people prepare for a future where traditional 9-5 jobs are vanishing?

Yuyan: Start small businesses early. Learn essential business skills: how to register an LLC, market products, balance your check book, and file taxes. Everything takes time to grow. Taking the risk today brings resilience tomorrow. And passion-driven work keeps people fulfilled, no matter how much technology changes.

The Five C's for the AI Age

Mike: When you spoke at Toastmasters, you shared the "Five C's." Can you walk us through those again?

Yuyan: Certainly. The Five C's are:

1. Creativity – generating ideas machines cannot.
2. Communication – convincing clients, investors and bankers.
3. Compassion – empathy remains human and irreplaceable: AI cannot wipe your tears.
4. Collaboration – teamwork leads to sustainable growth.
5. Contribution – giving back defines purpose, not just profit.

These are core strengths to make us prevail in the AI era.

Purpose-Driven Prosperity

Mike: You often say CAPA NoVA is "purpose-driven, not profit-driven." What does that mean?

Yuyan: We aim to create legacy and community impact. Money follows purpose. When we do good work, opportunities and resources appear organically. CAPA NoVA wants to nurture leaders who create wealth responsibly and share it socially.

Young Role Models in Action

Mike: You have met my sons, Chris and Kevin. What stood out to you about their journeys?

Yuyan: Chris impressed me with his maturity — methodical decision-making and gratitude for your mentorship. He approaches homeownership with responsibility and humility, rare among teens. Kevin's story of buying a home at 18 proves what financial literacy education can achieve. Both show how early mentorship shapes disciplined investors.

The Meaning of Success

Mike: What does success mean to you, personally?

Yuyan: Success is about legacy, not possessions. It is seeing young people become confident, independent, and generous. CAPA NoVA's next vision includes entrepreneurship incubators, leadership camps, and innovation platforms — to help students exchange ideas, create jobs, and lead communities.

Final Thoughts

Yuyan reminds us that financial literacy is not about money. It is about mindset. Learn early, think boldly, and give back. Do not wait for the perfect time. The sooner you act, the better your future will be.

Chapter 21

The First House Is the Hardest: Interview with Fred Williams, Real Estate Pro

"Your first real estate purchase teaches you more than any book. Start small, keep reserves, and learn from each deal, because once you buy that first house, every next one feels easier."—Fred Williams, Real Estate Investor

About the expert: Mr. Fred Williams began investing in mutual funds at the young age of 8 and never looked back. After completing a bachelor's in finance and an MBA, he spent years honing his expertise in the industry before going all in as a successful full-time real estate, stock, and specialty asset investor.

Fred mentors his son in pursuing financial literacy, financial wisdom, and financial discipline. This father-son team is a living example of mind over matter in building wealth.

1. Every Real Estate Deal Has Its Own Story

Mike: Fred, thank you for joining me. Before we dive in, tell our readers a bit about your recent plans.

Fred: My plans changed at the last minute. I was going to look at a short-term rental in Maine, but it went under contract the same day it was listed. In popular areas — like the lake region of northern Maine — homes still move quickly, even in this market. Location really matters.

Mike: That is so true — location, location, location. Let us go a little deeper. You transitioned from financial investments into real estate. How did that happen?

Fred: During COVID, when everyone was stuck at home, I started watching a lot of real estate investing videos. I have always had an interest in real estate, but I came from a financial background, mostly stocks and bonds. When markets started to swing wildly during the pandemic, I realized I needed something steadier. People will always need a place to live, and that stability was very appealing.

I studied as much as I could in 2020 and 2021, learning about cash flow, appreciation, and tax benefits. By 2023, I pulled the trigger and bought my first investment property.

Mike: And how do you feel about it now? Any regrets?

Fred: Not really. The stock market has outperformed real estate recently, but it is also far more volatile. With property, you have cash flow that is almost tax-free and tangible value. Unless you buy at the absolute bottom — like 2008 levels — it is a real asset you can hold and improve over time. Real estate offers both appreciation and depreciation, as you like to say.

2. The Power of Stability and Leverage

Mike: Exactly. That combination of leverage and tax efficiency is one reason I love real estate. Tell me: how do you handle maintenance and the headaches that come with ownership?

Fred: Property managers manage long-term rentals. For small issues, tenants contact them directly. But larger repairs — like when I had to replace a century-old sewer line for $25,000 — fall to me. That is why I always keep a reserve fund. I typically set aside about 10% of monthly rents for maintenance. New roofs, plumbing, tenant wear, and tear: they are all part of the business.

Mike: Cash reserve, which is a lesson in liquidity. During the recent government shutdown, I saw people line up at food banks because they had no emergency savings. Real estate investors must plan differently.

Fred: Exactly. You always need cash on hand. Something will always break, sometimes at the worst time.

3. Exploring Property Management Careers

Mike: You mentioned property management earlier. Do you think it is a good field for young people to enter?

Fred: Absolutely. Property management is one of the most stable businesses out there because people always need housing. Managers charge 8–10% of monthly rent and have no ownership risk. It is also a fantastic way to learn real estate from the ground up.

Beyond management, appraisers and inspectors also do well without huge overhead. Each appraisal can run around $800. Inspectors charge $300–$500 for a few hours of work, and all they need is knowledge, licensing, and a laptop. Specialized licenses become entry points into lucrative careers.

Mike: Yes, licenses create opportunities. They serve as barriers to entry and as professional validation.

Fred: Exactly. Once you have one license, whether real estate, appraisal, or mortgage, you can turn that into income immediately.

4. Buying from the Inside and Building Networks

Mike: Earlier, you mentioned buying properties from your manager's network. How did that work?

Fred: That has been one of my most effective strategies. My Milwaukee property manager also manages homes for other investors. When some of them wanted to exit, he introduced me as a buyer. Because I already had access to rent rolls, maintenance records, and tenant history, there were no surprises. We closed quickly and saved everyone money. It was a win-win for all parties involved.

Mike: Fascinating. Inside knowledge and relationships are true leverage.

Fred: Right. Networking is everything in real estate. Once you build trust with agents, managers, and contractors, deals start coming to you.

5. Teaching the Next Generation

Mike: Parents like us often try to pass these lessons on to our children. Do you believe kids should shadow us in these deals?

Fred: Absolutely. Real estate involves layers of work — analyzing deals, calculating capitalization rates, understanding insurance, taxes, and maintenance. It is complicated at first, but teaching these skills early turns them into muscle memory. My son, Andy, has been learning these calculations with me. There is no substitute for watching a deal come together from start to finish.

Mike: That is the best kind of apprenticeship. It builds "rich dad" thinking instead of a worker's mindset.

Fred: Yes, and it is a mindset shift. My parents worked hard — my father was a mechanic, my mom sold insurance. They lived by the "40-hour" mentality. But to build wealth, your assets must do the work for you. School teaches obedience — bells telling you when to start, when to stop — because it was designed for workers, not owners. We must teach our children to think differently.

6. The Role of Emotion and People Skills

Mike: In your view, how important are people skills in real estate?

Fred: Extremely important. You cannot just negotiate over email. You must read the room—people's eyes, their tone. Something always comes up. Real estate is personal and emotional. I even change my watch depending on who I am dealing with: a Rolex for meetings with sellers, a cheap digital when negotiating with contractors. Presentation matters.

7. Technology, AI, and the Modern Investor

Mike: Now, let's shift to technology. How can AI tools help investors?

Fred: Some platforms are using AI to analyze nationwide listings. They apply filters like the 1% rule—checking sale price against possible rental income—to pinpoint profitable deals quickly. Instead of manually searching for 1,000 houses, you might only have to analyze 50. That efficiency is game-changing, especially if expanded to multi-family analysis. AI can help investors find needles in a haystack.

Mike: Agreed. Information is power. Those who leverage data gain an edge over traditional investors.

8. Taking the First Step

Mike: Every investment involves risk. How do you manage the risks of owning out-of-state properties?

Fred: I am personally conservative but realistic. I hold properties in LLCs for liability protection. Risk is unavoidable if you want growth. Even savings accounts barely outpace inflation. Real estate at least leaves you with something tangible. You might lose value temporarily, but properties persist. It is about being comfortable with managed risk.

9. Short-Term Rentals and Creative Strategy

Mike: That is inspiring. You mentioned short-term rentals as a strategy — how has that worked for you?

Fred: Short-term rentals can outperform long-term leases, especially in the right market. You can host professionals like traveling nurses or temporary contractors. The key is flexibility. Short stays reduce tenant rights risks and usually yield higher monthly income. Platforms like Airbnb and VRBO handle marketing, making the process streamlined and scalable.

Final Thoughts

Fred's message to new investors who are afraid to start is direct: stop overthinking and take the first step. Real estate can feel overwhelming at first: so many steps, variables, and numbers, but your first purchase teaches you more than any book. Start small, keep reserves, and learn from each transaction. Once you buy that first house, every next deal feels easier.

Chapter 22

Build A Strong Generation: Interview with Home Restoration Expert Alexander Samuel

"Strong men create good times. Good times create weak men. Weak men create hard times. And hard times create strong men." – Michael Hopf, Novelist

About the expert: Alexander is the owner of New Generation Restoration, a second-generation restoration company specializing in water damage and property recovery. His father began the trade after immigrating to the U.S. in 1985, and Alexander stepped in to lead the company in 2020, determined to carry that legacy forward with modern systems, structure, and purpose.

Through professional certification and hands-on experience, he learned to combine technical excellence with empathy, as restoration is as much about rebuilding people's peace of mind as it is about repairing their homes.

Alexander's mission is to grow in every dimension (spiritually, mentally, physically, and financially) while building businesses that create opportunities for others. He believes in patience over instant gratification, humility over entitlement, and systems over shortcuts. Every project is a chance to model discipline, gratitude, and generational strength for those who will come after us.

1. Introduction: Building Financial Literacy Through Real Stories

Mike: Alexander, thank you for joining me in the interview. I really appreciate your willingness to help with *FLY: Financial Literacy for Young People.* As an accountant, I have learned that no matter how much financial knowledge we gain, it is meaningless if we do not pass it on to the next generation.

This book is about teaching young people the power of wealth accumulation and delayed gratification — how to own a rental property before age 25. You are a great example of someone who took practical skills and turned them into a thriving business.

Alexander: It's my honor to participate in this exciting book project.

2. Lessons from His Father: Humility and Hard Work

Mike: How did your dad shape your work ethic?

Alexander: He is my greatest mentor. He even worked with the FBI and CIA at Guantanamo Bay. His father worked for the IMF and World Bank, so discipline runs deep.

My dad taught me to show up, be on time, and use common sense. Growing up, I realized YouTube cannot replace real-world experience. He pushed me to do small things well before chasing big ones.

3. From Family Trade to Entrepreneurship

Mike: Tell me, how did you get into the restoration business?

Alexander: It all began with my father. When he came to the U.S. in 1985, he started doing carpet cleaning. By 2010, one of his mentors introduced him to water damage restoration, and he became certified through the Floor Covering Institute.

As I grew up, I helped him with jobs and learned the trade hands-on. During the COVID pandemic, business slowed down, so at age 20, I stepped in to reorganize operations. I started learning business systems, taking college courses, and focusing on running the business.

4. Reinventing the Family Business

Mike: That is what I call a growth mindset. You took what you learned and built a better version.

Alexander: Thank you. I wanted to make everything systematic. We built standard operating procedures (SOPs) and earned a certificate at Institute of Inspection, Cleaning and Restoration Certification (IICRC) in water damage and mold remediation. That training helped; all my field experience made sense.

We also focused on communication and transparency with clients. When people's homes flood, it is traumatic. Being calm, empathetic, and professional made all the difference.

5. The Four Cs: Skills AI Cannot Replace

Mike: Exactly. AI can take white-collar jobs, but it cannot replace the *four Cs: compassion, communication, collaboration, and credibility*. You have all four, and that is why you stand out.

If young people cannot find tech jobs, what trades would you recommend?

Alexander: Service-based trades are both AI- and recession-proof. Water damage restoration is a great start. The IICRC Water Restoration Technician course costs under $700, and the startup investment is modest compared to the return.

Other great fields include HVAC, plumbing, drywall repair, and painting. Expert one, subcontract the rest. There is a lot of personal freedom in skilled trades that get paid well if the job is done professionally.

6. Delayed Gratification vs. Instant Gratification

Mike: A typical American family is already in the top 5% globally measured by income, yet many people live paycheck to paycheck because of instant gratification.

Alexander: Exactly. Social media and consumer culture make us crave instant rewards. But success is like a bamboo tree—it grows underground for years before shooting up. Business works the same way. Patience compounds. Small, consistent effort beats quick thrills.

7. Small Business Mindset: Survive to Thrive

Mike: In both accounting and restoration, most small businesses fail within three years. If you survive, you will thrive.

Alexander: Absolutely. The first years are the hardest. But I learned to live within my means and reinvest profits into my business and education. Too many people increase spending as income grows.

Mike: Yes, my son Kevin runs a junk removal business. He sees how much useless stuff people accumulate over the years. That is money that could've been invested and compounded nicely.

Alexander: Exactly. If you cannot afford something four or five times over, do not buy it. Focus on appreciating assets, not depreciating toys — that is straight out of *Rich Dad, Poor Dad.*

8. Wealth, Wisdom, and the Power of Reflection

Mike: Real wealth comes from balance. In FLY, I teach the Five Fs: *faith, family, fitness, finance, and field of career.*

Every December, I write a personal "annual report" reviewing progress in those five areas — like Warren Buffett's letters to shareholders. It is my way of leaving wisdom for future generations.

Alexander: That is incredible. I might start doing that myself. Reflecting helps keep you accountable and humble.

9. Vision for the Future

Mike: Where do you see yourself in 5–10 years?

Alexander: Continuing to grow spiritually, mentally, physically, and financially. I want to build systems that generate passive income, eliminate financial stress, and let me serve others while scaling new ventures.

Mike: That is the FLY spirit: turning vision into legacy. You are already ahead of most of your generation.

10. Raising the Next Generation Right

Mike: If you have kids one day, how would you teach them these values?

Alexander: By giving them appreciation, not entitlement. My family came from Pakistan, and as a Christian family to survive in Pakistan, we often faced social and economic discrimination, and we had to work hard and keep a low profile. I want my future children to stay humble, grateful, and resourceful, even if they grow up in comfort.

Closing Thoughts

Mike: Alexander, thank you for sharing your story and wisdom. You have given young readers a powerful example of grit, gratitude, and growth.

Alexander: Thank you, Mr. Nie. It was an honor. I hope our conversation helps more young people see that financial independence starts with discipline and purpose.

Final Thoughts

This interview reminds us that financial literacy is not just about money. It is about mindset. Alexander's journey from helping his father clean carpets to running a professional restoration company proves that hard work, humility, perseverance, and consistency can turn any trade into a path to financial freedom.

Case Study 1

Chris's Rental Analysis: Campus House Investment and Rental

"*Every college student pays for housing, but the smart ones get paid from their housing.*"—Chris

1. The Vision

At age 18, Chris purchased a townhouse near his college campus in Daytona Beach, Florida. Instead of paying rent to someone, he turned his housing expense into an investment. His plan was simple: live in one room, rent out the others, and use the rental income to cover most (or all) of his mortgage.

2. House overview: 3 Bedrooms • 2.5 Bathrooms • 1,800 Sq Ft • Built in 2023

Just minutes from shopping, dining, and the world-famous Daytona Beach, this modern yet elegant two-story, all-block construction townhouse features granite countertops, stainless-steel appliances, and 18"x18" ceramic tile in all main living areas. The spacious open-concept design connects the kitchen, dining, and great room, perfect for both entertaining and family living.

The upstairs includes three bedrooms and a versatile loft space, ideal for a study or media nook. The primary suite offers a walk-in closet and ensuite bath, while two secondary bedrooms provide ample space for guests or student rentals. Energy-efficient upgrades include a high-efficiency HVAC system, dual-pane low-E windows, and modern insulation standards to keep utility costs low.

A covered patio extends the living space to the outdoors, overlooking a low-maintenance yard. Residents enjoy the convenience of an attached garage and the reliability of a builder warranty from a nationally recognized builder.

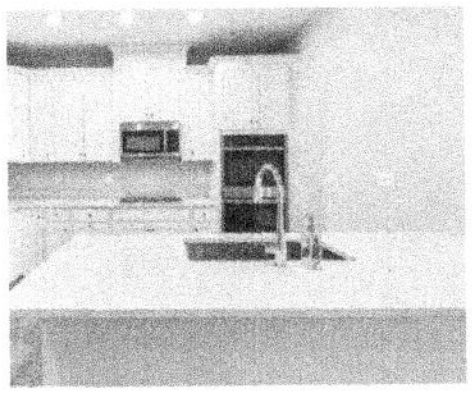

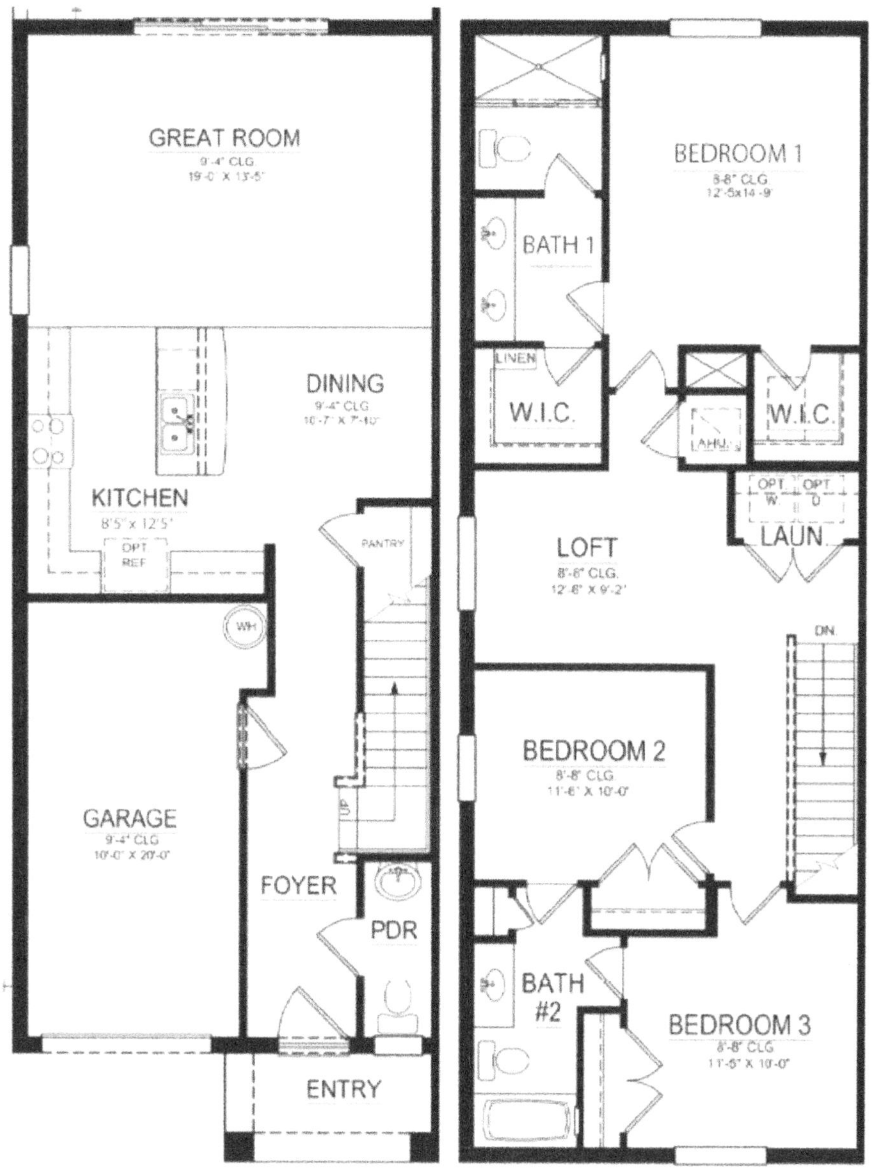

First Floor   Second Floor

3. **Loan Overview**

Item	Detail
Property Address	888 Main Street, Daytona Beach, FL 33333
Purchase Price	$325,990
Loan Type	Conventional 30-year fixed
Loan Amount	$309,690 (95%)
Interest Rate	5.5% (30-year fixed rate mortgage)
Monthly Principal & Interest	$1,758

Item	Detail
Total Estimated Monthly Payment (with taxes, insurance, HOA)	$2,339
Down payment	$16,300 (or 5%)

Note: loan information is for illustration only. Consult your licensed mortgage broker for details.

4. Understanding the Numbers

The mortgage estimate shows a total monthly payment of $2,339, which includes:

- Principal and interest: $1,758
- Mortgage insurance: $93
- Escrow for taxes & insurance: $488

This is the total cost of ownership before any rental income kicks in.

5. The Campus Real Estate Strategy

Chris used a "house hacking" model. House hacking is a real-estate strategy where you live on a property and rent out part (or all) of it so the rent helps pay your mortgage, taxes, and utilities Instead of buying a single-bedroom condominium, he purchased a three-bedroom townhouse, and applied a plan below:

Bedroom	Occupant	Monthly Rent
Bedroom 1	Chris (owner)	$400 (to be covered by his earned income) Partial space: Home office for his flight instruction business
Bedroom 2	Renter #1 (a SpaceX employee	$1,050
Bedroom 3	Renter #2 (college friend)	$950 (to be covered by his 529 distribution)
Total Fund Collected		**$2,000**

To make the numbers work, Chris contributed $500 monthly from his own income as a pilot instructor.

Total Rent + Self-Funding	$2,500
Mortgage & Expenses	$2,339

Total Rent + Self-Funding	$2,500
Net Monthly Cash Flow	$+61 (break-even or slightly positive)

6. Lessons from the Case

- Start early: Buying before age 25 means decades of appreciation and tax advantages.
- Leverage roommates: Turn extra bedrooms into a cash-flowing machine.
- Keep a cushion: Even break-even cash flow can build equity through principal paydown.
- Tax benefit: As owner-occupant, Chris can deduct mortgage interest and property taxes, while reporting rental losses on Schedule E. The rental loss is mainly driven by mortgage loan interest and mortgage insurance (down payment below 20%), depreciation, and ordinary and necessary rental expenses. Up to $25K losses are available to offset Chris's other income.

7. Long-Term View

In five years, even modest appreciation (3% annually) can raise the property value to around $378,000. Meanwhile, renters effectively pay their mortgage. By graduation, Chris will have built:

- Equity: $60,000–$70,000
- Credit history: perfect on-time payments
- Experience: real-world property management skills

8. Key Takeaway

"Every college student pays for housing. But the smart ones get paid *from* their housing." This case study proves that young people can achieve financial freedom through smart real-estate choices—by learning, planning, and taking early action.

Case Study 2

Kevin's Condo Investment

"Most people wait for the right time to buy. The smart ones create it."—Kevin

Property: 6666 Michael Jackson Avenue, Manassas, VA 22222. Community: AI Innovation Town Center Condos

1. The Vision

At just 19 years old, Kevin entered the Northern Virginia real estate market, one of the most competitive housing regions in the country. His goal was not simply to live in a high-end community near Washington D.C., but to convert his residence into a future income-producing property. This case study illustrates how careful planning, tax awareness, and shared ownership strategies can make a six-figure property accessible to young investors.

House description: 3 Bedrooms • 2.5 Bathrooms • 1,600 Sq Ft • Built 2025

On Zillow and Redfin, Kevin posts his rental as such: "Welcome to the newly built two-level condo which blends luxury finishes with functional living spaces in the heart of Manassas. The open-concept floor plan showcases a state-of-the-art kitchen with stainless-steel appliances, granite counters, and a sleek island overlooking a bright great room. Upstairs, spacious bedrooms and full baths offer privacy and comfort, highlighted by premium hardwood and tile flooring throughout.

Enjoy year-round efficiency with central A/C and heat-pump heating, plus the convenience of in-unit laundry. The home includes a one-car attached garage, driveway parking, and additional community parking."

2. Transaction Overview (with data revised for illustration purpose)

Item	Details
Purchase Price	$483,970
Loan Amount	$475,204
Down Payment / Cash to Close	$14,519 (3%)
Points Paid (1.5 %)	$7,128 (FHA loan)
Mortgage Insurance Premium	$8,173

Item	Details
Settlement Agent	First Title, LLC
Credits Received	$25,000 Seller Credit & Lender Credit

3. Estimated Monthly Costs

Component	Approx. Amount (USD)
Principal & Interest (30-yr fixed 6.5%)	$2,720
Property Taxes (annual $6,000 /12)	$500
Homeowners Insurance	$42
HOA + Condo Fees	$444
Total Monthly Payment	**$3,700 – $3,800**

4. Shared Ownership and Rental Plan

To make the purchase financially sustainable, Kevin structured the property with a co-ownership and partial rental strategy:

- The townhouse's three bedrooms + den allow for one owner's suite and two rentable rooms.
- Each room rents for $1,200 – $1,300/month in the AI Innovation Town Center area (based on 2025 market rates).
- Gross potential rent: $2,400 – $2,600/month.
- Owner's contribution (covering remaining mortgage/HOA): $1,200 per month. Kevin sells some of the stocks gifted by parents to cover his mortgage portion, without paying capital gain taxes because (1) he is a full-time college student, (2) he earned income more than half of his support (in-state college); (3) the gifted stocks appreciated value nicely in 2025; and (4) he filed his tax return including Form 8949. Based on a study by the State Council of Higher Education for Virginia, for the upcoming 2025-26 academic year at baccalaureate institutions, room and board charges averaged about $13,671 per year on campus. Kevin manages the stock selling at the right price level and at the right time.

This creates a near break-even or slightly positive cash flow, while the mortgage principal steadily builds equity.

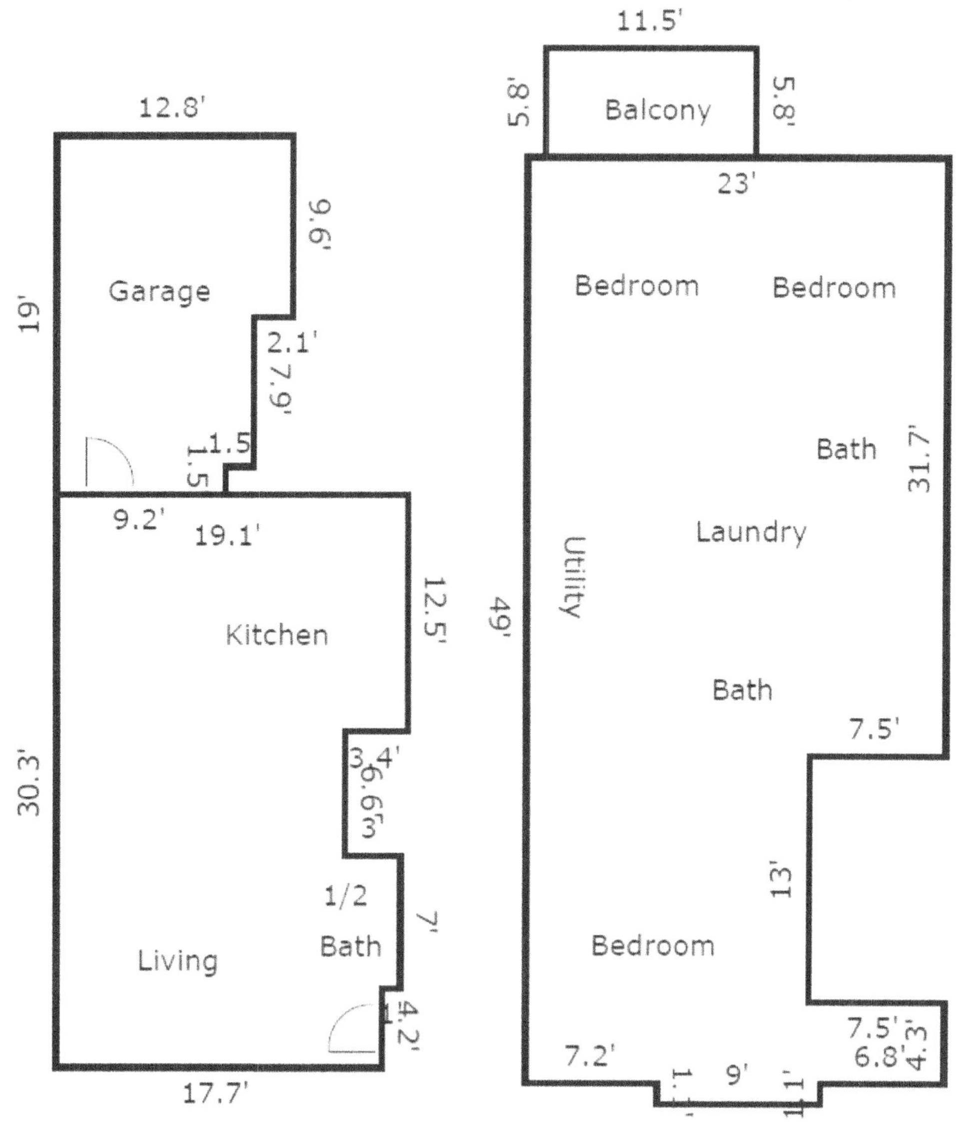

5. Community and Amenities

The AI Town Center offers a walkable lifestyle—steps from restaurants, retail, and the NVA University Science and Technology Campus. Amenities include:

- Modern clubhouse and fitness center
- Pool and playground areas
- Virginia Railway Express (VRE) Manassas Commuting Line to Union Station, DC (walking to VRE station in community)
- Quick access to I-66 and Route 28 (commuting to Tysons Corner or D.C.)
- Assigned parking and EV-ready garage infrastructure
- 1.7 miles (or seven minutes) to Costco, Target, and Walmart Superstore

6. Tax and Investment Considerations

- Mortgage Interest & Property Tax Deductions: Co-owners can allocate deductions proportional to ownership.
- Depreciation on Rented Portions: Kevin can claim depreciation on rented rooms via Schedule E while still occupying part of the home.
- HOA and Condo Fees: Deductible portion applies to rented areas.
- Future 1031 Exchange Eligibility: Once fully rented, the property can roll gains into a new investment tax-deferred.

7. Five-Year Projection (2025–2030)

Assumption	**Estimate**
Appreciation	5% per year. Value $600 K by 2030
Principal Reduction	$40K (through loan payments)
Total Equity by Year 5	$200K – $250K
Cash Flow Improvement	Positive as rents rise 3–5 % per year

8. Lessons Learned

1. Credits can be powerful: $25,000 in seller and lender credits reduced Kevin's actual out-of-pocket costs and closing burden.
2. HOA awareness: In multi-layer associations (condo + master HOA), budget carefully for dual fees.
3. Live and learn: Managing roommates and maintenance teaches real-world financial discipline.
4. Parental partnership: Co-buying with parents accelerates approval and credit building while retaining youth ownership benefits.

9. Key Takeaway

You do not have to wait until 40 to own property in Northern Virginia. You just need a plan. Kevin's story proves that strategic partnerships, careful tax planning, and smart use of credits can turn a six-figure townhome into a financial launchpad for anyone under 20.

Kevin graciously shares his brand-new condo pictures below. If you happen to know a reliable tenant moving to Manassas area, please call Kevin!

Case Study 3

Kevin's Bachelor Tax Return

"Age does not lower my tax bill. Strategy does." – Kevin

Background Story

At just 19 years old, Kevin exemplifies the next generation of financially literate real estate investors. As a single tax filer (full-time student, owner of a house junk removal business, and part-time employee at a local pizzeria), Kevin earns between $30,000–$40,000 annually from his W-2 job while managing his first rental property, generating passive income and building equity.

Though young, Kevin strategically integrates his income, investments, and education expenses into a tax-efficient plan. His approach demonstrates how smart filing, intentional deductions, and disciplined reinvestment can accelerate wealth creation even before age 25.

The following table summarizes 12 key tax planning lessons from Kevin's real estate and financial life.

Table 1: Tax Planning Strategies

#	Strategy	How Kevin Applies It	Tax Advantage / Principle
1	Optimize Form W-4 Withholding	Kevin sets zero or low federal and state withholdings since he expects sizable deductible real estate losses. See an example below.	Minimize W-2 salary withholding. Avoid giving the government an interest-free loan; maximize cash flow during the year.
2	Leverage Passive Loss from Rental Property	His rental generates up to $25,000 in deductible losses through depreciation and operating costs.	Offsets active W-2 income or other income with up to $25,000 real estate loss allowance (IRC §469) for active participants.
3	Use Bonus and Cost Segregation Depreciation	Accelerates depreciation on building components and fixtures.	Creates large paper losses to reduce taxable income—supported by the "One Big Beautiful Bill" provisions for 100% bonus depreciation.

4	Maximize 529 Plan Benefits	Make an annual contribution of $4K in Virginia State college savings account (i.e., VA 529) to receive state income tax credit (assuming Kevin pays VA state income in scenario 2, 3 and 4 below).	Withdraw from a 529 college savings plan to pay tuition and educational costs. Withdrawals are tax-free when used for qualified education expenses.
5	Claim the American Opportunity Tax Credit (AOTC)	Pays Virginia college tuition personally, carving out $4,000 of expenses not covered by 529 funds.	Qualifies for up to $1,000 in refundable credit—if there is no double counting. With proof of earned income more than half of his support.
6	Convert Lifestyle Costs into Legitimate Schedule E Deductions	Engages his girlfriend for help managing the rental—decorating, receipts, showing units, and meetings.	Convert eligible costs (meals, design, management) into Schedule E expenses, reducing taxable income.
7	Run a Side Business on Schedule C	Operates a junk removal business that supports his real estate activities.	Deducts business expenses (home office, mileage, tools, insurance) while building self-employment income.
8	Set Up a Solo 401(k)	Uses E*TRADE's Solo 401(k) plan after earning business profit.	If business is profitable, defers up to $24,500 (employee) + 20% (employer) contributions and can borrow up to $50,000 for future property investments.
9	Fund a Roth IRA Early	Contributes $7,000 in 2025 ($7,500 in 2026) annually from earned income.	Allows tax-free growth and post 59.5 withdrawals—compounding into over $2 million by retirement age.
10	Establish and Fund an HSA (Health Savings Account)	Covered under a family high-deductible plan, he contributes up to $8,550 in a Fidelity HSA.	Triple tax benefit: deductible contributions, tax-free growth, and tax-free medical reimbursements later. File Form 8606 to reflect that.
11	Track Home Office Expenses	Deduces part of his home used for business and rental management.	Convert personal expenses into legitimate business deductions (utilities, rent, Wi-Fi, etc.) in Schedule C.
12	Think Like a Long-Term Investor	Uses his rental equity and Solo 401(k) borrowing feature to fund the next property.	Applies the "Buy, Borrow, and Build" strategy to compound

			assets without triggering immediate tax.

Tax Pro Advice: Kevin's approach shows how young professionals can legally and ethically use the tax code to strengthen their financial foundation. Even on a modest income, he demonstrates how understanding the rules, W-4 optimization, depreciation, credits, and retirement accounts, can lead to thousands in annual tax savings.

His case underscores a universal truth: financial literacy is not about age; it is about awareness. By combining education with execution, Kevin proves that with planning, discipline, and strategic use of real estate, a 19-year-old can start building generational wealth now, not later.

Tax planning tip 1: Optimize Kevin's *W-4*

Below is how Kevin completed is 2025 Form W-4 to minimize or eliminate withholding. Note that the social security number is a fictitious one (xxx-xx-8888).

Form **W-4**
Department of the Treasury Internal Revenue Service

Employee's Withholding Certificate

Complete Form W-4 so that your employer can withhold the correct federal income tax from your pay.
Give Form W-4 to your employer.
Your withholding is subject to review by the IRS.

OMB No. 1545-0074

2025

Step 1: Enter Personal Information	(a) First name and middle initial: Kevin	Last name: Nie	(b) Social security number: 222-22-8888
	Address: 1234 Main St #88		**Does your name match the name on your social security card?** If not, to ensure you get credit for your earnings, contact SSA at 800-772-1213 or go to *www.ssa.gov*.
	City or town, state, and ZIP code: Fairfax VA 22030		

(c) ☑ **Single** or **Married filing separately**
☐ **Married filing jointly** or **Qualifying surviving spouse**
☐ **Head of household** (Check only if you're unmarried and pay more than half the costs of keeping up a home for yourself and a qualifying individual.)

Complete Steps 3–4(b) on Form W-4 for only ONE of these jobs. Leave those steps blank for the other jobs. (Your withholding will be most accurate if you complete Steps 3–4(b) on the Form W-4 for the highest paying job.)

Step 3: Claim Dependent and Other Credits	If your total income will be $200,000 or less ($400,000 or less if married filing jointly): Multiply the number of qualifying children under age 17 by $2,000 $ 0 Multiply the number of other dependents by $500 . . . . . $ Add the amounts above for qualifying children and other dependents. You may add to this the amount of any other credits. Enter the total here	3	$ 0
Step 4 (optional): Other Adjustments	**(a) Other income (not from jobs).** If you want tax withheld for other income you expect this year that won't have withholding, enter the amount of other income here. This may include interest, dividends, and retirement income	4(a)	$ 0
	(b) Deductions. If you expect to claim deductions other than the standard deduction and want to reduce your withholding, use the Deductions Worksheet on page 3 and enter the result here	4(b)	$ 25000
	(c) Extra withholding. Enter any additional tax you want withheld each **pay period** . .	4(c)	$

Step 5: Sign Here	Under penalties of perjury, I declare that this certificate, to the best of my knowledge and belief, is true, correct, and complete. Kevin Nie **Employee's signature** (This form is not valid unless you sign it.)	07/01/2025 **Date**

Employers Only	Employer's name and address	First date of employment	Employer identification number (EIN)
	Mama's Pizzeria 888 Main St. Fairfax VA 22030	07/01/2025	99-8888888

For Privacy Act and Paperwork Reduction Act Notice, see page 3. Cat. No. 10220Q Form **W-4** (2025)

Note: The $25,000 deduction in line 4(b) is based on (1) the rental loss (up to $25,000); (2) AOTC (up to $2,500), and (3) HSA contribution (up to $8,550).

Assume Kevin's W-2 salary for 2025 is $40K; and his rental property produces a $25,000 loss, which can be used to offset his W-2 earned income. This leads to AGI around $15K. With a $15,750 standard deduction, he will owe zero income tax to the IRS and VA state. Therefore, a $25K deduction will be entered in the W-4 box 4(b). If Kevin's salary increases to different levels, his W-4 will be adjusted accordingly.

See table below as a demonstration of different levels of W-2 income:

Kevin's Income	**Scenario 1**	**Scenario 2**	**Scenario 3**	**Scenario 4**
W-2 at Mama's Pizzeria	$40,000	$50,000	$100,000	$150,000
Rental loss (up to)	-$25,000	-$25,000	-$25,000	Phased out
AGI	$15,000	$25,000	$75,000	$150,000
Standard deduction (2025), subject to inflation indexing	$15,750	$15,750	$15,750	$15,750
Taxable income	$0	$9,250	$59,250	$134,250
Income tax (Fed)	$0	$925	$7,953 (1)	$25,072 (2)
Income tax (VA)	$0	$333	$3,147	$7,458 (3)
W-4 box 4(b)	$25,000	$25,000	$20,000	$0

Note (1): here is how the federal income tax $7,953 is derived:

Tax Bracket	**Taxable Income Range**	**Calculation**	**Tax for Bracket**	**Cumulative Tax**
10%	$0 – $11,925	$11,925 × 10%	$1,192	$1,192
12%	$11,926 – $48,475	($48,475 – $11,925) × 12% = $36,550 × 12%	$4,386	$5,582
22%	$48,476 – $59,250	($59,250 – $48,475) × 22% = $10,775 × 22%	$2,370	$7,953

Note (2): here is how $25,072 is derived:

Tax Bracket	Taxable Income Range	Calculation	Tax for Bracket	Cumulative Tax
10%	$0 – $11,925	$11,925 × 10%	$1,192	$1,192
12%	$11,926 – $48,475	($48,475 − $11,925) × 12%	$4,390	$5,582
22%	$48,476 – $103,350	($103,350 − $48,475) × 22%	$12,073	$17,656
24%	$103,351 – $134,250	($134,250 − $103,350) × 24%	$7,416	$25,072

Note (3): here is how Virginia state income tax $7,458 is derived:

Tax Bracket	Taxable Income Range	Tax Rate	Tax Calculation	Tax Owed	Cumulative Tax
1	$0 – $3,000	2%	$3,000 × 2%	$60	$60.00
2	$3,001 – $5,000	3%	($5,000 − $3,000) × 3%	$60	$120.00
3	$5,001 – $17,000	5%	($17,000 − $5,000) × 5%	$600	$720.00
4	$17,001 – $134,250	5.75%	($134,250 − $17,000) × 5.75%	$6,738	$7,458

Income	1a	Total amount from Form(s) W-2, box 1 (see instructions) W-2 work at Mama Pizza	1a	33,333
Attach Form(s) W-2 here. Also attach Forms W-2G and 1099-R if tax was withheld.	b	Household employee wages not reported on Form(s) W-2 W-2 internship at AI Inc.	1b	
	c	Tip income not reported on line 1a (see instructions)	1c	
	d	Medicaid waiver payments not reported on Form(s) W-2 (see instructions)	1d	
	e	Taxable dependent care benefits from Form 2441, line 26	1e	
If you did not get a Form W-2, see	f	Employer-provided adoption benefits from Form 8839, line 31	1f	
	g	Wages from Form 8919, line 6	1g	

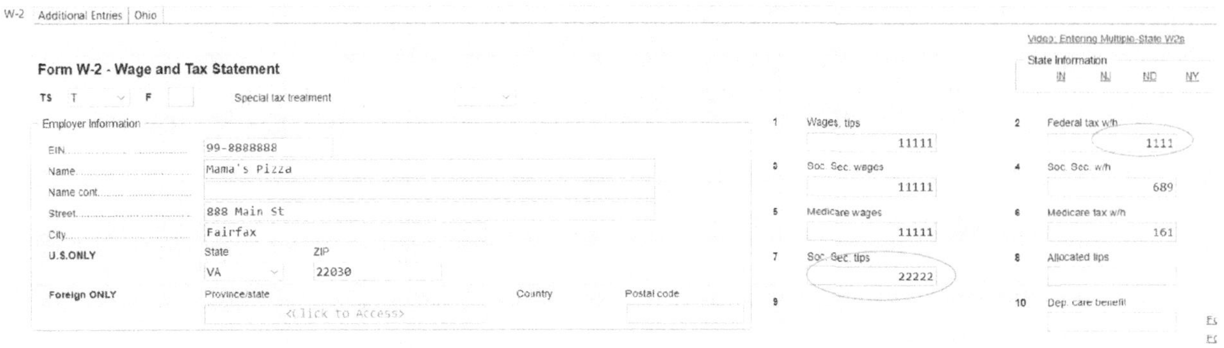

Kevin did not file his W-4 form correctly when he joined Mama's Pizza as a part-time waiter. He could have added a deduction (equivalent to his standard deduction $15K and other deductions such as HSA contribution and rental losses) on the W-4 box 4b in order to minimize the withholding and then reduce the need to ask for refund.

Tax planning tip 2: Rental losses up to $25,000

IRC §469 has a $25,000 special allowance for rental real estate, which Kevin can fully enjoy, if his AGI is below $100,000. He can enjoy a partial allowance if his AGI is between $100,000 and $150,000.

Even if Kevin's W-2 rises to $150,000, he can consider the following ways to reduce the AGI below $100,000 to fully enjoy the $25K rental losses. Selected strategies include:

Deduction Type	2025 Max (single)	Tax Rule	New MAGI
Traditional 401(k) (employee deferral)	Up to $23,500	Reduces W-2 taxable wages	$150,000 – 23,500 = $126,500
Traditional IRA	$7,000 in 2025 ($7,500 in 2026)	Deductible if not phased out by employer plan	$126,500 – 7,000 = $119,500
HSA (HDHP) *	$8,550 under family plan	Above-the-line deduction (Form 8889)	$119,500 – 8,550 = $110,950
Small business loss	$16,000 loss	IRC §168(k)	$94,950

* Kevin is under parent's HDHP family plan.

Tax planning tip 3: Use depreciation to create rental losses. Totally legal

When Kevin buys a property to rent out, the IRS lets the landlord write off part of its cost each year to reflect wear and tear, aging, and use. Kevin can depreciate the building, appliances, flooring, cabinets, and improvements. But he cannot depreciate land (because it does not wear out). Based on county appraisal value, the land may account for 15% of property value, with the remaining 85% ($410,550) being depreciable. The tax code stipulates a 27.5-year schedule; Kevin will record annual depreciation of $14,929 ($410,550 / 27.5).

FLY Tax Term: The 1986 Tax Reform Act made the residential rental property life 27.5 years and commercial rental life 39 years. In other words, you recoup the construction cost of your house at the end of 27.5 years. In reality, you may have to replace or fix many parts of your house much sooner.

Assuming Kevin's rental produces strong cash flows, his rental may be profitable, adding more taxable income. Now, he may consider cost segregation of his rental.

FLY Tax Term: Cost segregation is a tax strategy that lets real-estate owners accelerate depreciation—deducting a large portion of a property's value much faster than the standard 27.5 years. Instead of depreciating the whole building slowly, a study reclassifies parts of the property into shorter-life categories (100% bonus depreciation for components with 5, 7, or 15 years), creating much bigger deductions up front.

He acquired the rental and began renting out in late 2025, eligible for 100% bonus depreciation for ten-year or shorter-lived property assets. Kevin hires a qualified cost segregation vendor (such as Cost Segregation Services, Inc. (CSSI)), who produces a 60-page cost segregation report. Here is an excerpt:

Asset Category	Typical Recovery Period (MACRS)	Estimated Allocation %	Cost Basis Allocation ($)	Bonus Depreciation Eligibility	Description / Examples
Land (non-depreciable)	N/A	15 %	$75,000	No	Lot value, landscaping base soil
Building Structure (Real Property)	27.5 yrs	70 %	$336,000	No	Walls, roof, framing, foundation
5-Year Property (Tangible Personal Property)	5 yrs	8 %	$38,400	Yes (100 % from 2025 under §168(k))	Appliances, carpets, cabinets, blinds, ceiling fans

Asset Category	Typical Recovery Period (MACRS)	Estimated Allocation %	Cost Basis Allocation ($)	Bonus Depreciation Eligibility	Description / Examples
7-Year Property (Tangible Personal Property)	7 yrs	2 %	$9,600	Yes	Furniture, built-in shelving, some fixtures
15-Year Land Improvements	15 yrs	5 %	$24,000	Yes	Driveways, walkways, decks, fences, landscaping, lighting
Total		100 %	$483,000		

If Kevin decides to do cost segregation in the future (say year 2030), he is electing the change of depreciation accounting method from straight line (27.5 years) to accelerated depreciation. He will need to fill Form 3115, which is a specialized tax topic available in my book *SMART Family Tax Guide* (Chapter 18).

Year	**Without Cost Segregation** **(straight-line deprecation of 27.5 years)**	**With Cost Segregation in 2030 (catch-up)**
2025 – 2029	$14,929 (1)	NA
2030	$12,218 (2)	$84,218 ($12,218 + $72,000 bonus). Note: $72,000 is the sum of 5-year property bonus depreciation $38,400, 7-year $9,600, and 15-year $24,000). Fill Form 3115 to change to accelerated depreciation
2031 and beyond	$12,218	$12,218

Note: (1) The straight-line depreciation from 2025 to 2029 ($14,929) is calculated by 85% of house cost basis ($410,550) divided by 27.5-year.

(2) The post-2031 straight line depreciation of $12,218 is derived by: $336K Building Structure divided by 27.5 years.

A large depreciation amount emerges in 2030, but Kevin's tax return can only offset up to $25K rental losses (including depreciation). Assuming Kevin's AGI for 2031 and forward is below $100K, his unused bonus depreciation will be applied toward year 2031 and beyond against his AGI to lower his taxes for these years.

Section B - Assets Placed in Service During 2024 Tax Year Using the General Depreciation System

(a) Classification of property	(b) Month and year placed in service	(c) Basis for depreciation (business/investment use only-see instructions)	(d) Recovery period	(e) Convention	(f) Method	(g) Depreciation deduction
19a 3-year property						
b 5-year property						
c 7-year property						
d 10-year property						
e 15-year property						
f 20-year property						
g 25-year property			25 yrs.		S/L	
h Residential rental	01-2024	483,000	27.5 yrs.	MM	S/L	16,833
property			27.5 yrs.	MM	S/L	
i Nonresidential real			39 yrs.	MM	S/L	
property				MM	S/L	

Tax planning tip 4: State 529 plan

Virginia's 529 program is called "Virginia529," and is one of the most generous state programs in the U.S. because it allows unlimited carryforwards of state deductions and tax-free withdrawals for education expenses. This is how it works:

- No federal deduction for contributions (same as all states).
- Tax-free growth: Earnings in your 529 account are not taxed while they grow. A total equity index investment option produces the highest return (10-year average 12%) with the lowest expense ratio (0.07% per year), much better than a target-day 529 plan. (See chart below.)
- Tax-free withdrawals: If used for *qualified education expenses*, withdrawals are not subject to federal income tax.

PORTFOLIO	E.R.	% EQUITY	10YR PERFORMANCE
Global Equity	0.36%	100%	N/A
Stable Value	0.09%	0%	1.97%
Total Stock Market Index	0.07%	100%	12.01%
Total Bond Market Index	0.08%	0%	1.26%
Total International Stock Index	0.12%	100%	3.95%
Inflation Protected Securities	0.12%	0%	1.76%
REIT Index Fund	0.15%	100%	5.23%

Source: https://www.invest529.com/

- Virginia State Tax Benefits: Virginia residents can deduct contributions to any Virginia529 account from their Virginia state taxable income.
- Deduction limit:
    - $4,000 per account, per year, per taxpayer
    - If you contribute more than $4,000, you can carry forward the excess indefinitely to future years. A better strategy is to open multiple accounts, up to $4,000 each. Then you can have more state income tax deduction in the current year.
    - Virginia's top income tax rate = 5.75%, so a $4,000 contribution saves about $230 per year per account on your state return. If you contribute for multiple children (or accounts), the deduction multiplies.

Total Subtractions	7.				Interest	20.
Deductions	8A.	104	VA 529	4000.	Total Adjustments	21.
	8B.					
	8C.					
Total Deductions	9.			4000.		

Tax planning tip 5: Claim the American Opportunity Tax Credit (AOTC)

Tax term: The American Opportunity Tax Credit (AOTC) helps college students and their parents pay for higher education by reducing their taxes or even giving them money back if they owe little or no tax. It became effective in 2009.

The credit can be worth up to $2,500 per year, per student, including up to $1,000 refundable credit. Qualified college expenses include tuition, required fees, and books, supplies, and course materials (even if bought off-campus or online). Make sure you have proved earned income that exceeds half of your support.

Kevin used his credit card and paid $4,000 in tuition to Northern Virginia University. The school sent Kevin Form 1098-T, which shows $4,000 tuition paid that year. He filled out Form 8863, attached to his tax return 1040. If Kevin owes more than $2,500 in federal tax (in Scenario 3 and 4), he will get full AOTC credit; if he owes less than $2,500 in federal tax, he still gets up to $1,000 as a refund.

Payments	25	Federal income tax withheld from:				
	a	Form(s) W-2	25a			
	b	Form(s) 1099	25b			
	c	Other forms (see instructions)	25c			
	d	Add lines 25a through 25c			25d	
If you have a qualifying child, attach Sch. EIC.	26	2024 estimated tax payments and amount applied from 2023 return			26	
	27	Earned income credit (EIC) NO	27			
	28	Additional child tax credit from Schedule 8812	28			
	29	American opportunity credit from Form 8863, line 8	29	1,000		
	30	Reserved for future use	30			
	31	Amount from Schedule 3, line 15	31			
	32	Add lines 27, 28, 29, and 31. These are your **total other payments and refundable credits**			32	1,000

Tax planning tip 6: Convert Lifestyle Costs into Legitimate Schedule E Deductions

Kevin dates his high school sweetheart, Helen, an internal design college major, while studying hard and managing his rental. By hiring her to manage and maintain the rental, Kevin can ordinary and necessary business expenses from his Schedule. Kevin (1) signs a service contract with Helen; (2) ensures Helen indeed does her job; (3) keeps records and payments; and (4) issues a 1099 NEC to Helen at year end.

Let's assume the rental income is $36,000 and Helen is paid $300 per month, or $3,600 annually. That is about 10% of total rental income.

Personal or romantic spending (like dates, gifts, or vacations) cannot be deducted. Helen will report such income in her Schedule C (with reasonable expense deductions on her end, such as auto, cell phone, supplies, and home office).

#	Expense Category	How Helen Can Help	Deducted on Kevin's Schedule E
1	Property management / coordination	Helen schedules maintenance, communicates with tenants, handles lease renewals.	Management fees or outside services
2	Bookkeeping / admin support	She tracks rent payments, utilities, receipts, and mileage logs.	Legal and professional services
3	Tenant screening	She runs background checks or interviews applicants.	Advertising and tenant-screening costs
4	Marketing / listing work	She photographs the unit, writes ads, posts listings online.	Advertising expense
5	Design & staging	She selects paint colors, arranges furniture, or decorates for showings.	Supplies or maintenance expense
6	Cleaning & turnover prep	She deep-cleans between tenants or coordinates cleaning crews.	Cleaning and maintenance expense
7	Minor repairs supervision	She meets plumbers, HVAC techs, or delivery crews on site.	Repairs expense
8	Errands & purchasing	She buys filters, bulbs, locks, paint, or small tools.	Supplies expense

9	Travel / mileage	She drives to and from the property for inspections or errands.	Auto and travel expenses (mileage at IRS rate)
10	Recordkeeping / digital organization	She maintains Google Drive or accounting spreadsheets for receipts.	Office expense

Kevin is so lucky to have a beautiful, frugal and hardworking girlfriend. He can spend more time managing his junk removal business, and hunt for more rental properties. If Helen had her parents apply the same FLY strategy listed in this book, she may have purchased her first home and rented to her college friends as well. She can hire Kevin to work around the rental as a contractor and issue him a 1099.

	Federal Supporting Statements	2025
Name(s) as shown on return		Tax ID Number
Kevin Nie		22

Schedule E - Line 19 - Other Expenses Stat

Other Expenses		Property A	Property B	P
Contractor - xxx9999	Pay girlfriend	8,888		
Business meals (50%)		777		
Home office ($5/sqf)		750		
HVAC 1.263(a)-1(f)	$2,500 safe harbor	2,445		
Total		**12,860**		

Type of Property:

1 Single Family Residence	3 Vacation/Short-Term Rental	5 Land	7 Sel
2 Multi-Family Residence	4 Commercial	6 Royalties	8 Oth

			A
Income:			
3	Rents received	3	26,666
4	Royalties received	4	
Expenses:			
5	Advertising	5	222
6	Auto and travel (see instructions)	6	3,111
7	Cleaning and maintenance	7	555
8	Commissions	8	
9	Insurance	9	
10	Legal and other professional fees	10	555
11	Management fees	11	
12	Mortgage interest paid to banks, etc. (see instructions)	12	6,666
13	Other interest	13	
14	Repairs	14	
15	Supplies	15	
16	Taxes	16	7,777
17	Utilities	17	
18	Depreciation expense or depletion	18	14,928
19	Other (list) Statement #1	19	12,860
20	Total expenses. Add lines 5 through 19	20	46,674
21	Subtract line 20 from line 3 (rents) and/or 4 (royalties). If result is a (loss), see instructions to find out if you must file **Form 6198**	21	(20,008)

Note: "Pay girlfriend" is for FLY readers' understanding. Obviously, you do not add such notes in your tax return to the IRS.

Tax planning tip 7: Run a side business (home junk and goods removal)

Kevin has an SUV powerful enough to haul heavy items. He builds up a house clean and junk removal side business with an LLC (Gym and Home Operator LLC). As a single member LLC owner, Kevin enjoys at least ten tax saving benefits:

#	Tax Benefit	How It Works for Kevin	IRS Form / Code Section
1	Vehicle Deduction (SUV or Truck)	Kevin can deduct business use of his SUV—either actual expenses (gas, repairs, insurance) or standard mileage rate (70¢ / mile for 2025). If the SUV > 6,000 lbs GVWR, he may use §179 or bonus depreciation for an immediate write-off.	Form 4562 / §179 / §168(k)
2	Fuel, Maintenance, & Insurance	All business-related fuel, oil changes, tires, repairs, and vehicle insurance are deductible for the business-usage.	Schedule C Lines 9 & 10
3	Equipment & Tools	Dump trailers, dollies, bins, cleaning gear, gloves, safety equipment—all immediately deductible or depreciated.	Form 4562 / §162
4	Home Office Deduction	Kevin can deduct part of his rent, internet, and utilities for a workspace used exclusively to manage the business.	Form 8829 / §280A
5	Cell Phone & Internet	The business share of his phone and data plan counts as a communication expense.	Schedule C Line 25
6	Startup & Organization Costs	Up to $5,000 of startup costs (licenses, LLC filing, advertising) are deductible in year 1.	§195
7	Business Meals & Networking	When Kevin meets clients at coffee shops or lunches with junk business contractors, 50 % of those meals are deductible if business is discussed.	§274(n)
8	Hire girlfriend to work on marketing	Kevin hires Helen (a 1099 NEC contractor) to set up appointments, manage website and social media, and handle post-service survey	§162(a)
9	Retirement Plan (Solo 401(k))	As both "employer" and "employee," Kevin can contribute up to $24,500 (+ 20% of profit) pre-tax—sheltering large amounts from income tax.	§401(k) / Form 5500-EZ
10	QBI Deduction (20% Business Profit)	Under §199A, Kevin may deduct up to 20 % of his qualified business income (QBI) from taxable income.	Form 8995 or 8995-A

Tax planning tip 8: Set Up a Solo Traditional 401(k)

Kevin has made sizable profits in his home goods removal business. He sets up an E*TRADE Solo 401(k), including Traditional (pre-tax), Roth, and loan features, and applies a Roth conversion strategically during a market dip multiplying long-term tax benefits.

#	Strategy / Action	How It Works for Kevin	Tax Benefit / Effect
1	Open a Solo 401(k)	As a single-member LLC owner, Kevin qualifies to open a Solo 401(k) at E*TRADE since he has no full-time employees.	Creates a tax-sheltered retirement account just for his self-employment income.
2	Make Employee Deferral (Traditional)	He can contribute up to $24,500 (2026 limit) of his net self-employment income pre-tax.	Reduces taxable income now; defers tax until withdrawal.
3	Add Employer Contribution	As his own "employer," he can add up to 20% of net profit, bringing the total to about $66,000 max.	Larger tax-deferred contribution; lowers current-year AGI.
4	E*TRADE Loan Feature	He can borrow up to 50% of his vested balance (max $50,000) for business expansion or equipment.	Tax-free access to capital; interest paid goes back into his own 401(k).
5	Choose Roth or Traditional Sub-Account	E*TRADE Solo 401(k)s allow both Traditional (pre-tax) and Roth (after-tax) buckets.	Flexibility: lower taxes now (Traditional) or growth tax-free (Roth).
6	Roth Conversion During Market Dip	When stock values drop, Kevin can convert part of his pre-tax 401(k) to the Roth side while asset prices are low.	Pays tax on a smaller value → future rebound grows 100% tax-free.
7	Tax Bracket Control	Convert gradually in years when business income or market returns are lower to stay in a lower bracket.	Smooths tax liability; avoids pushing AGI into higher tiers.
8	Tax-Free Compounding (Roth Side)	Once in the Roth, future gains and withdrawals in retirement are tax-free if held 5+ years and after age 59½.	Zero tax on growth, dividends, or withdrawals later.
9	Business Deduction for Traditional Portion	Every pre-tax dollar contributed reduces Kevin's business income on Schedule C.	Lowers AGI, which may also restore rental-loss or AOTC eligibility.
10	Retirement + Liquidity Combo	By combining 401(k) loan + Roth conversion, Kevin can invest for the long term yet still tap funds if needed.	Keeps cash accessible while maximizing tax-advantaged growth.

Schedule 1 (Form 1040) 2025 Page 2

Part II Adjustments to Income

11	Educator expenses	11	
12	Certain business expenses of reservists, performing artists, and fee-basis government officials. Attach Form 2106	12	
13	Health savings account deduction. Attach Form 8889	13	8,550
14	Moving expenses for members of the Armed Forces. Attach Form 3903. If claiming only storage fees (see instructions), check here ☐	14	
15	Deductible part of self-employment tax. Attach Schedule SE	15	184
16	Self-employed SEP, SIMPLE, and qualified plans . . . Set up Solo 401(K)	16	2,370
17	Self-employed health insurance deduction	17	

Schedule C shows 20% company match to solo 401(k) – traditional

Part I Income

1	Gross receipts or sales. See instructions for line 1 and check the box if this income was reported to you on Form W-2 and the "Statutory employee" box on that form was checked ☐	1	22,222
2	Returns and allowances	2	0
3	Subtract line 2 from line 1	3	22,222
4	Cost of goods sold (from line 42)	4	
5	**Gross profit.** Subtract line 4 from line 3	5	22,222
6	Other income, including federal and state gasoline or fuel tax credit or refund (see instructions)	6	
7	**Gross income.** Add lines 5 and 6	7	22,222

Part II Expenses. Enter expenses for business use of your home **only** on line 30.

8	Advertising	8	666	18	Office expense (see instructions)	18	
9	Car and truck expenses (see instructions)	9	3,889	19	Pension and profit-sharing plans	19	20% match 593
				20	Rent or lease (see instructions):		
10	Commissions and fees	10		a	Vehicles, machinery, and equipment	20a	
11	Contract labor (see instructions)	11		b	Other business property	20b	
12	Depletion	12		21	Repairs and maintenance	21	
13	Depreciation and section 179 expense deduction (not included in Part III) (see instructions)	13		22	Supplies (not included in Part III)	22	
				23	Taxes and licenses	23	125
				24	Travel and meals:		
14	Employee benefit programs (other than on line 19)	14		a	Travel	24a	888
				b	Deductible meals (see instructions)	24b	278
15	Insurance (other than health)	15	1,111	25	Utilities	25	188
16	Interest (see instructions):			26	Wages (less employment credits)	26	
a	Mortgage (paid to banks, etc.)	16a		27a	Energy efficient commercial bldgs deduction (attach Form 7205)	27a	
b	Other	16b					
17	Legal and professional services	17	555	b	Other expenses (from line 48)	27b	11,333
28	**Total expenses** before expenses for business use of home. Add lines 8 through 27b					28	19,626
29	Tentative profit or (loss). Subtract line 28 from line 7					29	2,596
30	Expenses for business use of your home. Do not report these expenses elsewhere. Attach Form 8829						

Note: We have noted two different spaces to enter the 20% match suggested by tax advisors: (1) Schedule C line 19; or (2) Schedule 1 line 16. Readers should consult their tax pro for guidance.

Tax planning tip 9: Fund a Roth IRA Early

Kevin's $70K AGI is far below the Roth IRA phase-out range ($146K to $161K), so he can fully fund both a Solo 401(k) and a Roth IRA in the same year. The Solo 401(k) saves taxes today, while the Roth IRA gives him tax-free income later, the best of both worlds.

Kevin can contribute to a traditional IRA if his AGI is slightly over $100K. By doing so he can apply rental losses to offset his earned income up to $25K a year.

Factor	Solo 401(k)	Roth IRA

Type of account	Employer-based, self-employed retirement plan	Individual retirement account
Contribution source	Self-employment income	Earned income (can be wages or self-employment)
Tax treatment	Pre-tax (Traditional) or after-tax (Roth 401(k))	After-tax, tax-free growth
2025 contribution limit	$23,500 employee deferral (+25% profit sharing, total up to $66,000)	$7,000 (under 50)
Income phase-out (Roth IRA)	N/A	Phases out for single between $146,000–$161,000 AGI

Source: Data from Yahoo Finance, chart edited by author

Form **8606**

Department of the Treasury
Internal Revenue Service

Nondeductible IRAs

Attach to 2025 Form 1040, 1040-SR, or 1040-NR.
Go to *www.irs.gov/Form8606* for instructions and the latest information.

OMB No. 1545-0074
2025
Attachment Sequence No. **48**

Name. If married, file a separate form for each spouse required to file 2025 Form 8606. See instructions.			Your social security number
Kevin Nie			222-22-8888
Fill in Your Address Only if You Are Filing This Form by Itself and Not With Your Tax Return	Home address (number and street, or P.O. box if mail is not delivered to your home)		Apt. no.
	City, town or post office, state, and ZIP code. If you have a foreign address, also complete the spaces below. See instructions.		
	Foreign country name	Foreign province/state/county	Foreign postal code

Note: Except where stated otherwise, "traditional IRA" includes traditional SEP IRAs and traditional SIMPLE IRAs. "Roth IRA" includes Roth SEP IRAs and Roth SIMPLE IRAs.

Part I **Nondeductible Contributions to Traditional IRAs and Distributions From Traditional IRAs**

Complete this part only if one or more of the following apply.

- You made nondeductible contributions to a traditional IRA for 2025. Nondeductible contributions to a traditional IRA do not include employer contributions made to a SEP IRA pursuant to a SEP arrangement or to a SIMPLE IRA pursuant to a SIMPLE IRA plan.
- You took distributions from a traditional IRA in 2025 and you made nondeductible contributions to a traditional IRA in 2025 or an earlier year. For this purpose, "distributions" does not include rollovers (but does include certain 2025 retirement plan distribution repayments treated as rollovers (see instructions)). Also, it does not include qualified charitable distributions, one-time distributions to fund an HSA, conversions, recharacterizations, or returns of certain contributions.
- You converted part, but not all, of your traditional IRAs to Roth IRAs in 2025 and you made nondeductible contributions to a traditional IRA in 2025 or an earlier year.

1	Enter your nondeductible contributions to traditional IRAs for 2025, including those made for 2025 from January 1, 2026, through April 15, 2026. See instructions	1	7,000
2	Enter your total basis in traditional IRAs. See instructions	2	
3	Add lines 1 and 2	3	7,000
	In 2025, did you take a distribution — No — Enter the amount from line 3 on line 14.		

Tax planning tip 10: Establish and fund an HSA (Health Savings Account)

As Kevin's parent, I maintain a High-Deductible Health Plan (HDHP) through my employer. Kevin is in my family health insurance plan. Even though he is covered under my plan, he can open his own Health Savings Account (HSA) if he is not claimed to be my tax dependent (which is the situation when he claims AOTC under tax planning tip 5).

Why so? The IRS allows anyone who is covered by an HDHP and not listed as a dependent to have their own HSA. That means Kevin qualifies to set one up by his own name. Kevin can contribute to the family limit of $8,550 (2025) because the HDHP provides family coverage, not self-only coverage. The money that goes into Kevin's HSA can come from his own earnings (from work, tutoring, or his side business) or from a gift from me, his parents, or relatives. The IRS does not care whose money it is, only that it is contributed on Kevin's behalf into his HSA account. The funds belong to him personally and can grow tax-free for life.

Every dollar in Kevin's HSA gets a triple tax advantage:

- Contributions are tax-deductible (they reduce his taxable income if he files his own return).
- Earnings grow tax-free inside the account. Kevin invests his HSA money at Fidelity HSA brokerage account, investing in BRK.B or S&P 500 index fund (half and half).
- Withdrawals for qualified medical expenses, like doctor visits, prescriptions, or even future health premiums, are completely tax-free. Kevin can pay with his credit card or check, negotiating a discounted service price.
- Even better— if Kevin does not use the money for medical costs now, and rather uses his credit card with 5% cash back reward, he can let HAS money compound for decades and later use it as a tax-free retirement medical fund, effectively giving him one of the most powerful, early-start savings tools available under IRC §223.

Form **8889** — **Health Savings Accounts (HSAs)** — OMB No. 1545-0074 — **2025**

Department of the Treasury
Internal Revenue Service

Attach to Form 1040, 1040-SR, or 1040-NR.
Go to *www.irs.gov/Form8889* for instructions and the latest information.

Attachment Sequence No. 52

Name(s) shown on Form 1040, 1040-SR, or 1040-NR	Social security number of HSA beneficiary. If both spouses have HSAs, see instructions
Kevin Nie	222-22-8888

Before you begin: Complete Form 8853, Archer MSAs and Long-Term Care Insurance Contracts, if required.

Part I **HSA Contributions and Deduction.** See the instructions before completing this part. If you are filing jointly and both you and your spouse each have separate HSAs, complete a separate Part I for each spouse.

1	Check the box to indicate your coverage under a high-deductible health plan (HDHP) during 2025. See instructions		☐ Self-only ☒ Family
2	HSA contributions you made for 2025 (or those made on your behalf), including those made by the unextended due date of your tax return that were for 2025. **Do not** include employer contributions, contributions through a cafeteria plan, or rollovers. See instructions	2	8,550
3	If you were under age 55 at the end of 2025 and, on the first day of **every** month during 2025, you were, or were considered, an eligible individual with the **same** coverage, enter $4,300 ($8,550 for family coverage). **All others,** see the instructions for the amount to enter	3	8,550
4	Enter the amount you and your employer contributed to your Archer MSAs for 2025 from Form 8853, lines 1 and 2. If you or your spouse had family coverage under an HDHP at any time during 2025, also include any amount contributed to your spouse's Archer MSAs	4	
5	Subtract line 4 from line 3. If zero or less, enter -0-	5	8,550

It flows to Schedule 1 as a reduction of AGI.

Schedule 1 (Form 1040) 2025 Page 2

Part II **Adjustments to Income**

11	Educator expenses	11	
12	Certain business expenses of reservists, performing artists, and fee-basis government officials. Attach Form 2106	12	
13	Health savings account deduction. Attach Form 8889	13	8,550
14	Moving expenses for members of the Armed Forces. Attach Form 3903. If claiming only storage fees		

Tax planning tip 11: Track Home Office Expenses

Kevin can legitimately claim two different home office deductions if each space is used exclusively and regularly for a distinct business purpose:

- Schedule E: managing his rental property
- Schedule C: operating his junk-removal LLC (Gym and Home Operator LLC)

Below is a clear comparison table.

Category	**Schedule E (Rental Property)**	**Schedule C (Junk-Removal Business)**
Primary IRS Code	IRC § 212 – ordinary & necessary expenses for producing rental income	IRC § 162(a) – trade or business expenses
IRS Form / Worksheet	Schedule E + Form 8829 (optional) or manual allocation	Schedule C + Form 8829 (Home Office Deduction)
Purpose of the space	Office used exclusively for managing rentals: tenant communication, bookkeeping, repairs scheduling, etc.	Office or garage space used exclusively for running the junk-removal LLC: scheduling, website management, billing, records.
Exclusive-use rule	Must be used only for rental-management tasks	Must be used only for business-management tasks
Typical location	Small desk area or study	Separate workshop area, garage corner, or office
Common expenses allocable	Rent or mortgage interest, property tax, utilities, internet, depreciation, insurance (pro-rated by square-foot %)	Same expense categories, but based on separate exclusive-use area
Allocation method	% = (square feet of rental office ÷ total home sq ft)	% = (square feet of business office ÷ total home sq ft)
Tax impact	Reduces passive income from rentals on Schedule E	Reduces active business income on Schedule C, lowering self-employment tax too
Recordkeeping	Floor-plan sketch, dated photos, receipts for home expenses	Same evidence, plus proof of business activity in the space
Prohibition	Cannot double-deduct the same area or expense for both—each must be distinct and documented	Must not overlap with the rental-management area

To firm up our record keeping, the IRS allows multiple home-office deductions if each area is used exclusively and regularly for a different income-producing purpose. Kevin just needs separate, well-documented spaces: one for rental management and one for his business, and he can maximize both deductions safely.

Tax planning tip 12: Think like a long-term investor

Kevin strategically and selectively uses securities-backed line of credit (SBLOC), home equity line of credit (HELOC), life-insurance backed line of credit (IBLOC), and Solo 401(k) loan feature (up to $50K) to buy more rental property with a goal of one property every two years.

After owning six rentals, he claims himself as a real estate professional, another powerful tax planning tool for future wealth building. See my *SMART Family Tax Guide* for more information.

Loan Type	Collateral Type	Best Used For	When to Use	Typical Interest Rate (2025)	Tax Deductible if Used to Buy Rentals?
SBLOC	Brokerage investments (stocks, ETFs)	Down payment or short-term bridge	When markets are stable and you want to avoid selling investments	6%–7% variable	Yes, if funds are traced directly to rental purchase or improvement (Temp. Reg. §1.163-8T; report on Sched E). But the loan is not added to the at-risk limit.
HELOC	Primary home or rental property equity	Rehab, down payment, or acquisition	When you have sufficient equity	7%–8% variable	Yes, if funds are used for rental or business investment (IRC §163(h)(3); deductible on Sched E)
IBLOC	Whole life / IUL cash value	Opportunistic purchases or refinance reserves	When policy has strong cash value and good dividend performance	5%–6% fixed	Potentially, if traced to rental property or investment use (Temp. Reg. §1.163-8T; not deductible for personal use)
Solo 401(k) Loan	Retirement account balance (up to 50% vested, max $50K)	Entry-level liquidity, rehab, or down payment	When short-term cash is needed and you want to repay yourself	Prime + 1%	No, not deductible—but interest paid goes back into Kevin's own 401(k) account (not to a lender) (§72(p))

Note: Kevin reports interest income from the loan repayment on his Schedule 1 as other income, literally offsetting the business interest deductions from Schedule E. But the loan enables Kevin to claim real estate pro status, achieve 100% bonus depreciation, pay his girlfriend reasonable compensation, and apply rental losses against his active income. These benefits outweigh the interest expense deduction matter.

Final observations: Kevin, a full-time college student, earned W-2 income, ran a side business in junk removal, managed his rental while dating his girlfriend. He contributed to his Roth IRA, solo traditional 401(k), and funded his Health Savings Account and VA 529 account. He claimed AOTC refundable tax credit. His final tax burden is as below.

He repeats his tax savings year by year, works hard toward his SMART strategies: Start to Master Assets and Reduce Taxes.

	Total Income	Taxable Income	Total Tax	Refund	Balance Due	Payment Method
Federal	14,865	265	1,243	0	243	Check or CC
VA760	14,865	1,435	0	0	0	

Case Study 4

Kevin and Wife's Joint Tax Return

"*Marriage doubles the strategy, not just the income.*" – Mike Nie

Hypothetical Situation: Kevin and Helen married in their mid-20s, bound by shared faith and a vision for financial independence. While Helen pursued medical field and earned her M.D. from Johns Hopkins, Kevin began building a small real-estate empire — buying a new rental roughly every two years around the D.C. metropolitan area.

When Helen graduated and joined Inova Fairfax Hospital earning $440,000 a year, Kevin already managed several properties, handled repairs himself, and had recently earned his real-estate license. Their daughter, Helena, was born soon after, becoming the inspiration for a long-term financial plan.

With one spouse as a high-income W-2 earner and the other a real-estate professional, a tax pro helped the young family integrate rental ownership, tax efficiency, and generational wealth creation into one cohesive system.

Together, they implemented:

- Real Estate Professional (REP) status for Kevin to unlock rental loss deductions
- Bonus depreciation and cost segregation to shelter Helen's income
- UTMA account, Trump Account (after July 2026), Coverdell ESA, and 529 plans for Helena's education and first investment.
- Whole-life policies to fund future rentals via "Borrow–Buy–Build (BBB)" financing
- HSA family plan and SMART Family Foundation for charitable purposes.

By age 18, their daughter Helena is projected to control several accounts: (1) UTMA ($900K); (2) state 529 plan ($800 K); (3) Coverdell ($100K); (4) Trump account ($200K); (5) parent gifted stocks ($700K); (6) life-insurance cash value ($500K); and (7) minor Roth IRA ($100K). These accounts, if established early and invested in a low fee, high performance stock index fund, could amount to over $3.2M, enough for her to own rental, launch her career, and FLY high.

The table below outlines the tax situation and tax solutions under the OBBB.

#	Situation	Tax Solution (2025 OBBB)
1	W-2 Income: Helen is a physician at Inova Fairfax earning $440,000 W-2. Kevin is a Real Estate Professional (REP) with mixed income (rental + commissions).	• High W-2 income pushes MFJ into the 35%–37% bracket, making deductions extremely valuable. • Kevin's REP status allows rental losses to offset Helen's W-2 income (unlimited). • Strong incentive to do cost segregation + 100% bonus depreciation to reduce joint AGI.
2	Primary Residence + Vacation Home: Primary home in Northern VA; vacation home in Virginia Beach.	• Vacation home mortgage interest subject to $750K OBBB cap combined for both homes. • You can deduct two houses (primary residence and secondary home), such as taxes, mortgage interest, and points, on Schedule A to maximize the $40K state and local taxes (SALT) benefits.
3	Rental Properties: Kevin manages several rentals and sold one rental early 2025, generating a capital gain.	• If owned >1 year → long-term capital gain (LTCG) 15% or 20% + 3.8% net investment interest tax (NIIT) depending on your AGI. • Depreciation recapture taxed at 25%. • Sell crypto during 2025 crash → harvest capital losses to offset Kevin's property sale gains. • Buy back the crypto second day. No wash-sale rule.
4	Childcare Expenses + One Child Age 12	• Childcare expenses qualify for Child & Dependent Care Credit (20% credit for high-income MFJ). • Possible Dependent Care FSA if employer offers (up to $5,000 pre-tax for 2025, and increased to $7,500 in 2026).
5	Health Savings Account (HSA)	• If family HDHP, they may contribute $8,550 (family limit for 2025) • HSA reduces AGI. • Long-term triple tax advantage: deductible + tax-free growth + tax-free medical use.
6	Kevin's Small Business & Solo 401(k)	• Kevin can contribute: ‣ Employee deferral: the lower of net income and $23.5K (2025) ‣ Employer profit-share: up to 20% of net SE income • Contributions reduce Kevin's Schedule C income → lowers AGI and NIIT. • Real estate commissions may qualify for §199A QBI deduction (20%). • Vacation home can qualify for Section 280A (the Augusta rule): if rented <14 days → no need to report rental income on Schedule E, but can be deducted as business expense on Schedule C. Need a strong documentation such as business meeting minutes, event flyer, and daily rental agreement.

#	Situation	Tax Solution (2025 OBBB)
7	Energy Credit for Tesla Purchased in 2025	• If Tesla qualifies for 2025 rules → up to $7,500 Clean Vehicle Credit. • Use standard mileage method to ensure annual auto deduction (vs. using actual expense method with business portion of bonus depreciation).
8	Bonus Depreciation Taken on a Rental Property (2025)	• 2025 bonus depreciation = 100% • Kevin as REP can deduct losses fully against Helen's W-2. • Large depreciation deduction reduces AGI, reduces NIIT, and may reduce capital gains taxes.
9	April 2025 Tariff War Market Drop (-13% to -15%)	• Helen performs a Roth conversion during dip → ideal timing (tax paid on depressed value, long-term tax-free growth). • Consider converting $55K depending on AGI and REP losses shielding income. • Measure Roth conversion amount to avoid pushing marginal tax bracket from 24% to 32%, a huge jump.

1. Married Filing Jointly

By filing a joint tax return, Kevin and Helen move into broader tax brackets and claim a larger standard deduction — about $31,500 for 2025 (with future upward adjustment with inflation). Filing jointly also simplifies mortgage qualification for new rental purchases because lenders evaluate their combined credit and income. Helen's W-2 job as a doctor helps mortgage loan approval. The structure itself becomes the first layer of tax efficiency.

Table: Standard Deductions Across Various Tax Laws

Filing Status	Pre-TCJA 2017	TCJA 2025	OBBB 2025	OBBB 2026
Single	$6,350	$15,000	$15,750	Indexed
MFJ	$12,700	$30,000	$31,500	Indexed
MFS	$6,350	$15,000	$15,750	Indexed
HOH	$9,350	$22,500	$23,625	Indexed
QSS	$12,700	$30,000	$31,500	Indexed

Source: IRS. Table created by author.
Note: TCJA stands for the Tax Cuts and Jobs Act (TCJA), the tax law enacted during Trump's first term of presidency. OBBB stands for the One Big Beautiful Bill, which was signed into law during Trump's second term. It expanded and extended key tax benefits for businesses and families under the TCJA.

Filing status:

- Single – Unmarried and not eligible for another filing status.
- MFJ (Married Filing Jointly) – Married couples who file one combined tax return.
- MFS (Married Filing Separately) – Married individuals who file separate tax returns.

- HOH (Head of Household) – Unmarried (or considered unmarried) taxpayers who pay more than half the cost of supporting a qualifying dependent.
- QSS (Qualifying Surviving Spouse) – A surviving spouse with a dependent child who may use joint return tax benefits for up to two years after the spouse's death.

2. Optimize W-4 for Doctor Wife

Helen is aware of the importance of optimizing her W-4. Rather than claiming a large IRS refund in May of next year (providing no interest earned loan to the government), they maximize the deductions with one newly born child and Kevin's real estate professional status. See the example below.

> **Tax term: The IRS Form W-4** (Employee's Withholding Certificate) tells your employer how much federal income tax to withhold from your paycheck.
>
> It does not determine how much tax you owe for the year—it only affects cash flow during the year.

Form **W-4**

Department of the Treasury
Internal Revenue Service

Employee's Withholding Certificate

Complete Form W-4 so that your employer can withhold the correct federal income tax from your pay.
Give Form W-4 to your employer.
Your withholding is subject to review by the IRS.

OMB No. 1545-0074

2025

Step 1: Enter Personal Information

(a) First name and middle initial: Helen
Last name: Nie
(b) Social security number: 222-22-9999
Address: 123 Main St
City or town, state, and ZIP code: Fairfax VA 22030

Does your name match the name on your social security card? If not, to ensure you get credit for your earnings, contact SSA at 800-772-1213 or go to *www.ssa.gov*.

(c) ☐ ~~Single or Married filing separately~~
☑ Married filing jointly or Qualifying surviving spouse
☐ Head of household (Check only if you're unmarried and pay more than half the costs of keeping up a home for yourself and a qualifying individual.)

TIP: Consider using the estimator at *www.irs.gov/W4App* to determine the most accurate withholding for the rest of the year if: you are completing this form after the beginning of the year; expect to work only part of the year; or have changes during the year in your marital status, number of jobs for you (and/or your spouse if married filing jointly), dependents, other income (not from jobs), deductions, or credits. Have your most recent pay stub(s) from this year available when using the estimator. At the beginning of next year, use the estimator again to recheck your withholding.

Step 3: **Claim Dependent and Other Credits**	If your total income will be $200,000 or less ($400,000 or less if married filing jointly): Multiply the number of qualifying children under age 17 by $2,000 $ 2000 Multiply the number of other dependents by $500 . . . . . $ Add the amounts above for qualifying children and other dependents. You may add to this the amount of any other credits. Enter the total here	3	$ 0
Step 4 (optional): **Other Adjustments**	**(a) Other income (not from jobs).** If you want tax withheld for other income you expect this year that won't have withholding, enter the amount of other income here. This may include interest, dividends, and retirement income	4(a)	$ 0
	(b) Deductions. If you expect to claim deductions other than the standard deduction and want to reduce your withholding, use the Deductions Worksheet on page 3 and enter the result here	4(b)	$ 85000
	(c) Extra withholding. Enter any additional tax you want withheld each **pay period** . .	4(c)	$

Step 5: **Sign Here**	Under penalties of perjury, I declare that this certificate, to the best of my knowledge and belief, is true, correct, and complete. **Employee's signature** (This form is not valid unless you sign it.)		**Date**
Employers Only	Employer's name and address Inova Fairfax Medical Center, Fairfax VA 22030	First date of employment 01/01/2025	Employer identification number (EIN) 99-8888888

For Privacy Act and Paperwork Reduction Act Notice, see page 3. Cat. No. 10220Q Form **W-4** (2025)

Helen contributes $13.5K fully in her traditional 401(k), based on two factors: (1) max match and out: the employer Inova medical center matches 3% of the W-2 income. Her $444K salary will bring in company 401(k) matching of $13K; and (2) Helen contributes $13.5K in her traditional 401(k), and can use the remaining capacity (about $10K) in her solo 401(k) contribution, if she has a profitable side hustle.

Solo 401(k) program offered at E*Trade (now part of Morgan Stanley) provides the small business owner more investment options, including single name stocks, much wider options than corporate sponsored 401(k), which only offers index funds or high-fee low-performance mutual funds. In addition, E*Trade solo 401(k) has a loan feature, which provides Helen with more funding liquidity (up to $50K (if balance over $100K) per 401(k) plan) if any investment opportunity occurs in Kevin's real estate business.

With careful planning, her W-2 would read like a table below, and their 1040 tax return should be able to keep the tax due or tax refund within +/- $2,000 range.

The 1040 pro forma analysis shows this couple will receive IRS refund at $43K. Helen can either use the refund to buy cash value life insurance policies, or she could forfeit the refund by doing more Roth conversions in the current year.

In addition, Helen deducted $5,000 dependent care flexible spending account from her W-2 (box 10, code D), which helped reduce the income tax. Helen's W-2 box 1 has income at $430K ($444K minus $13.5K traditional 401(k) contribution).

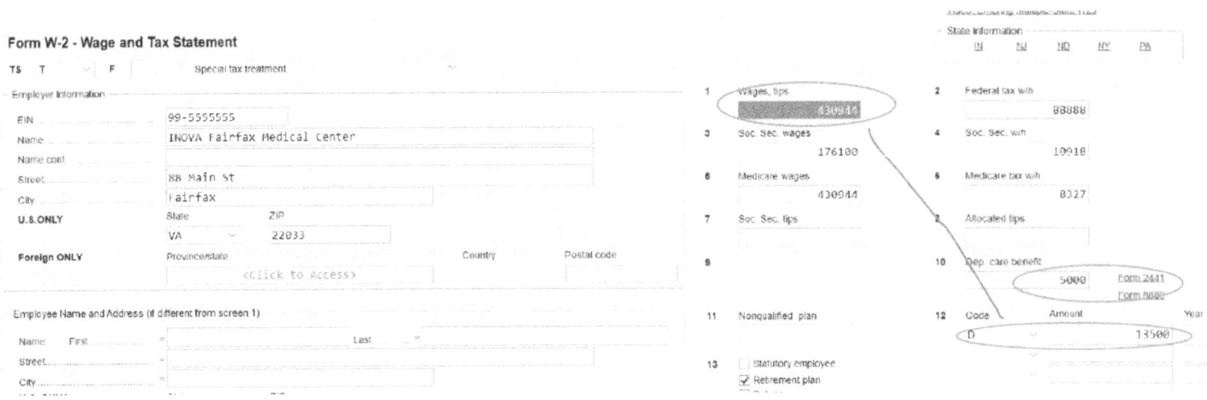

Form W-2 - Wage and Tax Statement

TS T | F | Special tax treatment

Employer Information

EIN	99-5555555
Name	INOVA Fairfax Medical Center
Name cont	
Street	88 Main St
City	Fairfax
U.S.ONLY	State: VA — ZIP: 22033
Foreign ONLY	Province/state: <Click to Access> — Country — Postal code

Employee Name and Address (if different from screen 1)

Name: First — Last
Street
City

State Information: IN NJ ND NY PA

1	Wages, tips: 430944	2	Federal tax w/h: 88888
3	Soc. Sec. wages: 176100	4	Soc. Sec. w/h: 10918
5	Medicare wages: 430944	6	Medicare tax w/h: 8327
7	Soc. Sec. tips	8	Allocated tips
9		10	Dep. care benefit: 5000 (Form 2441, Form 8889)
11	Nonqualified plan	12	Code: D — Amount: 13500 — Year
13	☐ Statutory employee ☑ Retirement plan		

3. Child and Dependent-Care Credits

Their new child qualifies the couple for two valuable credits: the child tax credit (up to $2,200 per child under 17) and the dependent-care credit (up to 35 % of eligible childcare expenses). Unlike deductions, credits reduce the tax bill dollar to dollar. For a dual-income family, these credits help offset the cost of professional childcare that allows Helen to continue her medical work, and allows Kevin to actively manages his home junk removal business and multiple rentals.

Sec. 70104. Extension and Enhancement of Increased Child Tax Credit

OBBB 2025	TCJA	Pre-TJCA
$2,200*	$2,000	$1,000

*Indexed for inflation.

With Kevin's real estate professional status, their AGI was able to drop to $343K, below the $400K phase-out threshold, and make the child tax credit fully available.

Form 1040 (2025) **Helen & Kevin Nie** 222-22-9999 Page **2**

Tax and Credits	Line	Description	Box	Amount
	11b	Amount from line 11a (adjusted gross income)	11b	343,291
	12a	Someone can claim ☐ You as a dependent ☐ Your spouse as a dependent		
	b	☐ Spouse itemizes on a separate return c ☐ You were a dual-status alien		
	d	**You:** ☐ Were born before January 2, 1961 ☐ Are blind		
		Spouse: ☐ Was born before January 2, 1961 ☐ Is blind		
Standard deduction for-	e	**Standard deduction or itemized deductions** (from Schedule A)	12e	56,442
• Single or Married filing separately, $15,750	13a	Qualified business income deduction from Form 8995 or Form 8995-A	13a	1,318
	b	Additional deductions from Schedule 1-A, line 38	13b	
• Married filing jointly or Qualifying surviving spouse, $31,500	14	Add lines 12e, 13a, and 13b	14	57,760
	15	Subtract line 14 from line 11b. If zero or less, enter -0-. This is your **taxable income**	15	285,531
	16	Tax (see instructions). Check if any from Form(s): 1☐ 8814 2☐ 4972 3☐	16	54,221
	17	Amount from Schedule 2, line 3	17	
• Head of household, $23,625	18	Add lines 16 and 17	18	54,221
	19	Child tax credit or credit for other dependents from Schedule 8812	19	2,200
• If you checked a box on line 12a, 12b, 12c, or 12d, see inst.	20	Amount from Schedule 3, line 8	20	7,500
	21	Add lines 19 and 20	21	9,700
	22	Subtract line 21 from line 18. If zero or less, enter -0-	22	44,521
	23	Other taxes, including self-employment tax, from Schedule 2, line 21	23	3,314
	24	Add lines 22 and 23. This is your **total tax**	24	47,835

SCHEDULE 8812 (Form 1040) Department of the Treasury Internal Revenue Service	**Credits for Qualifying Children and Other Dependents** Attach to Form 1040, 1040-SR, or 1040-NR. Go to *www.irs.gov/Schedule8812* for instructions and the latest information.	OMB No. 1545-0074 **2025** Attachment Sequence No. 47
Name(s) shown on return: Helen & Kevin Nie		Your social security number: 222-22-9999

Part I Child Tax Credit and Credit for Other Dependents

Line	Description			Box	Amount
1	Enter the amount from line 11a of your Form 1040, 1040-SR, or 1040-NR			1	343,291
2a	Enter income from Puerto Rico that you excluded	2a			
b	Enter the amounts from lines 45 and 50 of your Form 2555	2b			
c	Enter the amount from line 15 of your Form 4563	2c			
d	Add lines 2a through 2c			2d	
3	Add lines 1 and 2d			3	343,291
4	Number of qualifying children under age 17 with the required social security number	4	1		
5	Multiply line 4 by $2,200			5	2,200
6	Number of other dependents, including any qualifying children who are not under age 17 or who do not have the required social security number	6			
	Caution: Do not include yourself, your spouse, or anyone who is not a U.S. citizen, U.S. national, or U.S. resident alien. Also, do not include anyone you included on line 4.				
7	Multiply line 6 by $500			7	
8	Add lines 5 and 7			8	2,200
9	Enter the amount shown below for your filing status. • Married filing jointly-$400,000 • All other filing statuses-$200,000			9	400,000
10	Subtract line 9 from line 3. • If zero or less, enter -0-. • If more than zero and not a multiple of $1,000, enter the next multiple of $1,000. For example, if the result is $425, enter $1,000; if the result is $1,025, enter $2,000, etc.			10	0
11	Multiply line 10 by 5% (0.05)			11	
12	Is the amount on line 8 more than the amount on line 11? ☐ **No. Stop here.** You cannot take the child tax credit, credit for other dependents, or additional child tax credit. ☒ **Yes.** Subtract line 11 from line 8. Enter the result.			12	2,200
13	Enter the amount from **Credit Limit Worksheet A**			13	46,721
14	Enter the smaller of line 12 or line 13. **This is your child tax credit and credit for other dependents** Enter this amount on Form 1040, 1040-SR, or 1040-NR, line 19.			14	2,200

4. Can Kevin deduct vehicle and home office expenses?

Yes — under Schedule C, he deducts mileage, meals, supplies, home office, and training costs related to his brokerage and property-management activities. This further reduces self-employment income.

With a $59K gross income, Kevin made a net profit of $9K. Here are some tax saving strategies Kevin applied:

- Issue a 1099 NEC to his in-law, who helps with the rental open house every Sunday afternoon. The in-law is semi-retired with a low tax bracket and enjoys client interfacing activities.
- Kevin deducted the home office using the standard method.
- Kevin used a standard mileage approach for his car use.

3	Subtract line 2 from line 1	3	55,555
4	Cost of goods sold (from line 42)	4	
5	**Gross profit.** Subtract line 4 from line 3	5	55,555
6	Other income, including federal and state gasoline or fuel tax credit or refund (see instructions)	6	3,333
7	**Gross income.** Add lines 5 and 6	7	58,888

Part II **Expenses.** Enter expenses for business use of your home **only** on line 30.

8	Advertising	8		18	Office expense (see instructions)	18	
9	Car and truck expenses (see instructions)	9	standard mileage 6,222	19	Pension and profit-sharing plans	19	
				20	Rent or lease (see instructions):		
10	Commissions and fees	10		a	Vehicles, machinery, and equipment	20a	
11	Contract labor (see instructions)	11	Pay wife 1099 NEC 12,000	b	Other business property	20b	
12	Depletion	12		21	Repairs and maintenance	21	
13	Depreciation and section 179 expense deduction (not included in Part III) (see instructions)	13		22	Supplies (not included in Part III)	22	3,111
				23	Taxes and licenses	23	888
				24	Travel and meals:		
14	Employee benefit programs (other than on line 19)	14		a	Travel	24a	2,222
				b	Deductible meals (see instructions)	24b	500
15	Insurance (other than health)	15	1,111	25	Utilities	25	
16	Interest (see instructions):			26	Wages (less employment credits)	26	
a	Mortgage (paid to banks, etc.)	16a		27a	Energy efficient commercial bldgs deduction (attach Form 7205)	27a	
b	Other	16b					
17	Legal and professional services	17	555	b	Other expenses (from line 48)	27b	21,552

28	**Total expenses** before expenses for business use of home. Add lines 8 through 27b	28	48,161
29	Tentative profit or (loss). Subtract line 28 from line 7	29	10,727
30	Expenses for business use of your home. Do not report these expenses elsewhere. Attach Form 8829 unless using the simplified method. See instructions. **Simplified method filers only:** Enter the total square footage of (a) your home: 3,000 and (b) the part of your home used for business: 292. Use the Simplified Method Worksheet in the instructions to figure the amount to enter on line 30	30	1,460
31	**Net profit or (loss).** Subtract line 30 from line 29. • If a profit, enter on both **Schedule 1 (Form 1040), line 3,** and on **Schedule SE, line 2.** (If you checked the box on line 1, see instructions.) Estates and trusts, enter on **Form 1041, line 3.** • If a loss, you **must** go to line 32.	31	Profit margin 15%, audit safe 9,267
32	If you have a loss, check the box that describes your investment in this activity. See instructions.		

5. Active Real-Estate LLC

Kevin's separate real-estate sales and property management work runs through LLC. After deducting ordinary and necessary business expenses, Kevin has remaining profit that qualifies for the 20% qualified business income (QBI) deduction (§199A). The same income can fund a self-employed retirement plan, creating a bridge between business and personal finance.

Form 1040 (2025) Helen & Kevin Nie 222-22-9999 Page **2**

Tax and Credits	11b	Amount from line 11a (adjusted gross income)	11b	342,831
	12a	Someone can claim ☐ You as a dependent ☐ Your spouse as a dependent		
	b	☐ Spouse itemizes on a separate return c ☐ You were a dual-status alien		
	d	You: ☐ Were born before January 2, 1961 ☐ Are blind		
Standard deduction for-		**Spouse:** ☐ Was born before January 2, 1961 ☐ Is blind		
	e	**Standard deduction or itemized deductions** (from Schedule A)	12e	56,442
Single or Married filing separately, $15,750	13a	Qualified business income deduction from Form 8995 or Form 8995-A	13a	946
	b	Additional deductions from Schedule 1-A, line 38	13b	
	14	Add lines 12e, 13a, and 13b	14	57,388

Kevin makes a profit of $9K) in his Schedule C as a real estate agent, at a profit margin of 15%, a level reasonable to a real estate agent. After absorbing losses carried forward from prior year (Kevin's sole proprietorship with no LLC set up), his qualified business income is $6K, leading to a 20% QBI deduction of $946. In addition, Kevin's REP status successfully reduces their AGI below the QBI income phase-out threshold ($394K as of 2025, indexed with inflation annually), making the $946 QBI full deduction feasible.

Form **8995**

Department of the Treasury
Internal Revenue Service

Qualified Business Income Deduction Simplified Computation

Attach to your tax return.
Go to *www.irs.gov/Form8995* for instructions and the latest information.

OMB No. 1545-0074

2025

Attachment Sequence No. 55

Name(s) shown on return: Helen & Kevin Nie

Your taxpayer identification number: 222-22-9999

Note: *You can claim the qualified business income deduction* ***only*** *if you have qualified business income from a qualified trade or business, real estate investment trust dividends, publicly traded partnership income, or a domestic production activities deduction passed through from an agricultural or horticultural cooperative. See instructions.*

Use this form if your taxable income, before your qualified business income deduction, is at or below $197,300 ($394,600 if married filing jointly), and you aren't a patron of an agricultural or horticultural cooperative.

1	(a) Trade, business, or aggregation name	(b) Taxpayer identification number	(c) Qualified business income or (loss)
i	Schedule C: Gym and Home Operator LLC	11-5555555	8,612
ii			
iii			
iv			
v			

2	Total qualified business income or (loss). Combine lines 1i through 1v, column (c)	2	8,612		
3	Qualified business net (loss) carryforward from the prior year	3	(3,880)		
4	Total qualified business income. Combine lines 2 and 3. If zero or less, enter -0-	4	4,732		
5	Qualified business income component. Multiply line 4 by 20% (0.20)			5	946

5. Solo 401(k)

Through his LLC, Kevin may contribute up to $23,500 as an employee deferral (if his net profit on Schedule C exceeds this amount) and another 20% of net earnings as an employer contribution (up to $46.5K, if net profit is at $232K), roughly $70,000 total (with future inflation indexing available). These deposits reduce current-year adjusted gross income while building future retirement assets. The plan's loan feature (§72(p)) (offered by E*Trade) can later provide short-term, tax-free liquidity for property improvements.

Business owner solo 401(k) contribution: Line 16 of Schedule 1, including employee contribution ($9K, calculated based on net profit on Schedule C, deducting self-employment tax), and 20% company match.

Kevin figures out his solo traditional 401(k) (done by December 31 of current year) and company matching (done by tax filing date) based on the following formula:

Step 1: Compute Net Earnings from Self-Employment

The IRS says your self-employment income for retirement plan purposes equals:

Net earnings subject to SE tax
9,267×(100%-7.65%)=8,559

(to remove the employer portion of self-employment tax).

Step 2: Employee (Elective-Deferral) Contribution

Kevin can contribute up to $10K (Kevin did $8K contribution), but not more than the annual elective-deferral limit: $23.5K for 2025 (under age 50)

SE tax rate = 8,559×15.3%=1,310
Deductible half of SE tax
$1,310 ÷ 2 = $655

Step 3: Solo 401(k) Plan Compensation

This is the maximum base used for Solo 401(k) calculations.
$9,267−$655 = $8,612 (Kevin did $8K contribution)

Step 4: Employer (Profit-Sharing) Contribution

As the "employer," you can also add about **20% of net earnings** (after step 1).

8,612×20%=$1,722 (Kevin's match is $1.6K)

Step 4: Total Possible Solo 401(k) Contribution

Combine both parts (but capped by the IRS overall limit = $69,000 for 2025, $76,500 if 50+):

Component	Amount
Employee deferral	$8K (note)
Employer (20%)	$1.6K
Total Solo 401(k) contribution	**$9.6K**

Note: Kevin decides not to max out his 401(k) contribution. His $8K contribution is below the $10K capacity.

Schedule 1:

Schedule 1 (Form 1040) 2025 Page 2

Part II Adjustments to Income

11	Educator expenses	11	
12	Certain business expenses of reservists, performing artists, and fee-basis government officials. Attach Form 2106	12	
13	Health savings account deduction. Attach Form 8889	13	8,550
14	Moving expenses for members of the Armed Forces. Attach Form 3903. If claiming only storage fees (see instructions), check here ☐	14	
15	Deductible part of self-employment tax. Attach Schedule SE	15	655
16	Self-employed SEP, SIMPLE, and qualified plans Solo 401(K) - employee contribution	16	8,000
17	Self-employed health insurance deduction	17	

$8,550 + $655 + $8,000 = $18,205

This total amount flows to 1040 line 10 to reduce the AGI.

d	If you are married filing separately and lived apart from your spouse the entire year (see inst.), check here ☐		
7a	Capital gain or (loss). Attach Schedule D if required	7a	5,555
b	Check if: ☐ Schedule D not required ☐ Includes child's capital gain or (loss)		
8	Additional income from Schedule 1, line 10	8	(131,018)
9	Add lines 1z, 2b, 3b, 4b, 5b, 6b, 7a, and 8. This is your **total income**	9	361,036
10	Adjustments to income from Schedule 1, line 26	10	18,205
11a	Subtract line 10 from line 9. This is your **adjusted gross income**	11a	342,831

For Disclosure, Privacy Act, and Paperwork Reduction Act Notice, see separate instructions. Form **1040** (2025) Created 9/5/25

Form 1040:

Their AGI has been successfully down from $430K to $343K by a few powerful reductions:

(1) Real estate professional related rental losses (netting Kevin's real estate agent profits) ($140K loss offset by $9K Schedule C profit = $131K)

(2) HSA contributions ($8,550)

(3) Solo 401(k) contributions ($8K as employee contribution) plus company 20% match, ($8K x 20% = $1.6K)

6. Back-Door Roth IRA

Helen's high income exceeds the direct Roth IRA limits, but the couple can still gain Roth access by funding nondeductible traditional IRAs and immediately converting them to Roth.The conversion triggers minimal tax today and ensures future growth and withdrawals are tax-free under §408A.

The form excerpt is an example that Kevin made his $7,000 back-door Roth IRA contribution and invested in a brokerage account (S&P 500 index fund). His wife Helen did the same.

Kevin's form:

Form **8606** Department of the Treasury Internal Revenue Service

Nondeductible IRAs

Attach to 2025 Form 1040, 1040-SR, or 1040-NR.
Go to *www.irs.gov/Form8606* for instructions and the latest information.

OMB No. 1545-0074 **2025** Attachment Sequence No. **48**

Name. If married, file a separate form for each spouse required to file 2025 Form 8606. See instructions.	Your social security number
Kevin Nie	222-22-8888

Fill in Your Address Only if You Are Filing This Form by Itself and Not With Your Tax Return

Home address (number and street, or P.O. box if mail is not delivered to your home)		Apt. no.
City, town or post office, state, and ZIP code. If you have a foreign address, also complete the spaces below. See instructions.		
Foreign country name	Foreign province/state/county	Foreign postal code

Note: Except where stated otherwise, "traditional IRA" includes traditional SEP IRAs and traditional SIMPLE IRAs. "Roth IRA" includes Roth SEP IRAs and Roth SIMPLE IRAs.

Part I **Nondeductible Contributions to Traditional IRAs and Distributions From Traditional IRAs**

Complete this part only if one or more of the following apply.

- You made nondeductible contributions to a traditional IRA for 2025. Nondeductible contributions to a traditional IRA do not include employer contributions made to a SEP IRA pursuant to a SEP arrangement or to a SIMPLE IRA pursuant to a SIMPLE IRA plan.
- You took distributions from a traditional IRA in 2025 and you made nondeductible contributions to a traditional IRA in 2025 or an earlier year. For this purpose "distributions" does not include rollovers (but does include certain 2025 retirement plan distribution repayments treated as rollovers (see instructions)). Also, it does not include qualified charitable distributions, one-time distributions to fund an HSA, conversions, recharacterizations, or returns of certain contributions.
- You converted part, but not all, of your traditional IRAs to Roth IRAs in 2025 and you made nondeductible contributions to a traditional IRA in 2025 or an earlier year.

1	Enter your nondeductible contributions to traditional IRAs for 2025, including those made for 2025 from January 1, 2026, through April 15, 2026. See instructions	1	7,000
2	Enter your total basis in traditional IRAs. See instructions	2	
3	Add lines 1 and 2	3	7,000
	In 2025, did you take a distribution — No — Enter the amount from line 3 on line 14. Do not complete the rest of Part I.		

Helen's form

Form **8606** Department of the Treasury Internal Revenue Service

Nondeductible IRAs

Attach to 2025 Form 1040, 1040-SR, or 1040-NR.
Go to *www.irs.gov/Form8606* for instructions and the latest information.

OMB No. 1545-0074 **2025** Attachment Sequence No. 48

Name. If married, file a separate form for each spouse required to file 2025 Form 8606. See instructions.			Your social security number
Helen Nie			222-22-9999
Fill in Your Address Only if You Are Filing This Form by Itself and Not With Your Tax Return	Home address (number and street, or P.O. box if mail is not delivered to your home)		Apt. no.
	City, town or post office, state, and ZIP code. If you have a foreign address, also complete the spaces below. See instructions.		
	Foreign country name	Foreign province/state/county	Foreign postal code

Note: Except where stated otherwise, "traditional IRA" includes traditional SEP IRAs and traditional SIMPLE IRAs. "Roth IRA" includes Roth SEP IRAs and Roth SIMPLE IRAs.

Part I Nondeductible Contributions to Traditional IRAs and Distributions From Traditional IRAs

Complete this part only if one or more of the following apply.

- You made nondeductible contributions to a traditional IRA for 2025. Nondeductible contributions to a traditional IRA do not include employer contributions made to a SEP IRA pursuant to a SEP arrangement or to a SIMPLE IRA pursuant to a SIMPLE IRA plan.
- You took distributions from a traditional IRA in 2025 and you made nondeductible contributions to a traditional IRA in 2025 or an earlier year. For this purpose, "distributions" does not include rollovers (but does include certain 2025 retirement plan distribution repayments treated as rollovers (see instructions)). Also, it does not include qualified charitable distributions, one-time distributions to fund an HSA, conversions, recharacterizations, or returns of certain contributions.
- You converted part, but not all, of your traditional IRAs to Roth IRAs in 2025 and you made nondeductible contributions to a traditional IRA in 2025 or an earlier year.

1	Enter your nondeductible contributions to traditional IRAs for 2025, including those made for 2025 from January 1, 2026, through April 15, 2026. See instructions	1	7,000
2	Enter your total basis in traditional IRAs. See instructions	2	
3	Add lines 1 and 2	3	7,000
	In 2025, did you take a distribution — No — Enter the amount from line 3 on line 14.		

7. Family Health Savings Account

Because Helen is covered by INOVA Fairfax's High-Deductible Health Plan, the family can contribute up to $8,550 (2025 limit, subject to future inflation indexing) to an HSA. This account combines three tax benefits: contributions are deductible, growth is untaxed, and qualified medical withdrawals are tax-free. Unused balances roll forward indefinitely and can supplement medical costs in retirement.

See a sample form. Note that Line 2 reads "HSA contributions you made for 2025 (or those made on your behalf)." It means that HSA money can be Kevin and Helen's earned income or can be his loan drawn from SBLOC or IBLOC or can be gifted from their parents or relatives. But Kevin and family enjoy the tax savings. Such HSA contributions reduce their AGI from Schedule 1, and Form 1040.

Helen opts out the W-2 payroll deduction of her $8,550 contribution. Instead, she contributed her Fidelity HSA (no fee, both BRK.B and S&P 500 index fund available) with her take-home pay. Fidelity HSA seems a better choice for Helen, because the employer-sponsored HSA only offers a limited number, often high fee mutual funds. She reported the HSA contribution in Form 8889 below.

Form **8889** — Department of the Treasury, Internal Revenue Service

Health Savings Accounts (HSAs)

Attach to Form 1040, 1040-SR, or 1040-NR.
Go to *www.irs.gov/Form8889* for instructions and the latest information.

OMB No. 1545-0074 — **2025** — Attachment Sequence No. **52**

Name(s) shown on Form 1040, 1040-SR, or 1040-NR: Helen & Kevin Nie

Social security number of HSA beneficiary. If both spouses have HSAs, see instructions: 222-22-9999

Before you begin: Complete Form 8853, Archer MSAs and Long-Term Care Insurance Contracts, if required.

Part I **HSA Contributions and Deduction.** See the instructions before completing this part. If you are filing jointly and both you and your spouse each have separate HSAs, complete a separate Part I for each spouse.

Line	Description	Box	Amount
1	Check the box to indicate your coverage under a high-deductible health plan (HDHP) during 2025. See instructions	☐ Self-only ☒ Family	
2	HSA contributions you made for 2025 (or those made on your behalf), including those made by the unextended due date of your tax return that were for 2025. Do not include employer contributions, contributions through a cafeteria plan, or rollovers. See instructions	2	8,550
3	If you were under age 55 at the end of 2025 and, on the first day of every month during 2025, you were, or were considered, an eligible individual with the same coverage, enter $4,300 ($8,550 for family coverage). All others, see the instructions for the amount to enter	3	8,550
4	Enter the amount you and your employer contributed to your Archer MSAs for 2025 from Form 8853, lines 1 and 2. If you or your spouse had family coverage under an HDHP at any time during 2025, also include any amount contributed to your spouse's Archer MSAs	4	
5	Subtract line 4 from line 3. If zero or less, enter -0-	5	8,550
6	Enter the amount from line 5. But if you and your spouse each have separate HSAs and had family coverage under an HDHP at any time during 2025, see the instructions for the amount to enter	6	8,550
7	If you were age 55 or older at the end of 2025, married, and you or your spouse had family coverage under an HDHP at any time during 2025, enter your additional contribution amount. See instructions	7	
8	Add lines 6 and 7	8	8,550
9	Employer contributions made to your HSAs for 2025	9	
10	Qualified HSA funding distributions	10	
11	Add lines 9 and 10	11	
12	Subtract line 11 from line 8. If zero or less, enter -0-	12	8,550
13	**HSA deduction** (see instructions)	13	8,550

Form 8889 flows to Schedule 1 line 13, then to 1040 (line 10).

Schedule 1 (Form 1040) 2025 — Page **2**

Part II **Adjustments to Income**

Line	Description	Box	Amount
11	Educator expenses	11	
12	Certain business expenses of reservists, performing artists, and fee-basis government officials. Attach Form 2106	12	
13	Health savings account deduction. Attach Form 8889	13	8,550
14	Moving expenses for members of the Armed Forces. Attach Form 3903. If claiming only storage fees (see instructions), check here ☐	14	

8. **How can Kevin qualify as a Real Estate Professional (REP)?**
   He must spend >750 hours per year and >50% of his work time in real-estate activities (managing, staging, leasing, repairs, brokerage). Once qualified, rental losses from cost w and bonus depreciation can offset Helen's W-2 income under IRC §469(c)(7).

Kevin attaches this signed cover letter to their tax return
Real estate professional grouping letter Kevin Nie 123 Main St, Fairfax VA 22030 SSN: xxx-xx-8888

Pursuant to Treasury Regulation § 1.469-9(g), I hereby elect to treat all interests in rental real estate as a single activity for purposes of determining material participation under the passive activity loss rules of IRC § 469. I am a qualifying real estate professional under IRC § 469(c)(7).

The rental real estate activities grouped into this single activity include:

1. [Property Address 1]

2. [Property Address 2]

3. [Property Address 3]

[Add additional properties as needed]

Signed ______ Date April 12, 20xx

Kevin Nie

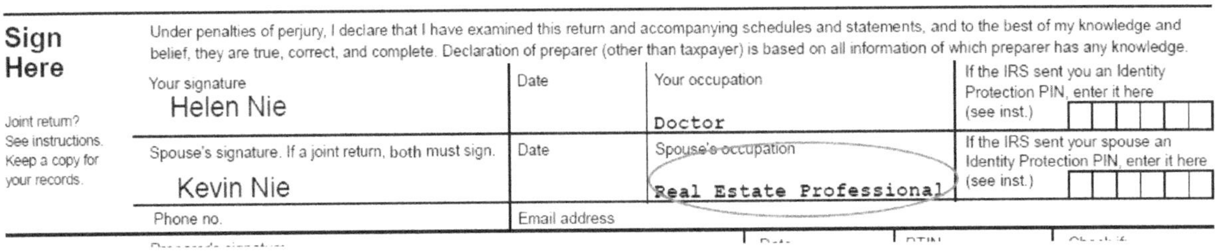
Sign Here

Joint return? See instructions. Keep a copy for your records.

Under penalties of perjury, I declare that I have examined this return and accompanying schedules and statements, and to the best of my knowledge and belief, they are true, correct, and complete. Declaration of preparer (other than taxpayer) is based on all information of which preparer has any knowledge.

Your signature	Date	Your occupation	If the IRS sent you an Identity Protection PIN, enter it here (see inst.)
Helen Nie		Doctor	
Spouse's signature. If a joint return, both must sign.	Date	~~Spouse's occupation~~	If the IRS sent your spouse an Identity Protection PIN, enter it here (see inst.)
Kevin Nie		Real Estate Professional	
Phone no.	Email address		

With REP status, Kevin's rental properties (two single family houses and one multi-unit apartments) generated $141K losses, property A and B using straight-line depreciation and property C using cost segregation and bonus depreciation. This loss was used to offset his Schedule C real estate agent net income and Helen's doctor W-2 income, achieving tax savings purposes.

SCHEDULE E (Form 1040)

Department of the Treasury Internal Revenue Service

Supplemental Income and Loss

(From rental real estate, royalties, partnerships, S corporations, estates, trusts, REMICs, etc.)

Attach to Form 1040, 1040-SR, 1040-NR, or 1041.

Go to *www.irs.gov/ScheduleE* for instructions and the latest information.

OMB No. 1545-0074

2025

Attachment Sequence No. 13

Name(s) shown on return: Helen & Kevin Nie

Your social security number: 222-22-9999

Part I Income or Loss From Rental Real Estate and Royalties

Note: If you are in the business of renting personal property, use **Schedule C**. See instructions. If you are an individual, report farm rental income or loss from **Form 4835** on page 2, line 40.

A Did you make any payments in 2025 that would require you to file Form(s) 1099? See instructions ☐ Yes ☐ No

B If "Yes," did you or will you file required Form(s) 1099? ☐ Yes ☐ No

1a	Physical address of each property (street, city, state, ZIP code)
A	123 Green St, Herndon, VA 20170
B	123 Red St, Vienna, VA 22180
C	123 Brown St Apartment, Fairfax, VA 22033

1b	Type of Property (from list below)		Fair Rental Days	Personal Use Days	QJV
A	1	A	365	0	☐
B	1	B	365	0	☐
C	2	C	365	0	☐

2 For each rental real estate property listed above, report the number of fair rental and personal use days. Check the QJV box only if you meet the requirements to file as a qualified joint venture. See instructions.

Type of Property:

1 Single Family Residence 3 Vacation/Short-Term Rental 5 Land 7 Self-Rental
2 Multi-Family Residence 4 Commercial 6 Royalties 8 Other (describe)

		Line	Properties: A	B	C
Income:					
3	Rents received	3	11,111	29,999	44,444
4	Royalties received	4			
Expenses:					
5	Advertising	5	1,111	999	2,222
6	Auto and travel (see instructions)	6	1,555	2,333	2,333
7	Cleaning and maintenance	7	999	888	3,333
8	Commissions	8			
9	Insurance	9	888	999	2,222
10	Legal and other professional fees	10	555	555	555
11	Management fees	11			
12	Mortgage interest paid to banks, etc. (see instructions)	12	3,333	4,444	8,888
13	Other interest	13	1,111	1,111	1,111
14	Repairs	14	888	2,222	2,222
15	Supplies	15	999	999	1,888
16	Taxes	16	3,333	8,888	19,999
17	Utilities	17			
18	Depreciation expense or depletion	18	12,120	16,692	91,950
19	Other (list) Statement #1	19	1,554	13,197	7,346
20	Total expenses. Add lines 5 through 19	20	28,446	53,327	144,069
21	Subtract line 20 from line 3 (rents) and/or 4 (royalties). If result is a (loss), see instructions to find out if you must file Form 6198	21	(17,335)	(23,328)	(99,625)
22	Deductible rental real estate loss after limitation, if any, on Form 8582 (see instructions)	22	(17,335)	(23,328)	(99,625)

		Line	Amount
23a	Total of all amounts reported on line 3 for all rental properties	23a	85,554
b	Total of all amounts reported on line 4 for all royalty properties	23b	0
c	Total of all amounts reported on line 12 for all properties	23c	16,665
d	Total of all amounts reported on line 18 for all properties	23d	120,762
e	Total of all amounts reported on line 20 for all properties	23e	225,842
24	**Income.** Add positive amounts shown on line 21. **Do not** include any losses	24	0
25	**Losses.** Add royalty losses from line 21 and rental real estate losses from line 22. Enter total losses here	25	(140,288)
26	Total rental real estate and royalty income or (loss). Combine lines 24 and 25. Enter the result		

This loss flows to Schedule 1 line 5, then to 1040 line 10.

SCHEDULE 1 (Form 1040) — Department of the Treasury, Internal Revenue Service

Additional Income and Adjustments to Income

Attach to Form 1040, 1040-SR, or 1040-NR.
Go to *www.irs.gov/Form1040* for instructions and the latest information.

OMB No. 1545-0074 — **2025** — Attachment Sequence No. **01**

Name(s) shown on Form 1040, 1040-SR, or 1040-NR: Helen & Kevin Nie — Your social security number: 222-22-9999

For 2025, enter the amount reported to you on Form(s) 1099-K that was included in error or for personal items sold at a loss . . . . . .

Note: The remaining amounts reported to you on Form(s) 1099-K should be reported elsewhere on your return depending on the nature of the transaction. See *www.irs.gov/1099k*.

Part I — Additional Income

1	Taxable refunds, credits, or offsets of state and local income taxes	1	
2a	Alimony received	2a	
b	Date of original divorce or separation agreement (see instructions):		
3	Business income or (loss). Attach Schedule C	3	9,267
4	Other gains or (losses). Check if any from Form(s): ☐ 4797 ☐ 4684	4	
5	Rental real estate, royalties, partnerships, S corporations, trusts, etc. Attach Schedule E	5	(140,288)
6	Farm income or (loss). Attach Schedule F	6	

Form 1040:

1a	Total amount from Form(s) W-2, box 1 (see instructions) · Gross pay $444K minus traditional 401(K)	1a	430,944
b	Household employee wages not reported on Form(s) W-2	1b	
c	Tip income not reported on line 1a (see instructions)	1c	
d	Medicaid waiver payments not reported on Form(s) W-2 (see instructions)	1d	
e	Taxable dependent care benefits from Form 2441, line 26	1e	
f	Employer-provided adoption benefits from Form 8839, line 31	1f	
g	Wages from Form 8919, line 6	1g	
h	Other earned income (see instructions). Enter type and amount:	1h	
i	Nontaxable combat pay election (see instructions) — 1i		
z	Add lines 1a through 1h	1z	430,944
2a	Tax-exempt interest — 2a; b Taxable interest	2b	
3a	Qualified dividends — 3a; b Ordinary dividends	3b	
c	Check if your child's dividends are included in 1 ☐ Line 3a 2 ☐ Line 3b		
4a	IRA distributions — 4a; b Taxable amount (Roth conversion)	4b	55,555
c	Check if (see instructions) 1 ☐ Rollover 2 ☐ QCD 3 ☐		
5a	Pensions and annuities — 5a; b Taxable amount	5b	
c	Check if (see instructions) 1 ☐ Rollover 2 ☐ PSO 3 ☐		
6a	Social security benefits — 6a; b Taxable amount	6b	
c	If you elect to use the lump-sum election method, check here (see instructions) ☐		
d	If you are married filing separately and lived apart from your spouse the entire year (see inst.), check here ☐		
7a	Capital gain or (loss). Attach Schedule D if required	7a	5,555
b	Check if: ☐ Schedule D not required ☐ Includes child's capital gain or (loss)		
8	Additional income from Schedule 1, line 10	8	(131,018)
9	Add lines 1z, 2b, 3b, 4b, 5b, 6b, 7a, and 8. This is your **total income**	9	361,036
10	Adjustments to income from Schedule 1, line 26	10	18,205
11a	Subtract line 10 from line 9. This is your **adjusted gross income**	11a	342,831

Privacy Act and Paperwork Reduction Act Notice, see separate instructions. — Form **1040** (2025) Created 9/5/25

9. How can Kevin use his REP tax status to help Helen perform Roth conversion strategically?

Helen watches the stock market closely. In April 2025, the S&P 500 declined 15%, then rebounded by 43% by December. Helen converted $55K traditional 401(k) to Roth 401(k), called "in-program conversion." She received a 1099-R form and recorded it in tax return accordingly. Her converted $55K now compounded to $78K, totally tax free in the Roth account.

If the stock market turned into a correction level again, Kevin could easily turn one more property into cost segregation and bonus depreciation to manufacture more losses to allow for Helen's more Roth 401(k) conversion while softening the tax blows. Kevin and Helen have full control over their finances, timing and taxes.

Chart 2: S&P 500 Index (October 2024 to December 2025)

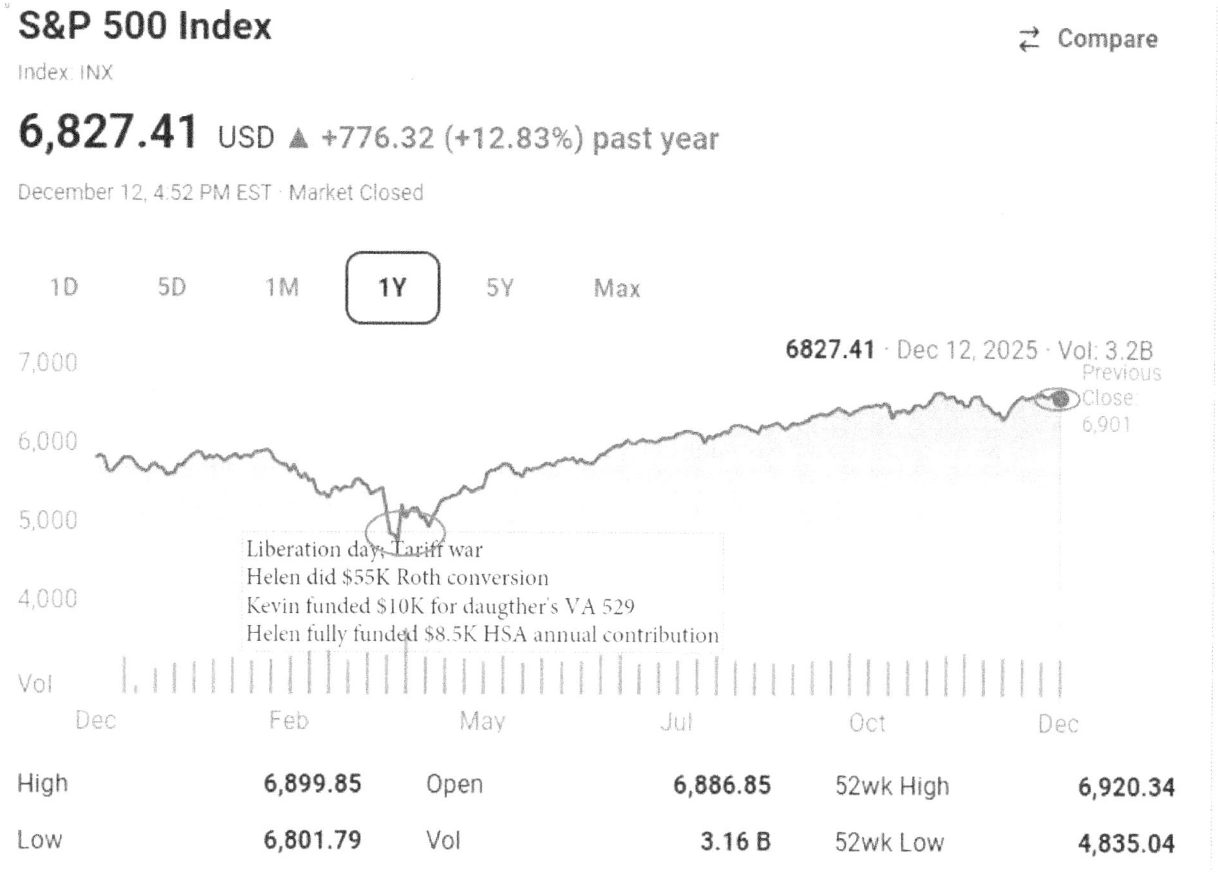

Source: Data from Yahoo Finance, chart edited by author.

10. **How does cost segregation reduce taxes?**
By reclassifying building components into 5-, 7-, or 15-year property lives, Kevin can take 100% bonus depreciation on short-life assets, producing paper losses that shelter Helen's salary. Kevin hired a licensed cost seg specialist who produced a report, with selected data in a table below:

Asset Category	Life (Years)	Typical Examples	Cost Basis	Bonus Depreciati on (100%)	Annual Depreciation (Straight-Line)
Land	N/A	Underlying lot, landscaping dirt	$72,450	NA	NA
5-Year Personal Property	5	Appliances (refrigerator, washer/dryer, dishwasher), carpets, blinds, ceiling fans, cabinetry, countertops, lighting fixtures	$51,417	$51,417	NA
7-Year Office / Furniture Assets	7	Furniture, desks, shelving, security systems, technology wiring (if rented furnished or used as home office)	$7,365	$7,365	NA
15-Year Land Improvements	15	Driveway, sidewalk, fencing, patio, exterior lighting, shrubbery, retaining wall	$29,381	$29,381	NA
27.5-Year Building Structure	27.5	Foundation, walls, roof, plumbing, HVAC, electrical system, windows, doors	$279,119	$0	(mid-month method) $3,807
TOTAL			**$439,000**	**$88,143**	**$3,807**

11. **Helen traditional 401(k) option**

    The couple purchased a Tesla Model X in February 2025, before the EV tax credit expiration date (September 30, 2025). They claimed EV credit via Form 8936, Clean Vehicle Credit.

13a	Qualified business income deduction from Form 8995 or Form 8995-A	13a	946
b	Additional deductions from Schedule 1-A, line 38	13b	
14	Add lines 12e, 13a, and 13b	14	57,388
15	Subtract line 14 from line 11b. If zero or less, enter -0-. This is your **taxable income**	15	285,443
16	Tax (see instructions). Check if any from Form(s): 1☐ 8814 2☐ 4972 3☐	16	54,200
17	Amount from Schedule 2, line 3	17	
18	Add lines 16 and 17	18	54,200
19	Child tax credit or credit for other dependents from Schedule 8812	19	2,200
20	Amount from Schedule 3, line 8 EV credit	20	7,500

12. **Use crypto with losses to offset rental sales gain**

    Kevin sold bitcoins with realized losses of $122K, and bought back the second trading date. No wash sale rule is applicable to him. The loss effectively offset his long term capital gain from his rental property sold in 2025.

Part II Long-Term Capital Gains and Losses - Generally Assets Held More Than One Year (see instructions)

See instructions for how to figure the amounts to enter on the lines below. This form may be easier to complete if you round off cents to whole dollars.	(d) Proceeds (sales price)	(e) Cost (or other basis)	(g) Adjustments to gain or loss from Form(s) 8949, Part II, line 2, column (g)	(h) Gain or (loss) Subtract column (e) from column (d) and combine the result with column (g)
8a Totals for all long-term transactions reported on Form 1099-B or Form 1099-DA for which basis was reported to the IRS and for which you have no adjustments (see instructions). However, if you choose to report all these transactions on Form 8949, leave this line blank and go to line 8b			Sold crypto with loss	
8b Totals for all transactions reported on Form(s) 8949 with **Box D** or **Box J** checked	111,111	233,333	Buy back second day	(122,222)
9 Totals for all transactions reported on Form(s) 8949 with **Box E** or **Box K** checked				
10 Totals for all transactions reported on Form(s) 8949 with **Box F** or **Box L** checked				

11 Gain from Form 4797, Part I; long-term gain from Forms 2439 and 6252; and long-term gain or (loss) from Forms 4684, 6781, and 8824 Capital gain by selling rental	11	127,777
12 Net long-term gain or (loss) from partnerships, S corporations, estates, and trusts from Schedule(s) K-1	12	
13 Capital gain distributions. See the instructions	13	
14 Long-term capital loss carryover. Enter the amount, if any, from line 13 of your **Capital Loss Carryover Worksheet** in the instructions	14	( )
15 **Net long-term capital gain or (loss).** Combine lines 8a through 14 in column (h). Then, go to Part III on page 2	15	5,555

For Paperwork Reduction Act Notice, see your tax return instructions. Schedule D (Form 1040) 2025 Created 10/6/25

13. Bonus deprecation recapture and decision making. For the rental sold in 2025, Kevin needs to pay tax (up to 25%) on depreciation recapture. See the difference below:

Deprecation method	**Straight line**	**Bonus / Cost Seg**	**Delta**
Depreciation recapture	$38,888	$88,888	$50,000
AGI	$343,000	$393,000	$50,000
Taxable income	$285,000	$335,000	$50,000
Tax due	$47,835	$59,835	$12,000
Tax refund	$43,131	$31,000	$(12,131)

Note: $12K/$50K = 24%, which is the couple's marginal tax bracket. Depreciation recapture tax rate is the lower of 24% and 25%.

14. Tax planning for Helena

- **Why is the UTMA account powerful for Helena?**
  Each parent gifts $19K annually ($38K total) into Helena's UTMA to invest in Berkshire Hathaway stock (BRK.B). Compound returns could reach $900K by age 18, which she can later pledge as collateral for her first rental loan under the BBB strategy. BRK.B does not issue dividend and therefore there is no kiddie tax concern.
- **What is the Coverdell ESA workaround for high incomes?**
  Since Helen and Kevin exceed the phase-out limit, Kevin gifts $2K to Helena's bank account, and Helena's parent (i.e., custodian of baby bank account) invests it in a Coverdell ESA under her own SSN — bypassing the income limit and keeping tax-free growth for education.

- **How do they triple-stack 529 deductions?**
  Virginia allows state deductions per taxpayer per beneficiary. They contribute $4K each for Kevin, Helen, and Helena (total $12K), saving state tax on each contribution ($5.75% Virginia state income tax rate times $12K), while building $800K over 18 years (assuming investing in the total equity index fund).

Total Subtractions		7.		Interest	20.
Deductions	8A.	101	3000.	Total Adjustments	21.
	8B.	104	12000.		
	8C.				
Total Deductions		9.	15000.		

Claiming More Adjustments - Schedule ADJS

PORTFOLIO	E.R.	% EQUITY	10YR PERFORMANCE
Global Equity	0.36%	100%	N/A
Stable Value	0.09%	0%	1.97%
Total Stock Market Index	0.07%	100%	12.01%

Note: E.R. means expense ratio, i.e., 0.07% meaning $7 annual expense per $10K 529 balance.

- **How can 529 funds repay Helen's student loans?**
  Up to $10K per borrower ($20K for couple) can be withdrawn tax-free to pay qualified student-loan principal or interest (SECURE Act 2019 expansion).
- **How does multi-generation 529 planning work?**
  Grandparent-owned 529 accounts for Helena do not affect FAFSA financial aid calculations, because they are not Helena's parental assets. The accounts can fund college, professional licenses (real-estate, acupuncture, electrician), and graduate programs.
- **Bonus: Cash-Value Life Insurance and IBLOC Access**
  Funding a whole-life policy builds protected cash value that can be borrowed through an Insurance-Backed Line of Credit (IBLOC). Loans against the policy are not taxable while the contract stays in force, providing a private reserve for future real-estate purchases or emergencies. Interest may be deductible if the borrowed funds are traced directly to business or rental investment use.
- **How does the whole-life policy fit the BBB model?**
  Kevin and Helen own policies totaling $4M in coverage. Cash value earns 4-5%, and can be borrowed against to buy more rentals while interest remains deductible under IRS tracing

rules if used for business purposes. They will report interest income in Schedule 1. So it is a "wash" with the interest expense deduction.

Moral of the Story

Kevin and Helen's story illustrates how tax pro-guided planning and smart tax strategy can turn a young family into a multi-generation financial dynasty before their children even graduate high school. By combining REP status, education funding, and the BBB method, they prove that financial freedom can begin at 18.

Appendix A

Why and How to Obtain Your Real Estate License

"Your real estate license is more than a credential—it is a compass. It points you toward income, independence, and impact for life."—Mike Nie, CPA

Part 1: Top 10 Reasons to Get a Real Estate License—Financial, Business & Tax Advantages

Having a real estate license is more than just selling homes; it is a gateway to financial control, tax efficiency, and entrepreneurial opportunity. For young professionals building their FLY Vision Board, it can fast-track independence, cut transaction costs, and open doors to investment deals others never see.

As technology and artificial intelligence transform the job market, many young people worry about job security and limited income opportunities. Yet, amid these changes, real estate remains one of the most human, tangible, and resilient industries. For college students and young professionals, earning a real estate license can be one of the smartest financial and business decisions they ever make.

Below are ten reasons why having a real estate license matters—not only as a source of income, but as a lifelong wealth-building and tax-advantaged strategy.

1. Real Estate Always Remains Essential

Even as technology evolves, people still need homes, workplaces, and land. Population growth and urban development guarantee long-term demand for real estate services. While some careers shrink with automation, licensed real estate agents stay indispensable, guiding families through life's biggest financial decisions—something AI cannot replicate.

2. Turn Downtime into Income

A license is one of the most flexible, high-earning side hustles for college students or early-career professionals. You can show properties on weekends or manage referrals for classmates and relatives. A few transactions a year can cover tuition, rent, or your next investment down payment. You set your schedule—and you control your earning power.

3. Built-In Backup Career

If you lose your main job, your license becomes an instant Plan B—or even your Plan A.
You already have the credentials, the skills, and the network. Many young entrepreneurs start part-

time, then scale into full-time business ownership. Real estate is one of the simplest entry points to entrepreneurship under 25.

4. Master Communication and Leadership Skills

The profession develops essential "people skills"—negotiation, emotional intelligence, persuasion, and confidence. Explaining contracts, resolving client concerns, and closing deals trains to lead in any career. These human-connection abilities are your most valuable long-term assets.

5. Tax Efficiency and QBI Deduction

As an independent contractor, you can structure your business to qualify for the 20% Qualified Business Income (QBI) deduction under IRC §199A. You can also deduct legitimate expenses—home office, mileage, marketing, phone, software, and continuing education—reducing taxable income while keeping more of what you earn.

6. Integrate Your License with Investing

Your license gives you direct access to MLS market data, comparables, and pricing trends. Represent yourself on purchases and save the buyer's commission—usually 2.5–3%. On a $400 K property, which is roughly $12 K in savings or income. You also spot undervalued "coming soon" properties before the public, enabling smarter buy-and-hold or flip strategies.

7. Unlock Real-Estate-Professional Tax Status

With active participation (≥ 750 hours / year), you may qualify as a Real Estate Professional (REP) under IRC §469(c)(7). That lets you use rental-property losses (from depreciation or cost-segregation) to offset W-2 or active income—a powerful tool for families or investors seeking to reduce taxes legally. In addition, you don't have to claim RE Pro status every year. Just make sure you claim it with well documented hour log in the year when your spouse happens to have a sizable income.

8. Build Business Credit and Banking Relationships

Operating under your license as an LLC helps establish business credit, HELOCs, and securities-backed credit lines. Lenders view licensed agents as informed industry participants, improving loan approval odds and leverage capacity—the engine behind long-term wealth in your FLY framework.

9. Expand Your Network and Influence

Being licensed puts you in daily contact with brokers, builders, title officers, and investors who create opportunities. This access often leads to partnerships, flips, or mentorships. You move from being a consumer to being part of the real-estate ecosystem that builds wealth.

You can also share your knowledge through workshops or social media, building a personal brand as an influencer and contributing to financial-literacy education—a direct reflection of the FLY mission.

10. Foundation for an Integrated Future

A real estate license connects naturally with careers in tax, finance, law, and investment management. You can structure a vertically integrated family enterprise—*Brokerage + Property Management + Investment LLC + Family Foundation*—where each branch supports the others. That creates multiple income streams and a legacy of financial independence across generations.

Part 2: Real Estate Agent Licensing Requirements by State

This table summarizes the requirements for obtaining and maintaining a real estate salesperson or agent license across ten selected U.S. states. It is arranged alphabetically and includes key information relevant to young professionals entering the field. FLYers can seek similar information from other states as appropriate.

Readers should always verify requirements directly with their respective state's Real Estate Commission or official government website before applying, renewing, or completing continuing education (CE) courses.

State	Min Age	Pre-License Education	CE	Renewal Cycle	License Fee	Annual / Renewal Fee	Notes
CA	18	135 hrs (3×45-hr courses)	45 hrs / 4 yrs	Every 4 years	$350	Varies	No reciprocity; fingerprinting required.
FL	18	63 hrs Sales Associate	14 hrs / 2 yrs	Every 2 years	Varies	Varies	First renewal requires post-licensing; state exam.
IL	18	Pre-license (Broker-level)	12 hrs / 2 yrs	Every 2 years	Varies	Varies	IL calls entry license 'Broker'; 12-hr CE mix required.
MA	18	40 hrs pre-license	12 hrs / 2 yrs	Every 2 years	$103	$103	Renew on birthday; complete CE before renewal.
MD	18	State-approved pre-license	15 hrs / 2 yrs	Every 2 years	$98	$78	Finish CE 30 days before renewal; upload delay possible.
NC	18	Provisional Broker course	8 hrs / yr	Annual (July–June)	Varies	Varies	Complete 4-hr Update + 4-hr elective by June 10.
NY	18	77 hrs salesperson course	22.5 hrs / 2 yrs	Every 2 years	$65	$55–$65	CE includes Fair Housing, Implicit Bias, and Ethics.
TN	18	Affiliate Broker pre-license	16 hrs / 2 yrs	Every 2 years	$75	$75	60-day grace; 1-year lapse = retest/reapply.

TX	18	180 hrs qualifying edu; 270 hrs SAE first renewal	18 hrs / 2 yrs	Every 2 years	Varies	Varies	First cycle 270 hrs; later cycles 18-hr CE.
VA	18	60 hrs pre-license + 30-hr post-license	11 hrs / 2 yrs	Every 2 years	$100	$100	First-year 30-hr PLE replaces CE; CE now 11 hrs.
WA	18	Broker pre-license; 90-hr first renewal	30 hrs / 2 yrs	Every 2 years	$304	$304	90-hr post-licensing before first renewal; 3-hr Core + Fair Housing.

Source: state department of professional licensing websites.

Real estate licensing laws and requirements vary by state and are subject to change. The information in this document is provided for general educational purposes only and may not reflect the most current regulations.

Additional Tips for Young Professionals

• Budget beyond the license (MLS dues, REALTOR® fees, lockbox access, marketing).

• Pick a broker that offers mentoring, technology tools, and reasonable commission splits.

• Mark CE deadlines in advance—some states require completion 30 days early.

• Expect background checks and fingerprinting before your license is issued.

• Confirm all requirements with each state's Real Estate Commission before applying.

Appendix B

Ten Wealth and Financial Books to FLYers Who Aspire to Invest In Real Estate

"Rich people do not have bigger brains—they just read better books and take action sooner."—Mike Nie, CPA

1. ***Real Estate Tax Secrets of the Rich*** **by Sandy Botkin (McGraw-Hill Education, 2006)**

After working as a tax attorney for the IRS, Sandy Botkin founded his own tax consulting business. He explains how real estate owners legally reduce taxes and keep more of their income while showing that the tax code rewards property owners who understand and use the rules correctly.

The main idea of the book is that taxes are not just a cost, but a planning opportunity. Botkin tells his readers how real estate investors use deductions, depreciation, exclusions, and tax-deferred strategies to increase cash flow and lower taxable income. Real estate can be one of the most tax-favored investments when managed properly.

Botkin stresses that real wealth comes from tax planning, not just tax filing. By planning ahead—before buying, operating, or selling property—investors can significantly improve after-tax returns. The book uses clear examples and practical explanations to make complex tax rules easy to understand and apply.

Overall, the book teaches that mastering real estate tax rules allows investors to protect income, grow wealth faster, and gain long-term financial freedom.

Notable Quotes

- "The tax law is written to reward those who understand it."
- "Real estate is one of the most powerful tax shelters available to investors."
- "Tax planning starts when you buy the property—not on April 15."

2. ***The Holy Grail of Investing*** **by Tony Robbins and Christopher Zook (Simon & Schuster, 2024)**

In *The Holy Grail of Investing*, Tony Robbins explores how ordinary investors can achieve financial freedom through disciplined, diversified, and risk-managed investing. Drawing on insights from world-class investors such as Ray Dalio, Warren Buffett, and Jack Bogle, Robbins presents a practical roadmap for building wealth that balances growth with protection.

The book's core principle is that the true "holy grail" of investing lies in diversification across uncorrelated assets—a strategy that reduces risk while maintaining strong long-term returns.

Robbins explains that most investors focus too heavily on stock-picking or market timing when the real power comes from asset allocation and emotional control. He advocates for a mix of equities, bonds, commodities, and alternative investments designed to perform in different economic climates.

Robbins also stresses the importance of compounding, low-cost index investing, and staying invested through volatility. Emotional decisions, he warns, destroy more wealth than bad market conditions. He calls on investors to automate their plans, focus on the long game, and remember that true wealth is not just money — it is freedom, peace of mind, and the ability to contribute to others.

Notable Quotes

- "The secret to wealth is not in chasing returns — it is in consistency and discipline."
- "Diversification is the one free lunch in investing."
- "You cannot control the markets, but you can control your decisions."

3. *The Latte Factor: Why You Don't Have to Be Rich to Live Rich* by David Bach and John David Mann (Atria Books, 2019)

The Latte Factor teaches that achieving financial freedom is not about earning more, but making smarter choices with the money you already have. Told through a simple story about a young professional named Zoey, the book reveals how small daily expenses — like a $5 latte — add up over time and prevent people from building wealth.

Bach's core idea is that anyone can become rich by paying attention to where their money goes and by investing consistently. He introduces the concept of "The Latte Factor" to show that small sacrifices, when redirected toward savings or investments, can grow into significant wealth through the power of compound interest. This message focuses on awareness and intentional spending rather than deprivation.

Through Zoey's journey, readers learn three timeless lessons: pay yourself first by automatically saving a portion of your income, make your money work for you through regular investing, and live rich now by aligning spending with your values instead of instant gratification. Bach emphasizes that financial freedom is available to everyone who commits to small, consistent habits over time.

Notable Quotes

- "You do not need to earn more to live rich — you need to spend smarter."
- "Small amounts of money, invested wisely, turn into financial freedom."
- "The secret to wealth is realizing you already have enough to start."

4. *Investing in Real Estate with No (and Low) Money Down* by Brandon Turner (BiggerPockets Publishing, 2014)

This book teaches that you do not need to be rich to start investing — you need creativity, strategy, and persistence. Turner breaks the myth that real estate is only for those with capital, showing how investors can use creative financing tools such as seller financing, partnerships, lease options, house hacking, private lending, and the "BRRRR" method to build wealth with little cash up front.

He reminds us that success depends more on resourcefulness than resources. By learning to leverage other people's money (OPM), find win-win deals, and build trust with partners and lenders, new investors can get started earlier and scale faster. Turner also cautions that while these techniques can reduce cash needs, they require discipline, due diligence, and risk management.

Notable Quotes

- "It is not about having money — it is about having the knowledge and creativity to find it."
- "The most successful investors are not the ones with the most cash—they are the ones who solve the most problems."
- "Do not wait to buy real estate. Buy real estate and wait."

5. ***J.K. Lasser's 1001 Deductions and Tax Breaks 2026: Your Complete Guide to Everything Deductible* by Barbara Weltman (Wiley, 2025)**

J.K. Lasser's 1001 Deductions & Tax Breaks 2026 by Barbara Weltman is a comprehensive, plain-English guide to every major tax deduction and credit available for the 2025–2026 filing season. It helps individuals, families, and small-business owners identify legitimate ways to reduce taxable income, maximize refunds, and plan year-round for tax savings.

The book explains hundreds of deductions — from home office and education costs to medical expenses, real estate, and retirement plans — along with eligibility rules, limits, and documentation tips. Updated for the latest IRS inflation adjustments and legislative changes, it encourages proactive planning rather than last-minute filing.

Weltman's central message is simple: smart taxpayers do not overpay; they prepare. By tracking spending, organizing records, and understanding the tax code, anyone can keep more of what they earn while staying fully compliant.

Notable Quotes

- "Save money—legally—on your 2025-26 taxes with easy, expert advice from a trusted source."
- "Each tax benefit is explained in simple, understandable language—along with eligibility requirements for claiming the benefit."
- "Tax planning is not just about filing; it is about preparing, tracking and structuring your financial life so Uncle Sam gets exactly what he is owed—and not a penny more."

6. ***Tax Strategies for the Savvy Real Estate Investor: Powerful techniques anyone can use to deduct more, invest smarter, and pay far less to the IRS!* By Amanda Han and Matthew MacFarland (BiggerPockets Publishing, 2016)**

This book is a practical guide designed to help investors use the U.S. tax code to their advantage. Written by experienced CPAs who specialize in real estate, the book breaks down complex tax concepts into clear, actionable strategies that enable investors to deduct more, invest smarter, and legally pay less to the IRS.

The central idea is that successful real estate investors do not just focus on finding good deals—they also plan their taxes strategically. Han and MacFarland explain how the tax code is written to encourage investment, not punish it. By understanding key principles such as depreciation, passive losses, and entity structuring, investors can turn ordinary expenses into powerful tax deductions.

The book covers practical techniques like maximizing write-offs for travel, home office, and property improvements; leveraging cost segregation to accelerate depreciation; and using Section 1031 exchanges to defer capital gains. It also highlights the advantages of operating through LLCs, partnerships, or S corporations, and how to qualify as a Real Estate Professional (REP) for greater tax benefits.

Beyond tactics, the authors stress the importance of proactive planning — working with a tax advisor before making big moves rather than reacting at tax time. Their message is that with the right structure, mindset, and recordkeeping, the average investor can achieve what the wealthy have done for decades: build long-term wealth while minimizing taxes legally.

Notable Quotes

- "You cannot control the tax laws, but you can control how you apply them."
- "Real estate investors who plan their taxes make money when they buy — and when they file."
- "The IRS rewards those who create housing and jobs, not those who wait until April 15 to think about taxes."

7. *SMART Family Tax Guide* by Mike Nie (Gifted Books, 2025)

The SMART Family Tax Guide by Mike Nie is a comprehensive, story-driven handbook that empowers families, business owners, and investors to take control of their financial destiny through intelligent tax planning. Written with clarity and real-life examples, the book turns the complex U.S. tax code into an accessible tool for building and preserving wealth across generations.

At its core, the guide introduces the SMART framework — a philosophy built on Strategy, Management, Assets, Retirement, and Trusts. Nie demonstrates how each of these pillars works together to minimize taxes legally while creating lasting financial security. Through detailed case studies, he shows how ordinary families can apply professional-level tax tactics—such as maximizing deductions, shifting income among family members, leveraging real estate and small business ownership, and using family foundations — to reduce tax liabilities and build generational wealth.

The book's storytelling approach connects tax strategy to life purpose. Nie explains how smart planning can fund education, support charitable giving, and ensure smoother estate transfers through trusts and legacy planning. He emphasizes that effective tax strategy is not about loopholes — it is about *alignment*: making every dollar work toward the family's long-term vision while staying fully compliant with the law.

Notable Quotes

- "SMART: start to master assets and reduce taxes."
- "You cannot build generational wealth with last-minute tax filing; you need year-round strategy."
- "The smartest families do not fear the tax code—they master it."

8. ***Lower Your Taxes - BIG TIME! 2023-2024* by Sandy Botkin (McGraw-Hill Education, 2023)**

Lower Your Taxes - BIG TIME! is a comprehensive tax guide written to help individuals and small business owners legally reduce their tax bills and keep more of their money. Written by a former IRS attorney, the book explains how the tax system really works and shows practical ways to take advantage of deductions, credits, and planning strategies that most taxpayers overlook.

The central idea of the book is that tax planning should be year-round, not just something you do at tax time. Botkin breaks down the tax code into understandable parts and teaches readers how to maximize savings. He covers a wide range of topics, including how to document business deductions properly, start and operate a home-based business, use tax-favored deductions for travel and meals, and take full advantage of recent tax code changes.

Botkin also explains advanced tax strategies for small businesses, such as choosing the best entity type and using fringe benefits to reduce taxable income. Throughout the book, he focuses on practical tips and real examples so that readers can immediately apply the ideas to their own finances. By understanding how the tax laws work, taxpayers can save thousands of dollars each year and protect their wealth more effectively.

Notable Quotes
- "Tax planning is not something you do only at the end of the year — it's a year-round strategy."
- "Most taxpayers overpay simply because they never learn how to take the deductions and credits they are entitled to."
- "Understanding the tax code is one of the best ways to keep more money in your pocket."

9. ***Tax-Free Wealth: How to Build Massive Wealth by Permanently Lowering Your Taxes* by Tom Wheelwright (RDA Press, 2013)**

This book teaches that the tax code is not meant to punish success — it is designed to reward behaviors that strengthen the economy. Wheelwright explains that by thinking like an investor or business owner, not an employee, anyone can legally reduce taxes and accelerate wealth.

The book shows how to use real estate, depreciation, business ownership, and strategic entity structures to transform ordinary expenses into powerful deductions. Wheelwright emphasizes proactive planning — changing your financial "facts" so you qualify for tax incentives, rather than reacting at filing time. His core idea is simple: you build wealth not by how much you earn, but by how much you keep.

Notable Quotes

- "The tax laws are a series of incentives — learn them, and you will pay less."
- "Depreciation is the king of deductions."
- "Change your facts, and you change your taxes."

10. ***The Art and Science of Real Estate Negotiation: Skills, Strategies, Tactics* by Gabrielle Dahms (Booksmart Press, 2020)**

The Art and Science of Real Estate Negotiation explains how investors and agents can negotiate better real estate deals. The book shows that strong negotiation skills help buyers save money, improve contract terms, and reach better agreements.

The main idea is that good negotiation requires preparation and clear communication. Successful negotiators understand their goals, learn what the other party wants, and focus on finding solutions that work for both sides. The book also teaches simple tactics such as asking good questions, listening carefully, and staying calm during discussions. It explains that confidence, patience, and clear communication often lead to better results than aggressive bargaining.

Overall, the book shows that negotiation is a skill anyone can learn. With preparation and practice, investors and buyers can negotiate stronger deals and make better real estate decisions.

Notable Quotes

- "Successful negotiations begin with preparation."
- "Listening carefully helps reveal the other side's priorities."
- "Clear communication leads to stronger agreements."

Appendix C

Ten Financial Freedom Quotes for FLYers

"Uncle Sam is Not Your Uncle."—Ed Slott, CPA, the Nation's #1 IRA Expert

Financial freedom begins not with money, but with mindset. These ten quotes, inspired by timeless wisdom and priceless real-life lessons, are designed to guide every young person toward independence, discipline, and lasting wealth.

1. "Uncle Sam is not your uncle."—Ed Slott, CPA

Taxes are life's unavoidable companion. From your first paycheck to your last retirement withdrawal, Uncle Sam always gets his share. April 15 is often called *Tax Liberation Day*—the date when the average American finally starts earning for themselves after paying federal, state, and local taxes.

Example: When Chris received his first W-2 at age 16, we reviewed his paycheck together. For every $100 he earned, about $20 went to taxes. He was shocked—but it taught him that tax planning is not optional; it is essential. We revised his W-4 withholding setup by factoring in HSA contribution, AOTC tax credit, traditional 401(k) contribution, and rental losses.

Lesson: Every financial move (marriage, investment, or even lottery winnings) has tax consequences. Always think with a "tax-smart" mindset.

2. "We do not need to impress people who do not care about us."

Many young adults fall into the trap of spending money to look successful. Keeping up with the Joneses can keep you broke.

Example: Kevin once spent $200 on a designer jacket just to "look cool." We sat down and talked about how real confidence comes from competence, not clothing. Two months later, he started his own moving business — and his pride came from his income producing results, not his wardrobe. Full disclosure: Kevin added "minimalism" to his 2026 vision board — a thoughtful declaration that every spending decision will be carefully evaluated.

Lesson: You do not win the wealth game by showing off. You win it by saving, investing, and staying humble.

3. "Begin with the end in mind."—Stephen Covey, Author of *Seven Habits of Highly Effective People*

Goals give direction; habits give momentum. Write down what financial success looks like to you.

Example: Chris created a *vision board* with a photo of a small Florida home he wanted to own by 20. Every time he thought about buying a new gadget or eating out, he asked himself: *Will this purchase delay my dream?* That one habit helped him save his down payment two years earlier.

Lesson: Be proactive. Your future wealth begins with today's small, intentional choices.

4. "Live with minimalism; Help others with maximalism."

True happiness does not come from accumulation—it comes from contribution.

Example: Kevin's junk removal business opened his eyes to how much people hoard. Garages filled with unused items were reminders that consumption does not create fulfillment. Instead, he began donating lightly-used shoes and clothes to families in need.

Lesson: Own less, give more. Live simply so others may simply live.

5. "Pay yourself first."—George S. Clason, *The Richest Man in Babylon*

Most people pay everyone else first—the government, credit cards, and bills—and then have nothing left to invest. Flip that order.

Example: When Chris received $500 from his pilot instruction part-time job, he immediately set aside $100 into a Roth IRA before spending a dime. Over time, that habit built a six-figure foundation by his 20s.

With the help of the family bank, Chris applies all his take-home pay and pays into his cash value whole life insurance policies in a form of paid up addition (compounding 5-6% annually), and he takes out policy loans to pay his mortgage and business expenses. If structured correctly, policy loan interest can be deductible business expenses. He pays back the policy loans to restore the cash value in the policies.

Lesson: Treat your savings like a bill you *must* pay. Your future self deserves to be your priority.

6. "Freedom is not free. It has a price tag on it."

Freedom—financial or otherwise—requires discipline, patience, and sacrifice.

Example: America's national debt grew from $3 trillion in 1997 to over $39 trillion when the book was published (April 2026). Source: https://www.usdebtclock.org/. The same pattern happens at home — too much borrowing today means less freedom tomorrow.

Lesson: Debt is a chain disguised as convenience. The more you borrow, the less you own your future.

7. "Delay instant gratification; display faithful appreciation."

Gratitude grows wealth faster than greed ever can.

Example: Every night, I write down ten things I am thankful for — from my family's health to the good weather. Chris and Kevin do the same. When you focus on appreciation instead of acquisition, you stop chasing happiness through purchases.

Lesson: Say "thank you" more often. The patient saver builds wealth; the impatient spender builds regret.

8. "Compound interest is the eighth wonder of the world."—Albert Einstein

Time turns small actions into extraordinary results.

Example: When Chris was born, I invested $19,000 into his UTMA account. By age 18, through consistent investing in S&P 500 index funds, which grew close to $900,000. That is the magic of compounding: small seeds, big trees. Then he uses the SBLOC to access the funds without paying capital gain tax or losing the future growth of underlying stocks.

Lesson: Start early. Even $100 a month can become a fortune if given enough time to grow.

9. "Do not put all your eggs in one basket."—Andrew Carnegie

Diversification protects you from uncertainty.

Example: Our family holds investments in real estate, stock index funds, and whole life insurance. When one market slows, another balances it out. This balance has kept our wealth stable through recessions and pandemics alike.

Lesson: Diversify your asset stocks, rentals, crypto, and cash flow businesses. Never let one storm sink your ship.

10. "Let Money work for you; not you work for money."

The goal is not to earn more. It is to earn smarter.

Example: Dr. Max, a real estate investor, told me that his client was a flight attendant in her late 60's, still working crazy hours simply to pay bills and mortgage. Instead, Dr. Max let his properties and investments generate income while he slept.

Lesson: Turn active income into passive income. Let your money become your employee, 24x7.

Final Thought

Financial freedom is a series of small, consistent decisions made with wisdom and intention. Each quote in this chapter is more than a saying — it is a mindset. If you are young, your greatest asset is not cash — it is time. Start early, stay disciplined, and always remember money is a tool, not an expert.

Appendix D

How Parents Design a Tax-Free Real Estate Legacy and Inheritance Planning

"Do not put your trust in money, but put your money in trust."—Oliver Wendell Holmes, U.S. Supreme Court judge

When parents own rental properties, they hold one of the most powerful financial tools available to a family. But without planning, that same tool can trigger unnecessary capital-gains tax, depreciation recapture, and estate tax. The good news: with proper structure, real estate can be passed to the next generation almost entirely tax-free.

This chapter explains how families can design a smart, compliant plan using the same principles wealthy investors rely on, step-by-step.

Disclaimer: This chapter discusses revocable living trusts and estate planning concepts. Readers should seek advice from a qualified estate planning attorney licensed in their state before implementing any strategies described herein.

1. Start with the Family Vision

Every plan begins with a shared purpose:

- Do the parents want the children to manage the properties, or sell them?
- Is the goal to create income, preserve legacy, or fund education?
- How involved are the children now?
- Is your child going through a contentious divorce?

Clarifying intent determines whether the strategy should focus on control, cash flow, or transfer. A "tax-free" plan does not mean any taxes ever; it means minimizing taxation at each stage while keeping family control intact.

2. The Foundation: Ownership and Entity Structure

A. Use the Right Entity

For parents with multiple properties:

- LLC (Limited Liability Company): Shields personal assets from lawsuits and allows flexible income allocation among family members.

- Family Limited Partnership (FLP): Excellent for gradual gifting—parents can retain control as general partners while gifting limited interests to children.
- Revocable Living Trust: Avoids probate and centralizes management.

Should each property be titled into its own LLC for liability protection purposes? It depends. A rule of thumb include: (1) bundle same state property into one LLC; (2) net market value (subtracting the mortgage loan) over $500K is a good threshold to set up an LLC; (3) be aware of the state and county taxes when you transfer real estate property titles to the LLC; and (4) all LLCs flow into a Family Holding Company, a top LLC owned by the family trust. Seek legal advice from real estate attorneys (such as KKOS).

3. Harvest Tax Benefits While Living

Even before thinking about inheritance, parents can reduce or eliminate taxes on rental income legally.

A. Accelerated Depreciation and Cost Segregation

Breaking property components into 5-, 7-, and 15-year assets allows faster write-offs under §168(k). This generates paper losses that can offset rental income—or even other income if one spouse qualifies as a Real Estate Professional under §469(c)(7).

B. 1031 Exchange—"Swap till Drop"

When selling a property, use an IRC §1031 like-kind exchange to roll gains into a new investment. This defers both capital gains and depreciation recapture indefinitely. You can repeat this process your entire life—turning real estate into a permanent tax-deferral machine. After parents' deaths, children inherit the rental properties at the step-up basis, and have the discretion to (1) sell the properties without paying capital gain taxes or deprecation recapture taxes; or (2) continue running the rentals with a real estate professional status (with a newly established basis value).

C. HELOCs and Cash-Out Refinancing

Borrowing against equity is not taxable. Parents can access property equity for retirement, business investments, or even funding children's down payments, all without triggering a sale. The OBBB permanently increases the estate and gift tax exemption to $15 million (indexed), effective for estates/gifts after 2025 (IRC §2010(c)(3), Sec. 70106). Parents can use HELOC, IBLOC and SBLOC borrowings to ensure the federal estate tax-free legacy planning. Relocate to states that are tax-friendly to trust and estate planning.

The borrowed money can (1) purchase state 529 plan (up to $95K per beneficiary, including children, spouses, grandchildren and so on); (2) gift to each family member up to $19,000 per year per person. If the senior citizen is married, such number doubles; or (3) donate to the family foundation as tax deductions.

Grandparent 529 plan value is excluded from their estate for the federal estate taxation purpose. In other words, if the grandfather passes away at the age 90 (owing $4M 529 plans with various children and grandchildren as beneficiary), this $4M is not part of the $15M lifetime estate exclusion amount. Seek your in-state financial advisor for state estate implications of such 529 plans. Add a successor owner of your 529 plan assets.

4. The Power of the "Step-Up in Basis"

This is the core of a tax-free inheritance strategy. When parents pass away owning real estate:

- The property's tax basis resets to its fair market value (FMV) on the date of death.
- That means all accumulated gains disappear for capital-gains purposes.

🔍 **Tax tip**: A rental purchased for $200,000 decades ago and now worth $900,000. You can inherit from your deceased parent and get a step-up basis to $900,000. If heirs sell immediately at that price, they owe zero capital-gains tax—and all past depreciation is wiped clean.

This "fresh start" makes the step-up basis one of the most powerful tax-free transfer tools in the entire tax code.

5. The Family Bank Strategy

Parents can create an internal Family Bank model by:

- Placing securities (invested in S&P 500 index and BRK.B stock) into the family-trust-owned brokerage account.
- Using SBLOC loans to help children buy additional properties or start small rentals. Execute a promissory note with repayment clauses required by the IRS.
- Charging IRS-compliant interest rates (the AFR rate), keeping interest income inside the family system instead of to outside banks.
- File tax form 1040 or 1041 (trust return) to report taxable interest income earned from the children who repay the loan to the family bank. Pay back SBLOC loan interest and principal to the brokerage firm.

This creates a private lending loop where wealth compounds within generations instead of leaving the family.

6. Using Gifting and Discounts

Parents can gradually gift membership units in their LLC or FLP to their children each year:

- Up to $19,000 per child per parent (2025 limit) without filing a gift-tax return.
- Discounted valuation methods (for minority interest or lack of marketability) allow even larger value transfers tax-efficiently.

Over time, ownership shifts from parents to children, without triggering capital-gains or gift taxes when done correctly.

7. Charitable and Foundation Integration

Families with philanthropic goals can integrate a family foundation.

- Donate appreciated stocks directly to the foundation → no capital-gains tax on the gift.
- Receive an immediate charitable deduction up to 20% of AGI.
- The family foundation can then sell stocks with 1.39% excise tax, creating a legacy of giving that also teaches youth stewardship.

8. Lifetime Planning vs. Death Planning

A true tax-free plan is not built at the last moment. Families should map out two horizons:

Timeline	Tools & Goals
While Living	1031 Exchanges, Cost Segregation, Family Loans, Gifts, Charitable Giving
After Death	Step-Up in Basis, Trust owned SBLOC or IBLOC, Estate Exclusion ($15M per person in 2026+)

By combining lifetime and death planning, parents can live tax-efficiently now while leaving properties tax-free later.

9. Involve the Next Generation Early

Tax-free planning works best when children understand the system. Parents can:

- Add adult children as property managers or trust co-trustees.
- Pay them for actually-performed management services, with earned income eligible for 401(k) or IRA contributions (either W-2 or 1099 NEC).
- Teach them property management, bookkeeping, and depreciation early.

This turns real estate into a family learning lab, not just an inheritance.

🔍 Tax Tip: The Nie Family Legacy Plan

Mike and Olga own four rentals in Virginia and Maryland worth $2 million with $800,000 total basis. They transfer them into a VA LLC and a MD LLC under their living trust. Each year, they gift 10% of LLC membership to their children through valuation discounts.

They use cost segregation to create $120,000 in paper losses and a HELOC to fund a family foundation that donates to youth education. When they eventually pass, the heirs receive the remaining assets with a full step-up basis: no capital gains, no recapture, and no estate tax due to the exclusion limit. Their children either sell the properties at fair market value, pay off the HELOC loan, and get the remaining fund tax free, or continue the rental business, claiming real estate professional tax status, continue 1031 exchange under their names and estates.

10. The FLY Lesson: Real Estate as a Living Legacy

For FLY readers, this chapter is not about death—it is about designing a living system that lets families enjoy, share, and transfer wealth without waste. Real estate becomes the classroom, the business, and the inheritance all in one.

Key takeaway: When parents plan intentionally—using trusts, 1031 exchanges, gifting, and the step-up basis—they can turn taxable property into a tax-free generational engine.

Summary Table: Tax-Free Real Estate Planning Tools

Strategy	Tax Benefit	Who Uses It	Code Reference
1031 Exchange	Defers capital gains & depreciation recapture	Parents	§1031
Cost Segregation	Accelerates depreciation deductions	Investors/Parents	§168(k)
Step-Up in Basis	Eliminates capital gains at parent death	Heirs	§1014
Real Estate Professional	Converts passive losses into active deductions	Parent/Spouse/Heirs	§469(c)(7)
Family LLC/FLP	Gift control units with valuation discounts	Parents/Children	Reg. §25.2512-3
Intra-Family Loans	Tax-free lending; retains family interest	Parents to Kids	IRS Applicable Federal Rate (AFR) rule
Family Foundation	Avoids capital gain; creates charitable deduction	Family	§501(c)(3)
Revocable Trust	Avoids probate; maintains control and management	Parents	State trust law

Final Thought

Tax-free real estate planning is not a loophole. It is financial design with purpose. Parents can live well, give well, and leave well, creating a structure where every brick continues to build wealth for generations. The smartest families do not just buy property. They build systems that make it last forever.

Appendix E

Using AI Tools to Build Real Estate Portfolio Wealth With Tax Saving Strategies

"AI won't replace humans—but humans with AI will replace humans without AI." – Karim Lakhani, Professor at Harvard Business School

Artificial intelligence (AI) has become the new financial partner for smart investors. Where past generations relied on instinct and spreadsheets, today's young professionals can use AI tools to analyze real estate markets, automate bookkeeping, identify opportunities, and even design tax strategies. For families and youths building long-term real estate wealth, AI is not science fiction; it is a financial accelerator.

In this appendix, we'll explore 10 use cases that show how today's investors (each under age 30) are using AI to grow their real estate portfolios, reduce taxes, and design multi-faceted strategies.

1. Portfolio Diversification with AI

Case Study: Emily Tran, Age 27

Emily, a recent MBA graduate, uses an AI-powered real estate analytics platform to identify undervalued multifamily properties in emerging neighborhoods. The AI tool analyzes rental trends, demographic shifts, and infrastructure projects, flagging three small apartment buildings across different cities.

By diversifying geographically, Emily reduces her risk exposure while securing long-term appreciation and steady cash flow. Her AI dashboard—integrated with Zillow Data API and ChatGPT Portfolio Assistant—provides monthly market updates and alerts for refinancing opportunities.

AI tools used:

- Reonomy AI – market heat maps and demographics
- ChatGPT Real Estate Analyst – cash flow projection and risk scoring

2. Tax-Loss Harvesting for Short-Term Rentals

Case Study: Marcus Lee, Age 29

Marcus owns several Airbnb units. His AI-driven accounting software tracks property values and rental occupancy in real time. When one property's fair market value drops, the system suggests selling it to realize a capital loss—offsetting gains from stock portfolio sales.

This strategy, called tax-loss harvesting, allows Marcus to lower his taxable income and reinvest his savings into a higher-performing rental.

AI tools used:

- QuickBooks AI + ChatGPT Tax Advisor – automatic gain/loss tracking
- TaxGPT – real-time tax projection and scenario simulation

3. Optimizing 1031 Exchanges

Case Study: Priya Patel, Age 25

Priya plans to sell her single-family rental and upgrade into a small retail plaza. She uses an AI 1031 Exchange Assistant that scans the national MLS and commercial listings for like-kind replacement properties, ensuring she meets IRS deadlines—the 45-day identification and 180-day closing rules under §1031.

The AI also flags related-party risks and calculates potential deferred taxes. Priya completes the swap seamlessly, deferring nearly $80,000 in capital gains.

AI tools used:

- RealNex Exchange AI – 1031 matching engine
- Turbotax Chat Pro (IRC §1031 Mode) – deferral and compliance modeling

4. Passive Activity Loss Optimization

Case Study: Jordan Smith, Age 30

Jordan, a part-time software engineer, invests in five rental homes. His AI tax software monitors his logged hours and recommends activities to meet the "active participation" test: marketing, management, and maintenance oversight.

By exceeding the required hours, Jordan qualifies for passive loss allowance under §469(i), offsetting part of his salary income.

AI tools used:

- TaxDome AI – activity tracker integrated with time logs
- ChatGPT REP Planner – IRS §469 eligibility review

5. Identifying Opportunity Zones

Case Study: Sofia Martinez, Age 28

Sofia uses an AI mapping system to find federally designated Opportunity Zones (OZ) with strong population and job growth. The tool overlays census data, school ratings, and projected appreciation, helping her select a mixed-use property in a revitalizing downtown district.

By investing through a Qualified Opportunity Fund (QOF), Sofia defers existing capital gains and, after a 10-year period, may pay zero tax on future appreciation.

AI tools used:

- ArcGIS AI + ChatGPT Map Analyst – OZ map overlay
- WealthGPT – QOF compliance and ROI modeling

6. Depreciation Recapture Planning

Case Study: Tyler Nguyen, Age 26

Tyler plans to sell one of his rental duplexes. His AI tax advisor calculates potential unrecaptured §1250 gain—the portion of profit taxed at 25% due to past depreciation. The software models different sale dates and capital-loss offsets, recommending that he delays the closing until next quarter to synchronize with a planned §1031 reinvestment. The timing adjustment saves him over $12,000 in taxes.

AI tools used:

- TaxGPT Advanced – recapture forecasting & scenario testing
- ChatGPT for Real Estate Investors – capital gain optimization

7. Family-Owned Business Estate Tax Exemption

Case Study: Jasmine Kim, Age 29

After inheriting her parents' rental portfolio, Jasmine uploads their property data into AI estate-planning software. The system checks eligibility for the Dynasty/GRATs): Transfer business interests to Generation-Skipping Trusts or Grantor Retained Annuity Trusts using exemptions, shielding future appreciation while retaining control/income.

AI analysis confirms that passive rentals normally do not qualify unless the family provides substantial services—prompting Jasmine to convert several units into short-term rentals managed actively, reclassifying them as a trade or business.

AI tools used:

- Relaw.ai– estate-planning and state GRATs
- Lexis+ AI – verifies local inheritance and estate-tax statutes

8. Automated Cost Segregation Studies

Case Study: Alex Johnson, Age 24

Alex acquires a duplex and uploads blueprints to a cost-segregation AI platform. In minutes, it categorizes assets into 5-, 7-, and 15-year property classes—identifying $68,000 of bonus-depreciable components under §168(k). The result: immediate deductions that improve cash flow and reduce taxable income for the year. Alex then engages a reputable cost seg company to issue a formal report with similar results.

AI tools used:

- EngineeredTax AI – image-based cost-seg modeling
- ChatGPT Accounting Copilot – verifies Form 4562 and depreciation schedule

9. Smart Entity Structuring for Liability and Tax

Case Study: Rachel O'Connor, Age 30

As Rachel's rental business grows, she wants protection and efficiency. Her AI legal advisor compares the impact of forming an LLC, or partnership based on her income, state tax, and risk exposure. It recommends an LLC taxed as a partnership—preserving pass-through treatment while limiting personal liability.

Rachel also uses AI to draft her operating agreement and auto-file with her state's corporate registry.

AI tools used:

- Harvey.ai – legal entity recommendation system
- TaxGPT – operating agreement & EIN checklist

10. AI-Driven Market Timing and Exit Planning

Case Study: Noah Williams, Age 28

Noah's AI dashboard tracks Federal Reserve data, local sales volume, and price momentum. The model predicts a 6% softening in its condo market. Acting early, Noah sells his unit, realizing long-term gains, and reinvests the proceeds into a higher-yield multifamily asset.

AI also schedules its sales to ensure 12+ months of holding, qualifying for long-term capital gain rates and avoiding short-term taxation.

AI tools used:

- MarketLens AI – predictive market cycle analyzer
- Dealmind AI– sale timing & reinvestment planning

The FLY Framework: How AI Builds Wealth

AI Function	Tax Code Reference	Real Estate Benefit	Key AI Tool
Market Research	§1014 Step-up awareness	Identifies undervalued markets	Reonomy, ChatGPT Analyst
Tax-Loss Harvesting	§1211–1212	Offsets capital gains	QuickBooks AI
1031 Exchange	§1031	Defers capital gains	RealNex, TurboTax AI
REP Status Tracking	§469(c)(7)	Converts passive to non-passive losses	TaxDome AI
Opportunity Zone Analysis	§1400Z	Eliminates appreciation tax	ArcGIS AI
Cost Segregation	§168(k)	Accelerates depreciation	EngineeredTax AI

Depreciation Recapture	§1250	Times gain recognition	TaxGPT Advanced
Entity Planning	§199A	Reduces business tax burden	Harvey.ai
Estate Tax Planning	§2032A, QFOBI	Preserves family assets	TrustGPT
Market Timing	§1222	Maximizes long-term gain rates	MarketLens AI

Real Estate AI Tools and Costs

AI Tool	Function/Code Reference	Website	Typical Annual Fee (2025)
Reonomy	Identifies undervalued markets	https://www.reonomy.com	~$3,588/year (approx $299/mo, confirmed quote needed)
ChatGPT Analyst	Analyst/Market/Tax Function	https://openai.com/chatgpt	$240/year (ChatGPT Plus), Team: $300/user/year (annual billing)
QuickBooks AI	Tax-Loss Harvesting (§1211–1212)	https://quickbooks.intuit.com	$420–$3,300/year (Simple Start: $35/mo, Advanced: $275/mo)
RealNex	1031 Exchange (§1031), CRE Deals	https://www.realnex.com	Contact for quote; est. ~$1,500/year
TurboTax AI	1031 Exchange (§1031), Filing	https://turbotax.intuit.com	$89–$210/year (per return, not SaaS)
TaxDome AI	REP Status (§469(c)(7))	https://www.taxdome.com	~$600/year (Pro plan)
ArcGIS AI	Opportunity Zone (§1400Z)	https://www.arcgis.com	~$500–$5,000/year (tiered per org)
EngineeredTax AI	Cost Segregation (§168(k))	https://engineeredtaxservices.com	Custom/per-project, annual support available
TaxGPT Advanced	Depreciation Recapture (§1250)	https://taxgpt.ai	Estimate ~$600–$1,000/year (subject to confirmation)

Harvey.ai	Entity Planning (§199A)	https://harvey.ai	Contact for quote; legal AI platform
TrustGPT	Estate Tax (§2032A, QFOBI)	https://trustgpt.com	Estimate ~$499/year (estate legal AI)
MarketLens AI	Market Timing (§1222)	https://marketlens.ai	Contact for quote

Note: AI tool subscription fee could be deducted from Schedule C or E as legitimate business expenses.

Final Reflection: AI as the Fifth Asset Class

In the modern financial world, AI itself becomes an asset class—not one you buy, but one you use. By integrating AI with:

- Real estate (hard assets),
- Tax strategy (soft savings), and
- Automation (time leverage).

Young professionals can achieve exponential efficiency. AI does not replace judgment—it amplifies wisdom. For the FLY generation, mastering AI is the new frontier of financial independence.

Your AI is your new CFO—if you train it to think like one.

Appendix F

One Big Beautiful Bill Helping FLYers

"*The true beauty of the One Big Beautiful Bill is not in the code—it is in the freedom it gives young people to dream bigger and FLY higher.*"—Mike Nie, CPA

The passage of the One Big Beautiful Bill Act marks a transformative moment for American families seeking to maximize their financial well-being. With sweeping reforms that make the 2017 tax cuts permanent, expand the child tax credit, boost the standard deduction, and introduce innovative savings tools like Trump Accounts, this legislation delivers unprecedented opportunities for families to keep more of what they earn and build lasting wealth.

From eliminating taxes on tips and overtime pay to enhancing 529 education savings and providing new incentives for estate planning, the Act empowers families at every stage of life to make smarter, more strategic tax moves. This chapter unveils ten actionable, FLYer-focused tax strategies, each designed to help you navigate the new landscape, reduce your tax burden, and secure a brighter financial future under the One Big Beautiful Bill Act.

Disclaimer: You are advised to visit IRS.gov for updated tax forms and schedules. Some states may choose not to amend the state tax codes to reflect the federal level tax law changes. Seek tax advice from the CPAs that are licensed in your state(s).

Unless otherwise noted, AGI thresholds are for 2025 and may be indexed for inflation in future years. For married couples, joint filing is often advantageous for phase-out thresholds. Taxpayers should consider timing income, deductions, and major purchases to maximize benefits under any phase-out rules. Consult a tax advisor for personalized planning, especially if your AGI is near a phase-out threshold.

No.	Tax Change/ Provision	Description	Impact on FLYers	Tax Planning Tip
1	No tax on qualified tips	Allows a deduction of up to $25,000 per year for cash tips received in occupations that customarily received tips before 2025, subject to income phaseouts and reporting requirements.	FLY workers in service industries (restaurants, salons, etc.) can reduce taxable income by excluding tips, lowering their tax bill.	Keep detailed records and ensure all tips are properly reported to maximize the deduction and avoid IRS issues.
2	No tax on overtime pay	Permits a deduction of up to $12,500 ($25,000 joint) per year for overtime compensation required under the Fair Labor Standards Act, with income phaseouts.	Young workers putting in extra hours can reduce taxable income, making overtime more financially rewarding.	Track overtime hours and ensure employers report overtime pay separately on W-2s for deduction eligibility.
3	Enhanced standard deduction	Increases the standard deduction, effective 2025.	Most FLYers will benefit from a higher standard deduction, reducing taxable income even if they do not itemize.	Compare itemized deductions to the new standard deduction each year to choose the most beneficial option.
4	Expanded child tax credit	Increases the child tax credit to $2,200 per child, with inflation adjustments and stricter SSN requirements.	Young parents will receive a larger credit per child, increasing refunds or reducing tax owed.	Ensure both you and your child have valid SSNs and file early to claim the credit.
5	Permanent above-the-line student loan interest deduction	Makes the deduction for up to $2,500 of student loan interest permanent and subject to inflation adjustments. AGI $200,000 (joint) phase-out applies.	FLYers graduates repaying student loans can continue to reduce taxable income, lowering their tax bill.	Make at least the minimum payments on student loans to maximize the deductible interest each year.
6	Employer student loan repayment exclusion	Makes permanent the exclusion from income for up to $5,250 per year in employer-paid student loan repayments, with inflation adjustments.	FLYer employees can receive tax-free student loan payments from employers, reducing both tax and debt.	Seek out employers offering this benefit and coordinate with HR to ensure payments are

No.	Tax Change/ Provision	Description	Impact on FLYers	Tax Planning Tip
				structured for tax-free treatment. Parents' businesses can hire children via payroll so that children and other employees equally enjoy such tax-free fringe benefits.
7	Expanded 529 plan qualified expenses	Broadens 529 plan distributions to cover more K-12 (including home schooling) and postsecondary credentialing expenses and increases the annual K-12 limit to $20,000.	FLYers students and parents can use 529 funds for a wider range of educational expenses, including job training and certifications.	Use 529 funds strategically for both college and qualified non-degree programs to avoid taxes and penalties.
8	Refundable portion of adoption credit	Up to $5,000 of the adoption credit is now refundable, with inflation adjustments.	FLYers adopting children can receive a cash refund even if they owe no tax, easing the financial burden of adoption.	File for the adoption credit once eligible and keep all documentation to support the claim.
9	Increased dependent care assistance exclusion	Raises the exclusion for employer-provided dependent care assistance to $7,500 ($3,750 MFS).	FLYing parents can receive more tax-free assistance for children or dependent care, reducing out-of-pocket costs.	Enroll in employer dependent care programs early in the year to maximize the exclusion.
10	Creation of Trump Accounts for children	Establishes new tax-advantaged savings accounts for children under 18, with a $5,000 annual contribution limit and a $1,000 government-funded pilot for newborns (2025–2028).	FLYers can jumpstart savings for their children's future, with tax-deferred growth and potential government contributions.	File Form 4547. Open a Trump Account for your child. Ask your employer for fringe benefit (up to $2,500 annual contribution from the employer).

Appendix G

Readers' Feedback for *The SMART Family Tax Guide*

"Tax Planning for Small Businesses: Mike Nie's Smart Family Tax Guide is more than a resource, it's a roadmap for families who want clarity and confidence in their financial future. Mike, a dedicated practitioner at our Hot Yoga studio, brings the same thoughtfulness and discipline to this book that he brings to his practice. He takes complex tax laws and turns them into clear, actionable steps that help small businesses/families keep more of what they earn and plan with purpose. A truly empowering guide."

—Lara Atella, Director of Hot Yoga Capitol Hill (https://www.hotyogacapitolhill.com/)

******

"Your book is SUPERB—so, it's my pleasure. I'm hoping to get a few copies for my friends and relatives because it's probably the most useful material I've ever seen on taxes!"

—Frances A. Chiu, Ph.D. Editor of ten award-winning books (2023-2025); Author, *The Routledge Guidebook to Paine's Rights of Man*; Dissertation/thesis coach; 41x boosted writer on Medium; Smith College A.B.; and Oxford University, Ph.D.

******

"I really like the heart behind your book—it feels grounded in real life, and that's going to connect well with families who are trying to make smarter moves but don't know where to start. My suggestion would be to keep things as plain and accessible as possible—add more breakdowns in layman's terms where the content gets heavy. Maybe also break up some of the longer chapters or use formatting to highlight your main tips. Overall, it's valuable, but a few structural changes will make it even more approachable to non-tax professionals."

—Lori Correa, Ex-Training Program Manager, Drake Software, Professional Tax Solutions

******

"Mike holds many licenses: CPA/CFP/CFA/EA, and in my more than 20 years of professional career, I have rarely encountered a peer with so many professional certifications.

In recent years, he has persistently conducted volunteer financial education seminars for our CAPA Chinese community every month, tirelessly sharing what he has learned and applied with everyone.

As a fellow professional, I admire his comprehensive knowledge system, envy his efficient execution ability, and appreciate his sincerity and chivalry. Now he has launched his first new book, and I am fortunate to be one of the three recommenders, so of course I have to support him in my social circle.

Mike Nie's book 'The Smart Family Tax Guide: 101 Ways to Keep More of Your Earned Money' is more than just a guide—it's a blueprint for wealth planning for middle-class families. With a father's heart and a strategist's mind, Mike demonstrates that vision boards are not just for dreamers—they are tools for planners. Each chapter translates tax law into actionable steps for wealth accumulation. This book reflects what I have always believed: true financial planning starts with a vision and ends with results."

—Yinan Fenley, CPA, FINRA RR | Former Deloitte Auditor | Tax Strategist for High-Net-Worth Families

******

"A Practical, Legacy-Building Playbook: As a long-time advocate for family and charitable growth, Mike Nie delivers exactly what busy, values-driven families need: clear, actionable tax advice with a larger purpose. The Smart Family Tax Guide isn't just about saving money—it's about building a legacy.

Nie's strength lies in his real-world teaching style: thoughtful, conversational, and rich with live examples. Whether you're planning for retirement, managing rentals, or launching a family foundation, his 101 strategies are to-the-point and doable.

What makes this guide warm and personal is its focus on family impact. The foundation chapters illuminate how smart tax planning can align with your giving goals—without sacrificing compliance or financial soundness.

Overall, this is a must-read for any family serious about financial responsibility and long-term legacy. Easy to understand, deeply practical, and inspiring—well-suited for anyone who wants to teach their kids more than just tax code."

—Suzanne S. Elliott, MA, Ed.
H.O.T. YOGA on the Island (https://yogaontheisland.com/)
Healing. Original. Therapeutic.
Founder/Director/Lead Teacher/Professor
USA Yoga, Non-Profit Board Member
H.E.A.R.T., Non-Profit, Inc. Board Member
F.I.T. Fun Innovative Training &
W.A.Y. Wild About Yoga, Creator/Founder/Master Trainer/Coach

******

"As a CPA, I found this book to be extremely helpful. It's well-organized, resourceful, and full of practical insights on tax planning and tax strategy. It breaks down complex U.S. tax law concepts into clear, actionable steps, with real-life examples and useful resources throughout. Go FIRE! Highly recommended!"

—Yuping P, Texas CPA

******

"In *The Smart Family Tax Guide*, Mike Nie demystifies the complexities of taxation. It is organized thoughtfully as a practical handbook for strategizing, actioning, and realizing true tax savings. He shares numerous personal examples in easy to understand language – many great strategies and ideas I wish I had taken action on sooner with my family. His insights into common pitfalls and frequently overlooked opportunities help readers avoid costly mistakes and maximize their returns.

The Smart Family Tax Guide is a must-read for anyone seeking clarity and confidence in managing their taxes. It undoubtedly has empowered countless families to navigate their financial journeys with these goals in mind. Thank you for inspiring many families with your knowledge and passion."

—Mike Seelig, Board member, Trustee, and Audit Committee Financial Expert; "re-wired" PwC Partner

******

"Mike breaks down intricate real estate tax strategies into clear, actionable steps suitable for investors at any level. This impactful book masterfully navigates and simplifies complex tax laws and regulations. Each page delivers game-changing advice, enriched with real-life case studies that bring the strategies to life."

—Fred W., Real Estate Professional

******

"This book is a spiritual and financial blueprint, brilliantly merging vision, clarity, and action. In the tradition of transformational guides like *The Soul of Prosperity,* Mike Nie invites you to create not just a vision board—but a living covenant with your family's financial future. Through stories, practical steps, and heartfelt reflection, this work reminds us: we don't just build wealth—we become it."

—Rev. Jim Webb, Author of *Create a Self-Manifesting Vision Board and The Soul of Prosperity*

******

"As a CPA with over 20 years of experience, I find this book to be beneficial. My daughter is going to college this year, and I believe this book would make the perfect gift for her. She has been asking me about how to manage her personal finances and establish a retirement account. I was surprised by how the younger generation is an avid learner and wants to be financially savvy. I could not explain all these better than what Mike did in this book. Good job, Mike, for providing the younger generation with tools to reach personal finance goals and build wealth at a young age."

—Tracy Yuan, CPA, Financial Executive

******

"As a graduate student navigating the intersection of academics, career building, and financial independence, I found the *FLY Guide to Real Estate* to be both timely and genuinely inspiring. What sets this book apart is its voice. The dialogue between Mike and his sons Chris and Kevin reads less like a textbook and more like a conversation you wish you had been part of. The father-son dynamic gives the financial guidance warmth and authenticity.

For anyone in high school or college wondering whether financial literacy is relevant to them right now, I believe this book is the answer. It guides young readers exactly where they are and gives them a concrete roadmap forward. I would recommend it without hesitation and hope it inspires future generations to come."

—Jenelle Soo, MPH Candidate, UC Berkeley

Afterword

A Message to My Future FLYers

When you finish this book, you will find yourself living through an unprecedented moment in history. I want to speak to you honestly — especially to young people who are preparing to FLY solo or duo.

At the national level, we are carrying a burden that your generations will bear unknowingly and unwillingly. The United States now holds more than $39.1 trillion in national debt, a number that compounds every single day. When you break it down, that debt represents more than $110,000 per person in this country — an invisible weight already placed on your shoulders before your life has fully begun. You will face lifetime higher taxes, reduced government services, or a combination of both.

At the same time, we see warning signs everywhere.

- Gold price and oil price are at record highs because investors worldwide are worried about the dollar, a fiat money.
- Bitcoin, once celebrated at $120,000 per coin, has fallen nearly 50%, reminding us how fragile speculation can be.
- Our nation feels divided—not only politically, but structurally. Some states are increasingly in tension with the federal government, struggling with irreconcilable differences in values, taxes, and governance.
- Wealthy families are quietly leaving high-tax states, voting with their feet. Meanwhile, society itself is splitting into two worlds: the top 0.1% (the super-rich) vs. everyone else, including many FLYers. These two groups no longer live the same reality.

And then there is artificial intelligence. AI is transforming everything—our work, our economy, even how we think. It can increase productivity, but it can also hollow us out if we let it. AI can take away jobs. It can take away certainty. If we are not careful, it can take away our heart, our purpose, and our sense of meaning.

That is why, for young people, having a strong foundation is no longer optional. It is essential. This book, *FLY Guide to Real Estate,* is written for you. But understand this clearly: this is only the beginning, not the destination.

Before you fly higher, I want to leave you with three guiding principles to help you navigate chaos, uncertainty, and opportunity — all without regret.

1. Build Your Life on Faith

Faith is not something reserved for one day a week. Christian faith, for me, is not only worship—it is a way of living. When Christ becomes the rock of your life, you gain something priceless: moral clarity, resilience, and purpose.

With faith, you are less likely to drift into unknown territory. You are anchored. You understand *why* you work, *why* you build, *why* you serve, and *why* you spend. In a world that constantly pulls you in every direction, faith keeps you grounded.

2. Develop a Growth Mindset

Stanford professor Carol Dweck famously wrote about the power of a *growth mindset.* This idea is more relevant today than ever before. AI can take away knowledge, AI can take away certain jobs, and AI can even disrupt education. But AI can never take away your curiosity. It cannot take away your creativity. And it cannot take away your desire to learn, unless you give it up yourself.

A growth mindset means learning how to learn. That mindset shaped my own life. It is why I pursued so many financial, accounting, and professional certifications over 27+ years. Not because I needed more titles—but because continuous learning keeps your mind sharp, adaptable, and relevant. In the future, those who know how to learn will always outpace those who only know what they learned once.

3. Build a Better World Through Kindness and Good Deeds

One day, my son Kevin asked me a simple but powerful question: "Dad, how do you measure a good day? And how do you measure a good life?"

I told him this: "A good day has two parts. First, you learn something new, something you didn't know yesterday. Second, you do something good for someone else: pick up trash, hold the door, offer help, or just smile kindly. If you repeat those two things every day, you are already living a good life."

There is a Chinese proverb that says: "*Do not ignore a good deed because it seems small.*
Do not commit a small wrongdoing because it seems insignificant." 勿以善小而不為，勿以惡小而為之。

Young people: Help yourself. Help your family. Help your friends. Help your community. This is how you build a life that matters.

A Final Word

As we conclude this chapter—and this book—thank you for walking with me on this journey.

If you believe in this message, I ask one small favor: Tell your friends about our book. If your friends are between 18 and 25 years old, this book is for them. I want them to receive it for free. The only request is that they leave an honest review on Amazon or social media—so more young people can be inspired to fly higher.

Confucius (551–479 BC), an ancient Chinese philosopher once said: 修身, 齐家, 治国 , 平天下. Translate into English: Cultivate oneself → Regulate the family → Govern the state → Bring peace to the world.

All FLYers: This book is my way of guiding you through life:

Live your life with purpose;
Love others selflessly;
Smile daily with sincerity; and
Ride the AI wave with competence and confidence

Mike, Chris, and Kevin Nie

Apirl 2026
Gaithersburg, Maryland;, Daytona Beach, Florida; and Manassas, Virginia

About the Authors

Mike Nie is a Christian father, tax strategist, and financial educator with over 27 years of experience helping families turn everyday decisions into lifelong opportunities. His experience includes: (1) Audit and Advisory Director at PricewaterhouseCoopers LLC (PwC, 10+ years); (2) Audit Inspection Leader at the Public Company Accounting Oversight Board (4 years); and (3) Staff Accountant at a federal financial regulatory agency (12+ years).

His credentials include Certified Public Accountant (CPA), Certified Financial Planner (CFP®), Chartered Financial Analyst (CFA®), and Enrolled Agent (EA). Other credentials include Financial Risk Manager (FRM®), Sustainability and Climate Risk (SCR®), Risk and AI (RAI®), and Distinguished Toastmasters (DTM®).

Mike and his wife Olga live in the DC Metro area with four adult children: a blended and blessed family.

As the Owner of Smart 1040 LLC (www.Smart1040.us), Mike specializes in faith-based, family-centered tax planning, with a focus on proactive strategy, not just tax filing. He can be reached at Help@Smart1040.us.

****

Chris Nie, at just 21, earned his Certified Flight Instructor–Instrument (CFII) rating at Embry-Riddle Aeronautical University, one of the world's most respected aviation schools. He did not stop there—by 20, he had built his own brand as a teacher, investor, and financial storyteller.

Chris's life bridges two worlds: aviation and financial literacy. In the cockpit, he trains student pilots on precision, patience, and checklists. In finance, he applies the same principles – system, structure, and situational awareness – to money management and investing. His belief is simple but powerful: young people do not have to wait until 40 to FLY.

****

Kevin Nie is a college student, entrepreneur, and mentor from Fairfax, Virginia, representing the next generation of purpose-driven youth leaders. Kevin embodies the balance of discipline, intellect, and service that defines the FLY philosophy—Financial Literacy for Youth.

Kevin Nie began exploring entrepreneurship at an early age, founding Gym and Home Operator LLC (https://gym-operator.com/), where he coaches high school students in physical fitness, body strength, and mental resilience. Beyond business, Kevin serves as Marketing Manager of Smart 1040 LLC and Chief Operating Officer of the SMART Life Family Foundation (https://smartlifeusa.org/), helping families and students develop tax literacy, charitable values, and leadership skills. He has presented numerous youth financial workshops on Roth IRAs, real estate entrepreneurship, and purpose-based living—translating professional strategies into relatable lessons for his peers.

Smart 1040 LLC offers a $100 package for six hours of Zoom class recording with slides and Excel templates to help FLYers take off!

ohttps://smart1040.us/100-tax-tips-series

1. FLY vision board
2. Compounding interest strategies
3. Smart life insurance
4. AI era career planning
5. Ten things to do after your 18th birthday
6. Ten must-have tax deferred or tax-free asset accounts

Payment Options ($100):

- Venmo: @Mike-Nie-CPA
- PayPal: help@Smart1040.us
- Credit Card: https://pay.smart1040.us/tax_service

Acknowledgements

This book would not have come to life without the wisdom, support, and inspiration of several extraordinary individuals.

We are deeply grateful to **Coach Lucy Chen**, owner of Gifted Books, whose unwavering lessons on resilience helped shape not only the content of this book, but also the perseverance behind its creation. Her voice reminded me that every challenge is an opportunity to grow stronger.

Special thanks to my editor **Dr. Frances Chiu**, whose relentless focus on clarity, brevity, and specificity pushed me to distill complex tax strategies into language that speaks directly and powerfully to families. Her mentorship sharpened my message and made every word count.

This chapter lists all friends, families and supporters who make this book more reader friendly. Thank you all. Again, we are accountable for all errors in both content and grammar.

To each of you: this book carries your fingerprints. Thank you for believing in its purpose. Any omissions or errors are our fault.

FLYers	**Quotes about Money, Finance, Wealth, Value, Career, and Life**
Kevin Nie	"No money, no honey."
Chris Nie	"No pain, no gain. No pain, no champagne." "It is your attitude, rather than aptitude, that determines your altitude."
Olesia Soukhoveev	"Never let the rain ruin your sunshine. Learn to dance in it!"
Sasha Soukhoveev	"Let your actions reflect what's truly important in your heart and life."
Lucy Chen	"Financial literacy should be taught at a young age. Very useful."
Bryson Hart	"You miss all the shots you don't take."
Isabella Morano	"The challenges you face can give you the tools to help someone else."
Kolade Folorunsho	"Work harder & sleep harder so you can."
Varun Gullanki	"Don't hope for it, work for it."
Kendan Vu	"Create your own luck."
Stephen Kim	"I told 2025 to keep the change. In 2026, I'm here to collect the interest."
Elaine Ding	"Fund Roth IRA at the lowest of the stock market."
Rin Hayashi	"Time is money."
Emma Wang	"Be fearful when others are greedy. Be greedy when others are fearful."

Kevin An	"The more your money works for you, the less you have to work for money."
Yan Liang	"Let money work for you."
Theo Hall	"Time is money – to achieve freedom over time, you need freedom over your finances."
Kayla Ma	"Time is Money."
Jonathan Zhang	"For we brought no money into the world, and we cannot take any money out of the world."
Bella X.	"I want to make money moves like Cardi B."
Cindy Li	"Financial freedom is available to those who learn about it and work for it."
Alex Lau	"Time is money."
Maggie Ding	"Money isn't everything, but it definitely is important to know how to spend and save it!"
A. Q.	"Financial concerns are increasingly becoming a concern for young people as the cost of living increases at a rate faster than overall increase in income."
Philip Wang	"If you don't find a way to make money while you sleep, you will work until you die."
Ian W	"Always remember the magic of compounding."
Tommy Lin	"Don't be afraid to take risk when young, but know the difference between investing and gambling."
Chelsea C	"Never be greedy."
Oliver Wang	"Don't put all eggs in one basket."
Angie Shen	"Money is a good servant and a bad master."
Kevin Song	"Believe the power of compound."
Celina Li	"As a first generation immigrant, I was not taught money growing up. As I received more and more financial literacy, I have realized the importance of Personal Finance in our daily life. I am inspired to increase my knowledge in this area."
S Fei	"Invest in yourself – your greatest investment."
Ayla Zhang	"Save money; live better."
Megan Sawant	"Work hard; save smart."

Kathleen Liu	"Would like to achieve financial independence and freedom like Chris and Kevin."
Vladimir Volkov	"Money is the cause and effect of everything in the world."
Natalya Volkova	"Wealth is not about having a lot of money; it's about having a lot of options."
Benjamin Leong	"Money can't solve all your problems. But it can solve all your problems that are solvable with money."
Lance Tung	"Real estate is an efficient way for accumulating wealth."
Chao Li	N/A
Lin Xia	N/A
CK Ho	"The more you learn, the more you earn."
Kelly Zhao	N/A
Emily Li	"Money is a tool. Its power depends on the hands that use it."
Kevin An	"Invest early."
Roger An	"Learn how money works young."
Becky Cheng	"Have money in head not in heart."
Tyler MacGregor	"You must gain control over your money or the lack of it will forever control you."
Megan Yee	"It's not what you make, it's what you save."
Jay Cox	"To compare investments fairly, we must include taxes, time-value-of-money, & inflation. The real after-tax return on one 10% investment may be double that of another so-called 10% investment."
Elizabeth Ding	"Financial literacy is so important in an ever changing economy and world."
Melanie Ma	"If you work for money, you give the power to your employer. If money works for you, you keep the power and control it."—Robert Kiyosaki.
David Zeng	"The best investment most people can make is learning how not to lose money before trying to make more of it."
Amy Brown	"It's true money is not the most important thing in life, but if we don't have money, it then becomes extremely important." —A Dog called Money
Joshua Zeng	"Rich people act with fear, poor people let fear control them." "Starting your financial journey early is the first step to success."

Joseph Chen	"The more you learn, the more you earn." --Warren Buffett "I'm excited to share this book with my peers who are also looking to make money and better financial decisions."
Tim Kim	"The stock market is a device for transferring money from the impatient to the patient." — Warren Buffett "Yes, financial literacy is the most important thing to know. They don't teach this in school so take advantage of your resources."
Josh Rhee	Still search my money quote.
Daniel Saenz	"Chase your passions & money will come."
Ryan Pourshojae	"Price is what you pay. Value is what you get." - Warren Buffett
George Cashman	"Wealth is not about great possessions but instead few wants."
Tyler Carroll Carroll	"Money is a terrible master but an excellent servant."
Caleb Shirey	"Scared money doesn't make money."
Ben King	N/A
Camp Conner	"Money doesn't just grow it follows discipline, patience, and smart decisions."
Jake Goodson	"The key to making money is staying invested."
Evan Panepinto-Lande	"Keep money in your head, but not in your heart."
Aidan Edelson	"All of us are born for a reason, but all of us don't discover why" - Danny Thomas
Andrew Teicher	"Money isn't everything, but everything requires money."
Reid Davis	"The worst sin you can ever commit to yourself is to sit and wait for someone to give you money."
Liam Rush	"Money is a tool, if you learn how to make it work for you, it gives you options later." "Start paying attention to money earlier than you think you need to. Even small habits, saving a little, tracking what you spend, or learning how things like rent and bills actually work. Don't stress about being perfect, just focus on being consistent."
Patrick Benzer	"Wealth exists not in having great possessions, but in having few wants."

Early Praises for *A FLY Guide to Real Estate: Owning and Managing Property When You're Under 25*

A Must-Have Financial Guide

A must-have financial guide, covering in extensive detail the far too often overlooked power that comes from early planning and surviving in today's economic climate, where housing prices and student loans seem unaffordable. This book provides actionable ideas for general investing and buying real estate. This motivating book goes to great lengths to show readers that financial freedom can be achieved with initiative, drive, and being prepared when it comes to real estate investing.

Additionally, it's chock-full of statistics and examples to make it more easily digestible for its soon-to-be knowledgeable readers. In addition, the author's dedication and intentions are highly noble and well meaning, with a mission statement to especially help young adults with the confusion, uncertainty, and generally overwhelming feelings that come from the unfortunate lack of finance knowledge early in life. It also features many professionals in their respective fields. These interviews show the benefits of real estate ownership.

Reading this book might change your outlook if it was previously gloomy and maybe even give you hope for a more secure and prosperous life as you grow older. I would say it's easy to comprehend, explaining anything and everything related to real estate, the steps needed to take, and then some, as it holds your hand through it all. Useful strategies, loopholes, tips, and it isn't just a few with some long-winded wording to pad it out, it's jam-packed with it, and from a professional tax advisor and investor, truly genuine advice.

Andy W., High School Senior

****

Stop Waiting For the Right Moment, and Start Building Toward It

When I first became Mike Nie's teaching assistant, I thought I was signing up to help students understand financial literacy. I didn't realize I was also signing up for a two-year masterclass in how to think about money, responsibility, and the future.

Over the course of working alongside Mike—through his Family Foundations course, his AI in Business program, and everything in between—I watched him teach learners of every age, background, and starting point. A teenager figuring out their first budget. A parent rethinking how their family talks about wealth. A professional trying to understand where AI is reshaping their industry. What struck me every time wasn't just how much Mike knew. It was how naturally he met each person where they were, and how consistently he left them with something they could actually use.

That's rarer than it sounds. A lot of financial education tells you what to do. Mike's approach asks something harder: it asks you to take ownership. He doesn't hand students a script—he builds the thinking behind the script. Sitting in on his classes and supporting his instruction, I found myself revisiting my own assumptions, my own timelines, my own definitions of what financial independence could look like.

This book is a direct extension of that classroom. What Mike teaches about real estate isn't reserved for people who already have wealth or connections or decades of experience. It's a framework for families and young people willing to be intentional—to plan earlier, act smarter, and build something together. The same philosophy I watched change how students carried themselves after just a few sessions is the one woven through every chapter here.

I've seen what happens when people actually absorb what Mike is teaching. They stop waiting for the right moment and start building toward it. If that's where you want to go, this is the right place to start.

Isaac T., High School Senior

****

The Tone Is Grounded and Highly Practical Rather Than Purely Theoretical Ideals

As a 23-year-old who recently graduated and started a career in finance, I often find that the standard financial advice given to our generation feels a bit outdated. We are usually told to simply contribute to a 401(k), live with roommates or at home with parents to save cash, and maybe buy a starter home in our thirties. While safe, it's a very slow approach to building wealth.

That is why A FLY Guide to Real Estate is such a refreshing and necessary read for young professionals. The fact that this book is also co-authored by homeowners who are under 25 themselves sells its thesis perfectly. The tone is grounded and highly practical rather than purely theoretical ideals. They prove that real estate investing isn't just a milestone reserved for mid-career professionals; it is a viable, actionable strategy that young adults can execute right now.

The true value of this book lies in how it breaks down sophisticated financial strategies and shows why they are beneficial for someone just entering the workforce. Thanks to Mike Nie's CPA background, the guide goes beyond basic saving tips and explains the powerful tax advantages of real estate. For a young professional trying to maximize an entry-level W-2 salary, learning how to use property depreciation to offset taxable income or how to leverage 1031 exchanges to defer taxes is incredibly useful. The book clearly explains how to safely use leverage to acquire an appreciating asset, giving our generation a practical alternative to throwing away thousands of dollars a year on rent.

Additionally, the guide is highly realistic about the day-to-day challenges of property management. It provides a straightforward blueprint for "house-hacking"—arguably one of the best financial strategies for recent grads. By showing how to offset a mortgage by renting out spare rooms, the book teaches young adults how to drastically reduce their living expenses, freeing up capital to invest in index funds or other ventures. The sections on setting rules and managing tenants are excellent for anyone taking on a landlord role for the first time.

Overall, A FLY Guide to Real Estate provides a clear, step-by-step approach to achieving financial independence early. It shifts the focus from passive saving to active investing, offering a highly effective toolkit for young adults who want to take control of their financial trajectory and get a serious head start on their future.

Jack Rizzo

****

What Stands Out Most Is the Authors' Emphasis On Starting Early

Become a Homeowner and Real Estate Investor Before 25 is a very direct, guide aimed at making something that feels out of reach—buying a home young, actually seem doable. The biggest strength of this book is how clearly it breaks down the process. Instead of overcomplicating real estate or relying on abstract advice, it focuses on specific steps: financial discipline, tax strategy, and long-term planning. That makes it especially useful for beginners who are looking to learn more about these topics. What stands out most is the authors' emphasis on starting early.

The book consistently pushes the idea that age is an advantage if you use it correctly. Rather than waiting until you have a high salary, it shows how small, intentional decisions—saving, understanding credit, and using tax-advantaged strategies can compound quickly. This is where the book feels different from typical personal finance content that is spewed by gurus online; it's less about theory and more about execution. Another strong point is the real-life angle.

Knowing that the strategies come from people who actually built a real estate portfolio at a young age makes the advice feel more credible. The sections on tax planning are also surprisingly valuable, especially for a book targeted at younger readers. That's something most beginner guides ignore, but here it's treated as a key advantage. That said, the book can feel a bit optimistic at times.

While it lays out a clear path, it doesn't always fully address how difficult some of these steps can be depending on someone's financial situation or market conditions. Not everyone will be able to move as quickly as the examples suggest. A bit more discussion of risk and setbacks would make the guidance feel more balanced. Overall, this is a strong, beginner-friendly introduction to early real estate investing. It's best suited for motivated high school or college students who want a clear starting point and are willing to take action.

The main takeaway is simple: if you understand the system early and stay disciplined, getting into real estate before 25 is not unrealistic at all if you take the time to learn about it.

Josiah Ketchem

****

An Analytical Mindset to Personal Finance

As a senior physics major preparing for graduate school, much of my academic training has focused on understanding complex systems and long-term dynamics. A FLY Guide to Real Estate applies a similarly analytical mindset to personal finance, offering a clear and practical framework for how young people can begin building financial independence early in life.

What stands out most is the book's emphasis on starting young and thinking long-term. Mike, Chris, and Kevin present real estate not only as an investment, but as a powerful educational tool that teaches responsibility, planning, and strategic thinking. For students accustomed to rigorous problem-solving, the book's "four pillars of wealth" framework provides a simple but effective model for understanding how different financial assets work together over time.

The practical examples and case studies make the ideas accessible and grounded in real experience. Rather than promoting quick profits, the book encourages discipline, patience, and thoughtful decision-making—principles that resonate strongly with anyone trained in a scientific field.

At a time when many young people feel uncertain about their financial future, A FLY Guide to Real Estate offers a motivating and constructive perspective. It is a thoughtful introduction to financial literacy that encourages students and young professionals to take ownership of their long-term financial path.

Nicholas Rizzo

****

Bonus Chapter of A FLY Guide to Investing: Ten Must-Have Accounts Under 25

Chapter TBD: Real Estate Cost Segregation Meets Market Timing – Investing Smarter in Tax-Deferred Accounts

"*Be quick, but do not hurry. Timing is everything.*" – John Wooden, legendary basketball coach, UCLA

1. The Power of Timing and Structure

In wealth building, *what* you invest in matters—but *when* and *how* you invest can be even more powerful. This chapter explores how real estate cost segregation can synchronize perfectly with market-timed contributions to tax-deferred accounts such as IRAs, HSAs, 529 plans, and Solo 401(k)s. Together, these two strategies—one from real estate and one from the securities market—create a turbocharged path to financial independence and early retirement (FIRE).

2. The Ten Tax-Sheltered Accounts Every Family Should Use

A disciplined investor, like Kevin and Helen in our earlier case studies, can strategically fill ten types of accounts each year:

- Backdoor Roth IRA—$7,000 per spouse ($7,500 in 2026).
- Minor Roth IRA—For children with earned income (often from family business or rental work).
- Coverdell ESA—$2,000 per child per year.
- 529 Plan—E.g., $4,000 per person per account per year in Virginia, with state income deduction. Invest in S&P 500 or stock index fund with lowest fee and double-digit 20+ year cumulative returns.
- Solo 401(k)—If FLYer's small business is profitable, employee deferral up to $24.5K a year plus employer match up to 20% of Schedule C income.
- Trump Account—Family can contribute child's account up to $5K a year between zero and 18 years old. Invest and compound in broad based, low fee securities index, such as S&P 500 index.

- UTMA Account—$19K per parent per child gift to child for long-term stock investing. Invest in long proved record of high performing, broad-based, no dividend paying stocks.
- Health Savings Account (HSA)—$8,550 annual family contribution, triple-tax-free.
- Roth Conversions—Move pre-tax IRA or 401(k) funds into Roth during low-income years.
- Cash Value Life Insurance (BBB strategy)—Borrow-buy-build using policy loans for investing.
- Charitable or Family Foundation Accounts—For long-term legacy and deduction leverage.

Each account has its own annual limit and timing window. If combined, they represent roughly $50,000–$60,000 per year of new contributions—yet how and when those contributions are made determines whether returns soar or stagnate.

3. Three Funding Methods

- Front-Load (January 1) – Fully fund early in the year. This maximizes compounding time but risks investing before a correction.
- Dollar-Cost Averaging (Monthly) – Contribute gradually to smooth out market volatility.
- Strategic Timing ("All In" During Market Dips) – The most opportunistic approach: reserve cash or lines of credit to fully fund accounts during 10–20% market corrections.

Example: If the S&P 500 drops 20% after an event—say, an economic shock or tariff announcement—you can immediately deploy the year's remaining unused contribution capacity of IRA, HSA, and 529 contributions at discounted prices. When markets recover 30–35%, your gains grow tax-free within those accounts.

Chart 1: S&P 500 Index from COVID-19 to 2025

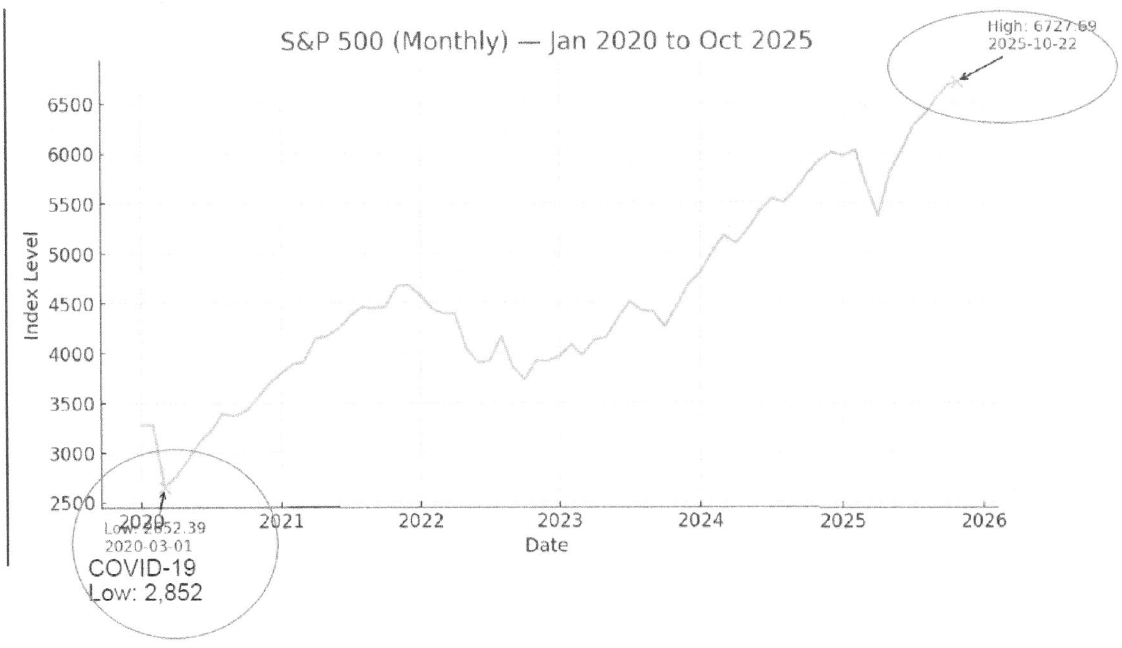

Source: Yahoo Finance. Chart created and edited by author

Note: Kevin and family had aggressively contributed to their tax-deferred account at the lowest point in recent memory (2,852), letting them compound to 6,727, producing tax-free or tax-deferred capital gain of 236% in five years, and achieving cumulative annual growth rate (CAGR) of 18.5%.

Account Type	**Maxed out Contribution (March 2020) Using 2020 IRS limit**	**Value at the high point (October 2025)**
1. Back-door Roth IRA (H – husband)	$6,000	$14,152
2. Back-door Roth IRA (W – wife)	$6,000	$14,152
3. VA 529 (H)	$4,000	$9,435
4. VA 529 (W)	$4,000	$9,435
5. VA 529 (C – child)	$4,000	$9,435
6. Coverdell Edu Savings Account	$2,000	$4,717
7. UTMA	$19,000	$42,457
8. Solo Traditional 401(k) – employee	$22,000	$51,891
9. 401(k) – company matching	$4,400	$10,378
10. HSA	$7,900	$18,634
SUM	**$78,300**	**$184,686**

In addition, $80K Roth IRA conversion would have produced future tax-free retirement savings of $189K.

4. Where to Find Capital During a Market Dip

During downturns, liquidity can tighten—margin lines and securities-backed credit (SBLOC) may get reduced. That is when alternative funding sources matter:

- Home Equity Line of Credit (HELOC) – Borrow tax-efficiently against your property.
- Whole Life Insurance Loans – Borrow from your policy's cash value at 5% interest, tax-free.
- Rental Property Cash Flow or Reserves – Redeploy passive income from your portfolio.

These funds can temporarily seed tax-deferred accounts, converting idle equity into compounding capital.

5. Real Estate Professional Status as a Tax Engine

Now comes the synergy. Real estate professionals like Kevin can use cost segregation and bonus depreciation to generate large paper losses that offset taxable income—especially when paired with Roth conversions.

For example, Kevin owns six rentals. By cost-segregating just two of them, he accelerates depreciation and creates tens of thousand dollars in more paper losses. These losses can fully offset the taxable income triggered by converting from his or wife's Traditional IRA to a Roth IRA during a market dip.

The result: a tax-free Roth conversion financed by real estate losses rather than cash tax payments. This "cookie jar" approach allows them to repeat the strategy across multiple properties over several years until most retirement funds are Roth-based. When they retire or are over 59.5, Roth IRA withdrawals are totally tax free.

6. Timing the Roth Conversion

The ideal Roth conversion window is when markets are down 20–30%. Why?

- You pay income tax on the depressed value of the converted assets.
- When the market rebounds, the growth inside Roth becomes permanently tax-free.
- Meanwhile, your bonus depreciation shelters the conversion's tax impact.

It is not just market timing—it is *tax timing*.

7. Example: Kevin and Helen's Strategic Year

- April 2025: S&P drops 20%.
- Kevin's cost segregation produces $150 K passive losses.
- They convert $150 K from their traditional IRAs to Roths.
- The losses offset taxable income, zeroing the tax bill.
- By December, the market rebounded by 40%.
- Their Roth accounts now show six-figure tax-free gains.

Meanwhile, all other accounts—529, Coverdell, HSA, UTMA—also benefit from low-point contributions. This synchronized timing between real estate and stock market investing becomes their wealth accelerator.

8. The Compound Effect of Coordination

By combining:

- Real estate cost segregation,
- Roth conversion timing,

- Strategic tax-deferred funding, and
- Conservative borrowing via life insurance or HELOC,

A young family can turn volatility into opportunity and tax law into leverage. Every correction becomes a moment of creation—not fear. The 2025 Liberation Day market turmoil provides an example of this strategy.

Chart 2: S&P 500 Index (October 2024 to October 2025)

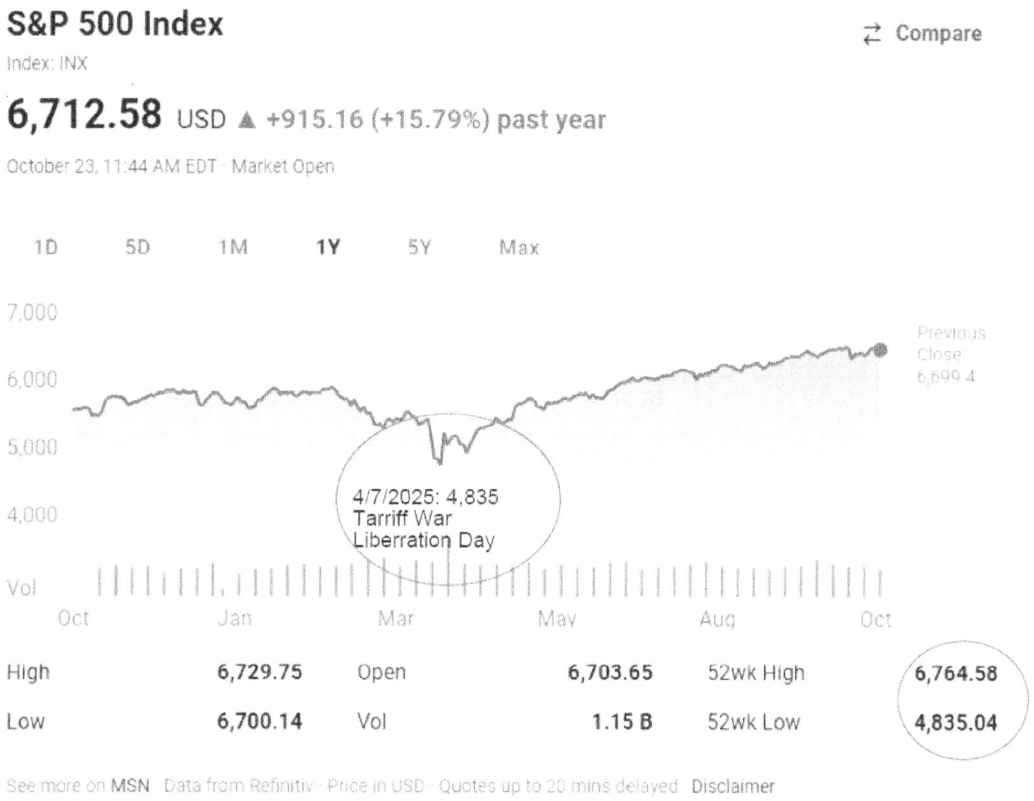

Source: Yahoo Finance. Chart created or edited by author.

April 2025 marked a significant market correction caused by the announcement of tariff war against main trading counties (China, EU, and Mexico). Kevin and his family strategically and systemically fund tax-deferred account fully at the low point. Six months later, the market reached 6,764, record high, producing 39.9% tax free or tax deferred capital gain in a half year. A quite decent market timing strategy!

Kevin's family total $83.7K account contribution for 2025 compounded to $117K in just six months. See table below.

Account Type	**Maxed out Contribution** **As of April 7, 2025**	**Value at the high point** **As of October 20, 2025**
1. Back-door Roth IRA (H – husband)	$7,000	$9,793

2. Back-door Roth IRA (W – wife)	$7,000	$9,793
3. VA 529 (H)	$4,000	$5,596
4. VA 529 (W)	$4,000	$5,596
5. VA 529 (C – child)	$4,000	$5,596
6. Coverdell Edu Savings Account	$2,000	$2,798
7. UTMA	$19,000	$26,580
8. Solo Traditional 401(k) – employee (assuming sufficient income earned by April)	$23,500	$32,876
9. 401(k) – company matching (up to 20%)	$4,700	$6,575
10. HSA	$8,550	$11,961
SUM	**$82,750**	**$117,163**

Assuming Kevin has no available cash to fund these accounts, he can secure a policy loan from cash value whole life insurance (IBLOC) with a fixed rate of 5%.

In addition, Helen did a $80K Roth conversion at low point, which ballooned to $112K in Roth balance (post-retirement tax-free withdrawal). Kevin applied one rental property cost segregation with about $80K bonus depreciations, offsetting the taxable income caused by the Roth conversion. The family tax burden was not affected.

9. Key Takeaways

- Be liquid before corrections. Keep cash or borrowing capacity ready.
- Use cost segregation strategically. Generate depreciation when you need Roth offset.
- Time conversions and contributions during 15–30% market declines.
- Avoid over-contribution. Exceeding limits causes a 6% penalty.
- Repeat annually. Each year is a new chance to realign tax brackets and market cycles.

10. Final Thought

Market cycles are inevitable, but how you respond determines your trajectory. By merging *tax-engineered real estate* with *market-timed investing*, you do not just ride the wave—you shape it. Each dip funds your future, each property shelters your gains, and each strategy layers upon the last—building a legacy of tax-free growth and generational stability.

Glossary

Numerical Terms

- **1031 Exchange**: think of this as a real estate "no-tax teleport" that allows you to sell one investment property and buy another without paying taxes on your profit right away. By rolling your gains into a new property, you can defer taxes indefinitely and grow your wealth faster.
- **401(k)**: a special retirement savings account often offered by employers that helps you save for when you are older. You can choose to put money in before taxes (Traditional) or after taxes (Roth), allowing your investments to grow over decades.
- **529 Plan**: also known as a Qualified Tuition Program (QTP), this is a tax-advantaged account designed to help families save for college costs like tuition and books. A unique "FLY" strategy involves using 529 funds to pay for room and board while living in a property your parents own as a half-time or full-time college student.
- **5-Year Property**: items in a rental property that the IRS says wear out quickly—like appliances, carpet, some cabinetry, and certain fixtures—and can be depreciated over five years instead of the full 27.5 years. These shorter lives often qualify for accelerated or bonus depreciation, creating big "paper expenses" early on. For FLYers using cost segregation, 5-year property is one of the main levers for front-loading tax deductions while the real estate itself may be rising in value.
- **Seven Habits of Highly Effective People**: a classic personal-development framework by Stephen Covey that teaches principles like being proactive, beginning with the end in mind, and putting first things first. It focuses on building character, taking responsibility, first understanding then being understood, and aligning your daily actions with long-term goals. For FLYers, these habits translate directly into money and real estate decisions—planning ahead, acting instead of reacting, and treating every property or account as part of a bigger life mission.
- **15-Year Property**: parts of a property that are considered land improvements rather than the building itself, such as driveways, sidewalks, fences, certain landscaping, and outdoor lighting. The IRS lets you depreciate these over 15 years, faster than the main structure but slower than 5-year items.
- **27.5-Year Depreciation Schedule**: the standard timeline the IRS uses to spread out the cost of residential rental buildings (not land) for tax purposes. Instead of writing off the entire building at once, you deduct a small portion each year over 27.5 years, which reduces your taxable rental income even if your real cash flow is strong. For FLYers, this schedule is the baseline—then cost segregation and bonus depreciation layer on top to pull more of those deductions into earlier years.

- **30-Year Fixed Loan**: a mortgage that lasts up to 30 years with an interest rate that never changes, so your principal-and-interest payment stays the same the whole time. The payment is lower than on a shorter-term loan, which makes it easier to qualify and leaves more monthly room for savings, repairs, or future investments. For FLYers, a 30-year fixed loan is like a long, predictable runway: it trades slightly more total interest over time for flexibility and safety while you are still building your career and portfolio.

A

- **Adjusted Gross Income (AGI)**: your total income after certain "above-the-line" deductions are taken out, such as HSA contributions, traditional 401(k)/IRA contributions, and some rental or business losses. It is the key number on Form 1040 line 11 that the IRS uses to decide whether you qualify for powerful tax breaks like education credits, rental loss allowances, and certain deductions. For FLYers, managing AGI is like managing the "scoreboard" of your tax life—lower AGI (legally) often means more benefits and fewer taxes.
- **ADU (Accessory Dwelling Unit)**: An ADU is a small, secondary home built on the same property as a main house—like a basement apartment, garage studio, or backyard tiny house. It usually has its own entrance, kitchen, and bathroom, so someone can live there independently. For young investors, an ADU can turn a regular home into a mini-duplex, adding rental income and boosting long-term property value.
- **Amortization**: the process of paying off a loan, like a mortgage, through regular monthly payments over a set number of years. Each payment has two parts: interest (the cost of borrowing) and principal (the amount that actually reduces your debt). In the early years, most of your payment is interest, but over time more goes to principal, slowly building your equity in the property.
- **Appreciation**: the increase in value of an asset, such as a house or stock, over time. When a property appreciates, it can be worth much more than you originally paid, especially if you used a small down payment and a mortgage. For FLYers, appreciation is one of the silent engines of wealth—your net worth can grow while you sleep, even if your monthly cash flow is only modest.
- **Asset Allocation**: the way you spread your investments across different categories, like stocks, real estate, cash value life insurance, and "fun money" assets such as crypto. The mix you choose affects both your potential return and your risk: more stocks can mean faster growth but bigger ups and downs, while more stable assets smooth the ride. A FLY-style allocation balances growth, safety, and income so you can stay invested through good and bad markets.
- **Asset Protection**: the set of legal and financial strategies you use to keep what you own safe from lawsuits, creditors, or accidents. This can include using LLCs for rentals, having umbrella insurance, and separating business and personal accounts. The goal is not hiding money; it is organizing your life so one mistake or lawsuit does not wipe out everything you and your family built.
- **Assessed Value**: the dollar amount your local government puts on your property to calculate your property taxes. It is not always the same as market value; in some areas it can be lower or lag behind current prices. Understanding your assessed value helps you estimate future tax bills and challenge them if they seem unfair compared with similar homes around you.

- **Augusta Rule**: a tax rule that lets you rent out your primary home for up to 14 days per year and pay zero income tax on that rent. Families often use it during business events (such as product promotion, software demo, board of advisor quarterly meeting), with business paying a reasonable rent. For FLYers and their parents, it can turn a well-located home into a part-time, tax-free income machine if planned and documented correctly.

B

- **Balance Sheet**: a simple financial report that lists what you own (assets), what you owe (liabilities), and the difference between them (equity). It is like a snapshot of your financial health at one point in time. For FLYers, reviewing a personal or family balance sheet helps you see if you are moving toward ownership and freedom or piling up debt and obligations.
- **Basis (Cost Basis)**: the starting value the tax system uses to measure your gain or loss on an asset, usually what you paid for it plus certain closing costs or improvements. When you sell, your taxable gain is the sale price minus this basis. For FLYers, tracking basis carefully—especially on rentals and stocks—can prevent surprising tax bills and unlock smarter decisions about when to sell, refinance, or 1031-exchange.
- **BBB Strategy (Buy, Borrow, and Build)**: a three-step wealth strategy where you buy appreciating assets, borrow against them instead of selling, and use that borrowed money to build small businesses or buy more assets (with interest cost potentially deductible as business expense). This lets your original investments keep compounding while you tap their value for new deals or opportunities. For FLYers, BBB is the opposite of consume-and-forget: it turns each good asset into a launchpad for the next one.
- **Buy and Hold**: a long-term investing approach where you choose solid assets, like broad stock index funds or good rentals, and keep them for years or decades instead of trading in and out. The focus is on compounding, cash flow, and tax efficiency rather than guessing short-term price moves. For FLYers, buy and hold means letting time, not constant trading, do most of the heavy lifting for your wealth.
- **Buy, Borrow, Die**: a strategy used by many wealthy families where they buy appreciating assets, borrow against them for cash instead of selling and paying capital gain taxes, and then let heirs inherit those assets with a stepped-up basis when they die. Because loans are not taxable income and the step-up can erase decades of gains, much of the growth may never be taxed. For FLYers, it is an end-of-life version of BBB that shows how tax law rewards planning across an entire lifetime, not just one year.
- **Bonus Depreciation**: a special tax rule that lets you write off a big portion of certain property items—like appliances, flooring, or land improvements—in the first year instead of slowly over many years. When combined with a cost segregation study, it can create very large "paper losses" that reduce your taxable income even while your rentals may be profitable in real life. For FLYers, bonus depreciation is one of the fastest ways to turn a new property into immediate tax savings that can fund more investment.
- **Brokerage Account**: an investment account that lets you buy and sell assets like stocks, ETFs, bonds, and sometimes options or funds. It does not have the same tax breaks as a 401(k) or Roth IRA, but it offers flexibility—you can invest or withdraw at any time without age restrictions. For FLYers, a low-cost brokerage account is the main "engine" for stock and index investing alongside real estate, especially when you automate monthly contributions, and FLYers can access the funds via BBB strategy to invest in other assets or businesses.

C

- **Capital Gains**: profit you make when you sell an asset—like a house or stock—for more than your cost basis (what you put in, plus certain expenses). The difference between the sale price and your basis is your gain, and the IRS may tax it at special capital-gains rates. For FLYers, managing when and how you realize real estate capital gains (for example, using 121 or 1031 rules) is a key way to keep more of your growth.
- **Capital Improvements**: major upgrades to a property that increase its value, extend its useful life, or change how it can be used, such as adding a bathroom, finishing a basement, or replacing a roof. These do not get deducted like simple repairs; instead, they are added to your cost basis. For FLYers, tracking capital improvements carefully can lower future taxable gains and support higher rents and appraisals.
- **Cap Rate (Capitalization Rate)**: a quick way to estimate a property's return based on its net operating income (NOI) divided by the purchase price or current value. A higher cap rate usually means more income relative to price but may come with more risk or a rougher area. For FLYers, comparing cap rates across deals helps you see whether a campus rental, condo, or duplex is giving you enough "rent for your risk."
- **Cash Flow**: the money left over each month after you collect rent and pay every property expense—mortgage, taxes, insurance, HOA, utilities (if you cover them), repairs, and reserves. Positive cash flow means the property is paying you to own it; negative cash flow means you are subsidizing it from your job or savings. For FLYers, focusing on steady, realistic cash flow keeps you from buying "Instagram deals" that look good on paper but drain your bank account.
- **Cash-Out Refinance**: a move where you replace your current mortgage with a new, larger loan and take the difference out in cash, using your built-up equity. Your debt goes up, but you get money you can use for another down payment, renovations, or paying off higher-interest loans. For FLYers, a smart cash-out refi can turn early appreciation into fuel for the next property—as long as you keep payments affordable and maintain strong reserves.
- **Cash Value Life Insurance**: a type of permanent life insurance (such as whole life) that includes both a death benefit and a savings or "cash value" component that grows over time. You can borrow against this cash value for things like down payments, emergencies, or business funding, usually without triggering tax as long as the policy stays healthy. For FLYers, cash value life insurance can act like a personal, long-term "family bank" when combined with other pillars like real estate and index funds.
- **Closing Costs**: all the fees and charges due at the end of a real estate transaction, such as lender fees, title insurance, recording fees, transfer taxes, and sometimes prepaid taxes or insurance. They often total 2–5% of the purchase price and must be paid in addition to your down payment (unless you negotiate seller or lender credits). For FLYers, understanding closing costs upfront prevents last minute surprises and helps you negotiate smarter with builders and sellers.
- **Collateral**: an asset you pledge to a lender as a back-up promise that you will repay your loan—like a house for a mortgage, or investments for a securities-backed line of credit. If you fail to pay, the lender can take the collateral to cover what you owe. For FLYers, managing collateral wisely lets you tap Other People's Money (OPM) without putting your entire financial life at risk.
- **Compounding**: the process where your money earns returns, and then those returns earn more returns, creating a snowball effect over time. It works with interest, dividends, rental

equity, and even tax savings if you reinvest them instead of spending them. For FLYers, compounding is the "cheat code" of wealth—starting early, even with small amounts, matters more than trying to catch up later with big amounts. Be aware of destructive compounding as well. Just watch the national debt ballooning to $38.7 trillion in the last decade.

- **Conventional Loan**: a standard mortgage that is not insured or guaranteed by the federal government, unlike FHA, VA, or USDA loans. It often requires a slightly higher credit score and a 3–20% down payment but can come with lower mortgage insurance costs once you have enough equity. For FLYers, a conventional loan is often the second or third property tool, after you use first-time-buyer or FHA programs to break into the market.

D

- **Debt-to-Income Ratio (DTI)**: the percentage of your monthly gross income that goes toward paying debts like student loans, car payments, credit cards, and mortgages. Lenders use DTI to decide how much house you can safely afford and whether to approve your loan. For FLYers, keeping DTI low—by limiting consumer debt—creates more room to qualify for good mortgages on real estate that actually builds wealth.
- **Deed**: the legal document that officially transfers ownership of a property from one person to another. It includes the names of the buyer and seller, a description of the property, and the way title is held. For FLYers, reading and recording the deed correctly is how you prove you truly own the house, not just the loan attached to it.
- **Depreciation**: an IRS-approved way to treat a building (not the land) as if it slowly wears out over time, even if your property is actually rising in market value. For residential rentals, the structure is usually written off over 27.5 years, creating annual "paper losses" that can reduce your taxable rental income. For FLYers, depreciation is a quiet superpower—tenants may be paying the mortgage while the tax code lets you report less income than you actually pocket.
- **Diversification**: the practice of spreading your money across different kinds of investments (such as real estate, stock index funds, cash value life insurance, and a small slice of speculative assets) so everything does not rise or fall together. When one area has a bad year, another may hold steady or grow, smoothing your overall results. For FLYers, diversification is your seatbelt for wealth building: it keeps one mistake or market crash from knocking you out of the game.
- **Down Payment**: the upfront cash you bring when you buy a property, such as 3–5% for some FHA or conventional loans, with the bank covering the rest through a mortgage. A smaller down payment means more leverage, while a larger one can lower your monthly payment and mortgage insurance. For FLYers, building a down payment is less about being rich and more about being intentional—using side hustles, Roth IRA first-home early withdrawal rules, and family planning to get into your first property years earlier.

E

- **Early Withdrawal Penalty**: a fee or extra tax you pay when you pull money out of certain accounts—like IRAs, 401(k)s, or some CDs—before the allowed age or time period. The IRS often charges an additional 10% on top of regular tax when you take retirement money out too early, unless you qualify for a special exception. For FLYers, planning ahead so you do not raid long-term accounts early keeps compounding intact and avoids receiving from Uncle Sam a "speeding ticket" on your savings.

- **Education Credits**: tax benefits that reduce your tax bill when you pay qualified college costs such as tuition, required fees, and course materials. Examples include the American Opportunity Tax Credit, which can even be partly refundable and put cash back in your pocket. For FLYers, using education credits in the right years—often by filing your own return as a student—can turn tuition payments into real tax savings that help fund investing or debt payoff. Make sure you have proved earned income that exceeds half of your support.
- **EIN (Employer Identification Number)**: a unique nine-digit number the IRS assigns to a business, trust, or organization, similar to a Social Security number for companies. You use it to open business bank accounts, file business tax returns, and give to clients on W-9 forms instead of exposing your SSN. For FLYers starting LLCs or side hustles, getting an EIN is a simple, powerful step to separate personal and business life and look more professional to banks and partners.
- **Emergency Funds**: cash you set aside in a safe, easy-to-reach place—like a savings or money market account—to cover surprise expenses such as car repairs, medical bills, or job loss. A common goal is three to six months of basic living costs, so you are not forced to use credit cards or sell investments when life goes sideways. For FLYers, an emergency fund is your first line of defense, making sure one bad month does not derail your long-term real estate and investment plan.
- **Emotional Intelligence**: the ability to understand and manage your own emotions and read other people's feelings so you can respond wisely instead of reacting impulsively. It shows up in how you negotiate, handle tenant conflicts, choose partners, and stay calm during market volatility. For FLYers, high emotional intelligence often matters more than test scores—it helps you avoid drama, build trust with tenants, and make steady, rational money decisions when others panic.
- **Entity Structuring**: the way you set up legal "containers" for your activities—such as LLCs, S-corps, and trusts—to hold rentals, businesses, and investments. Good structuring can protect assets from lawsuits, improve tax treatment, and make inheritance smoother for your family. For FLYers, choosing the right entities early is like drawing a smart blueprint: it does not change what you own, but it can change how safe, efficient, and future-proof everything is.
- **Equity**: the part of an asset you truly own, calculated as the market value minus any debt attached to it. In real estate, equity grows when you pay down the mortgage and when the property appreciates in value. For FLYers, building equity is how you move from being a forever renter to a true owner—it is also the foundation you later tap with HELOCs, cash-out refis, or lines of credit to fund new deals.
- **Escrow**: a special holding arrangement where a neutral third party keeps money or documents safe until all parts of a deal are completed. In real estate, escrow is used during closing to hold deposits and at least yearly to collect property taxes and insurance through your monthly mortgage payment. For FLYers, understanding escrow stops confusion: part of your "mortgage payment" is really the bank pre-saving your taxes and insurance for you.
- **Estate Tax**: a tax that may be charged on the total value of what someone owns at death before those assets pass on to heirs. In the current rules you use, only very large estates above the $15 million (indexed with inflation rate) lifetime exemption are affected, which means most families will not pay it but wealthy families must plan carefully. For FLYers, knowing how estate tax works explains why trusts, life insurance, and real estate are often used together to pass wealth with minimal taxes and maximum control.

- **ETFs (Exchange-Traded Funds)**: baskets of investments—like stocks or bonds—that trade on the stock market like individual shares. Many ETFs track broad indexes such as the S&P 500, giving you instant diversification with low fees and easy buying or selling. For FLYers, ETFs are a simple way to own hundreds of companies at once in a brokerage, while you focus your active energy on real estate and career building. You can also borrow against the ETF collateral up to 50-70% of the market value through a securities backed line of credit.
- **Ethical Investing**: choosing investments that match your values, such as avoiding companies involved in certain industries or favoring those that support the environment, fair labor, or faith-aligned missions. This approach still looks at risk and return, but it also asks, "What kind of world am I funding with my money?" For FLYers, ethical investing connects your financial life to your character so you feel good about both your profits and your impact.
- **Eviction**: the legal process a landlord uses to remove a tenant who has seriously broken the lease—often by not paying rent, causing major damage, or violating key rules. It usually requires proper notice, court filings, and documentation, and must follow local landlord-tenant laws closely. For FLYers, good screening, clear communication, and fair but firm boundaries are the best way to prevent evictions, which are stressful and expensive for everyone.
- **Exotic Assets**: higher-risk, less traditional investments such as crypto, private credit, pre-IPO shares, or certain collectibles. They can deliver big gains but also big crashes, and they often come with more complexity and less regulation. For FLYers, exotic assets belong in the "fun money" slice—5–10% of net worth at most—after your four core pillars (real estate, S&P 500 index fund, zero-dividend broad-based stocks, and cash value whole life insurance) are firmly in place.
- **Expense Ratio**: the annual fee a fund or ETF charges to manage your money, expressed as a percentage of the assets you have invested. A 1% expense ratio means you pay $100 per year for every $10,000 invested, whether the fund goes up or down. For FLYers, keeping expense ratios very low (usually 0.015 to 0.25%)—especially in index funds and 529 plans—matters hugely over decades because high fees quietly eat away a large chunk of your compound.

F

- **FAFSA**: the main federal form students fill out to report family income and assets so colleges can calculate financial aid. It helps determine eligibility for grants, work-study, and some student loans. For FLYers, treating the FAFSA like a yearly "money form" instead of just paperwork can unlock thousands of dollars that reduce the need for high-interest debt.
- **Fair Market Rent**: the amount a typical tenant would reasonably pay for a similar property in the same area, based on local supply, demand, and condition. It is obtained from Zillow, Redfin, Craigslist, or local property managers. For FLYers, understanding fair market rent helps you price units competitively—high enough to profit, but fair enough to keep vacancies low.
- **Family Bank**: an informal system where a family uses its own savings, investments, and cash value in whole life insurance policies to lend money to members for things like down payments, education, or business startups. Instead of paying interest to outside banks, the interest stays within the family and can be reused for the next generation. For FLYers, being

part of a well-run family bank can turn relatives into partners in wealth building, not just gift-givers.

- **Family Foundation**: a charitable organization funded and controlled by a family to support causes they care about over many years. It can provide tax deductions when funded and create a structured way for children to learn giving, governance, and stewardship. For FLYers, serving on a family foundation board is like a real-world MBA in generosity, leadership, and long-term planning.
- **Family LLC**: a limited liability company owned by family members, often used to hold rentals, businesses, or investments in one shared structure. It can protect assets from lawsuits, organize decision-making, and make it easier to transfer ownership shares gradually to children by taking advantage of the $19,000 annual gifting exclusion amount per parent. For FLYers, a family LLC is a training ground where you learn to read financials, vote on decisions, and think like a co-owner instead of just a consumer.
- **Federal Housing Administration (FHA)**: a government agency that insures certain mortgages, making it easier for first-time and lower-income buyers to qualify with smaller down payments and more flexible credit rules. FHA loans often allow as little as 3.5% down and can be combined with gifts or seller credits. For FLYers, FHA is one of the most practical doors into that crucial first property, especially when paired with a parent co-signer.
- **Federal Income Tax**: the tax the U.S. government charges on your income from jobs, businesses, investments, and some other sources each year. The system is progressive, meaning higher income is generally taxed at higher marginal rates. For FLYers, understanding how brackets, deductions, and credits work is the difference between just filing a return and running a tax strategy that keeps more money compounding for your future.
- **Financial Aid Eligibility**: the amount of help a student can receive for college costs based on formulas that look at income, assets, family size, and number of kids in college. Schools use data from FAFSA (and College Scholarship Service (CSS) for some private colleges) to award grants, scholarships, and loan packages. For FLYers, smart planning—like how assets are titled and whose income shows up—can preserve aid while still allowing early investing and real estate.
- **Financial Freedom**: the point where your passive income and assets produce enough cash flow that you no longer have to work just to cover basic living expenses. It does not always mean you stop working; it means you work by choice, not necessity. For FLYers, real estate, index funds, and tax-advantaged accounts are the three main engines that move you toward this level of freedom before traditional retirement age.
- **Financial Independence**: the stage where you control your money instead of your money controlling you, one anchored by low debt, strong savings, and multiple income streams. It is closely related to financial freedom but often emphasizes having options—where to live, what career to pursue, and how much risk to take. For FLYers, buying a first property before 25 is a powerful milestone on the road from dependence to true independence.
- **Financial Literacy**: the set of skills and knowledge that lets you understand, manage, and multiply money: budgeting, credit, debt, investing, taxes, and risk. It is not about being a math genius; it is about knowing how the system works so you can make it work for you. For FLYers, financial literacy turns confusing topics like "AGI," "1031," or "cost segregation" into everyday tools instead of scary jargon.
- **Financing Toolkit**: the collection of loan types and funding options you can use to buy or improve properties—conventional loans, FHA, VA, HELOCs, SBLOCs, IBLOCs, and even

seller financing. Each tool has its own rules, costs, and risks, and the art is matching the right one to each deal and stage of life. For FLYers, building a strong financing toolkit is like having multiple keys: you are not stuck waiting for just one door to open.

- **FIRE (Financial Independence, Retire Early)**: a movement where people aggressively save and invest—often 40–70% of their income—to reach financial independence decades before the traditional retirement age. Instead of working 40 years and retiring at 65, FIRE followers aim to build enough assets to step back in their 30s, 40s, or 50s. For FLYers, combining FIRE principles with real estate (steady cash flow) can make "retire early" less about quitting work and more about regaining control of your time.
- **First Home Fund**: a dedicated savings pool—often supported by family, gifts, or event contributions—set aside specifically for a young person's first down payment and closing costs. It might be funded at graduations, birthdays, or holidays instead of traditional presents. For FLYers, branding it as a "First Home Fund" turns vague saving into a concrete mission: helping you own instead of rent while your peers are still signing dorm leases.
- **First-Time Homebuyer Safe Harbor**: a special rule that lets first-time buyers withdraw up to a limited amount (like $10,000) from IRAs, without paying the usual early-withdrawal penalty when the money is used for a home. You may still owe regular income tax, but you avoid the extra 10% hit. For FLYers, this safe harbor can be a strategic bridge—used carefully—to turn early earnings into a real estate launchpad.
- **Five C's for the AI Age**: a modern skill checklist for thriving in a world reshaped by artificial intelligence—Creativity, Communication, Compassion, Collaboration, and Contribution. These are abilities machines cannot easily replace and that remain valuable even as technical tasks get automated. For FLYers, mastering the five C's makes you "AI-proof": you can lead teams, design solutions, and build communities around your financial and real-estate knowledge.
- **Five Golden Geographies**: five types of locations where rentals tend to stay in demand year-round: areas near mega-universities, major hospitals, military bases, big-box anchors like Costco, and growing tech or AI data-center hubs. These places attract a steady flow of students, staff, professionals, and families, which supports rents and reduces vacancy risk. For FLYers, hunting in these geographies is like fishing where the fish already are—demand is built into the map.
- **Fixed Income Market**: the part of the investment world made up of bonds and similar instruments that pay regular interest, like corporate bonds, government bonds, and some types of insurance company investments. Returns are usually lower than stocks but more stable, and they play a big role in how life insurers deploy their funds. For FLYers, understanding the fixed income market helps you see what sits behind products like whole life policies and why they behave differently than stocks or crypto.
- **Flexibility**: the ability to adjust your plans, budget, or strategy when life or markets change without blowing up your whole financial picture. It shows up in having cash reserves, multiple income streams, and loan structures that do not trap you. For FLYers, flexibility is a hidden asset: it lets you survive surprises (job loss, rate hikes, repairs) and still be ready when amazing deals or opportunities appear.
- **FLY Vision Board**: a visual roadmap that lays out your four core asset pillars—real estate, stock index investments, cash value life insurance, and a small slice of speculative assets—alongside your life goals and timelines. Instead of random money moves, it shows how each account, property, and policy fits into a bigger picture from age 18 to retirement and beyond.

For FLYers, the FLY Vision Board turns financial independence from a vague dream into a picture you can literally see on your wall and work toward each year.

G

- **Generational Wealth**: assets, skills, and values that are built in one generation and intentionally passed to the next, instead of being spent down in one lifetime. It includes real estate, businesses, investments, and also tax knowledge and family systems like trusts or LLCs. For FLYers, the goal is not just to make money once, but to design portfolios and plans that your kids and grandkids can build on—not start over from zero.
- **Gift Exclusion**: the amount you can give to another person in a year without triggering federal gift tax reporting or using up your lifetime gift and estate exemption. Parents and grandparents often use the annual exclusion to move money into UTMA accounts, 529 plans, or Coverdell education savings account for their children. For FLYers, understanding the gift exclusion lets you receive help for education or first homes in a tax-smart, IRS-approved way.
- **Grit**: the mix of passion and perseverance that keeps you going toward a long-term goal even when it is boring, hard, or slow. It shows up when you save month after month, fix tenant problems, study tax rules, or keep training for a license instead of quitting. For FLYers, grit is the "engine under the hood" of every success story—you do not need to be the smartest, just the most consistent.
- **Gross Yield**: the simple annual return from a rental before subtracting any expenses, usually calculated as yearly rent divided by purchase price. It is a quick way to compare deals, but it can be misleading because it ignores taxes, insurance, repairs, and vacancies. For FLYers, gross yield is a first filter ("Is this even in the ballpark?"), not the final answer; you still need to run real cash-flow numbers.
- **Gross Income**: your total income before any taxes or expenses are taken out, including wages, tips, business income, interest, dividends, and rents. Lenders and college aid forms often start with gross income before applying adjustments or deductions. For FLYers, tracking gross income helps you see your full earning power, while learning how to legally move from gross to a smarter AGI is how you keep more of what you make.
- **Gross Rent Multiplier (GRM)**: a quick rule-of-thumb metric that compares a property's price to its annual gross rent, calculated as purchase price divided by yearly rent. A lower GRM generally suggests you are paying less for each dollar of rent, but it still ignores expenses like taxes, insurance, and repairs. For FLYers, GRM can help you screen lots of deals fast—but you should always follow it with deeper analysis of net operating income and cap rate.
- **Guarantor**: a person—often a parent—who promises to step in and pay a loan if the main borrower cannot. Lenders may approve a young FLYer's mortgage or student lease more easily when there is a strong guarantor behind them. For both sides, being a guarantor is serious: it can help launch a young person's financial life, but it also means a FLYer's parent must trust their responsibility and have their own finances in order.
- **Government-Backed Loan**: a mortgage that is insured or guaranteed by a federal agency such as FHA, VA, or USDA, which reduces the lender's risk and allows for lower down payments or more flexible credit requirements. FHA loans serve many first-time buyers, VA loans support eligible veterans and service members, and USDA loans target rural areas. For FLYers, these government-backed options are often the gateway into their first property when a traditional conventional loan would be just out of reach.

H

- **Hand Up, Not Handout**: a mindset where parents and mentors provide opportunities, guidance, and structure instead of doing everything for a young person or endlessly rescuing them. The goal is to help the next generation build their own strength, skills, and confidence, not to create dependence or entitlement. For FLYers, a "hand up" might be co-signing a loan, funding a First Home Fund, or sharing tax strategies—while still expecting real effort, grit, and responsibility in return.
- **Health Savings Account (HSA)**: a special, tax-advantaged account you can use only if you are covered by a High Deductible Health Plan. Money you put in is tax-deductible, grows tax-free, and can be withdrawn tax-free for qualified medical expenses—often called a "triple tax benefit." For FLYers, an HSA is like a stealth retirement account: if you invest it and save your receipts, it can become a powerful long-term wealth and health tool.
- **HELOC (Home Equity Line of Credit)**: a revolving credit line secured by the equity in your home that works somewhat like a credit card with your house as collateral. You can borrow, repay, and borrow again up to a limit, usually at a variable interest rate. For FLYers, a HELOC is one way to tap Other People's Money by using your own equity as a springboard for renovations, down payments, or emergencies—if used with discipline and strong cash flow.
- **High Deductible Health Plan (HDHP)**: a type of health insurance with lower monthly premiums but higher deductibles you must pay before coverage kicks in. Only HDHPs qualify you to contribute to an HSA, unlocking those triple tax benefits. For FLYers, choosing an HDHP plus HSA can be a smart move when you are young and healthy, as long as you also build an emergency fund to handle that higher deductible if something goes wrong.
- **Home Office Deduction**: a tax break that lets you deduct part of your housing costs (such as real estate tax, mortgage interest, insurance, repair, depreciation, utilities, and HOA fees) when a specific area of your home is used regularly and exclusively for business. It can be claimed on Schedule C for a small business and sometimes allocated for rental management if done properly. For FLYers running side hustles or managing rentals, the home office deduction turns a corner of your room or apartment into a tiny tax-saving factory.
- **Homeownership Identity**: the shift in how you see yourself when you move from being a renter to being an owner who signs the mortgage, holds the deed, and makes the decisions. It often brings a new level of responsibility, maturity, and pride—suddenly you care more about maintenance, budgeting, and long-term planning. For FLYers, owning a home at 18 or in your early 20s is not just a financial milestone; it's a new identity as a builder, not just a consumer.
- **House Hacking**: a strategy where you live in part of a property and rent out the rest—such as extra bedrooms, a basement unit, or a duplex half—so your tenants help pay (or completely cover) the mortgage. Done right, it lets you live for very low cost or even for free while you build equity and landlord experience. For FLYers, house hacking turns the classic "college housing expense" into a learning lab in business, tax, and leadership.
- **HUD Settlement Statement**: an official closing document (also called a closing disclosure in newer formats) that lists all the money flows in a real estate transaction—purchase price, loan amounts, fees, taxes, and who pays what. It is the detailed receipt for your deal and becomes part of your long-term records for basis, deductions, and future sales. For FLYers,

reading the settlement statement carefully teaches you where every dollar goes at closing and how much of your cost can later help you at tax time.

I

- **IBLOC (Insurance Backed Line of Credit)**: a line of credit you get from a bank (such as Bancorp), or from a life insurance company, with the cash value of a life insurance policy as collateral instead of borrowing against your house or stock portfolio. You can borrow a percentage (up to 95%) of the policy's cash value, usually at a competitive rate, without touching the actual investments inside the policy. For FLYers, an IBLOC is like a quiet backup tank of liquidity that can help fund down payments or emergencies while your policy keeps compounding.
- **Identity Theft**: when someone steals your personal information—such as your social security number, credit card numbers, or login details—and uses it to open accounts, take out loans, or make purchases in your name. It can damage your credit, drain your accounts, and create a mess of fraudulent records that take time to fix. For FLYers, freezing your credit, using strong passwords, and checking your reports regularly is as important as locking your front door.
- **Income Shifting**: moving income from a high-tax person to a lower-tax family member in legal ways, such as hiring your teenager in a real business or paying a spouse a fair wage for real work. The same dollars then get taxed at a lower rate, freeing up more cash for saving and investing. For FLYers, income shifting (done properly with documentation) turns your family into a coordinated financial team instead of everyone fighting the tax code alone.
- **Independent Contractor**: someone who works for themselves rather than as an employee, getting paid on 1099s instead of W-2s, and responsible for their own taxes and benefits. They have more freedom but also more responsibility: tracking expenses, paying quarterly taxes, and often buying their own insurance. For FLYers, being an independent contractor through an LLC or sole proprietorship can unlock powerful deductions, but it also demands discipline and good record-keeping.
- **Index Fund**: an investment fund that simply tries to match the performance of a market index—like the S&P 500—instead of trying to beat it. Because it is not paying managers to pick stocks, costs are usually very low, and you get instant diversification across many companies. For FLYers, a low-fee index fund is often the default "set-it-and-grow" choice in brokerage, Roth IRA, 401(k), and even 529 accounts.
- **Inflation**: the gradual rise in prices over time that makes each dollar buy a little less, year after year. It quietly erodes the value of cash sitting under a mattress or in low-interest accounts, which is why long-term savers need growth investments. For FLYers, owning assets that tend to outpace inflation—like real estate and broad stock indexes—helps make sure your future lifestyle is not shrunk by rising costs.
- **Insurance Premium**: the amount you pay an insurance company—monthly, quarterly, or yearly—to keep your policy in force, whether it is health, auto, home, or life insurance. In return, the company promises to cover certain risks described in the policy, like accidents, illness, or death. For FLYers, premiums are not just "bills"; they are part of risk management, and choosing the right coverage level keeps one bad event from becoming a financial disaster.
- **Interest Tracing Rule**: a tax principle that says the deductibility of interest depends on how you actually use the borrowed money, not what the loan is secured by. If you borrow against stocks or a house and use the money for a rental property or business, that interest may be

deductible on those activities; if you use it for vacations or clothes, it is usually not. For FLYers, mastering interest tracing turns HELOCs, SBLOCs, and IBLOCs into precise tax tools instead of blunt instruments.

- **Intergenerational Wealth**: wealth that is intentionally built and structured to move smoothly from parents to children and then to grandchildren through thoughtful planning. It combines assets like rentals, policies, and portfolios with legal structures like trusts, LLCs, and foundations, plus education so the next generation knows how to handle what they receive. For FLYers, intergenerational wealth means you are not just trying to "get rich"; you are designing a system your future kids can step into and grow.
- **Internal Revenue Code (IRC)**: the main body of U.S. tax law, organized into sections (like §1031, §121, or §469) that spell out what is taxable, what is deductible, and what special rules apply. CPAs, tax attorneys, and serious investors refer to specific code sections when planning moves like 1031 exchanges, real estate professional status, or depreciation strategies. For FLYers, you do not need to memorize the whole code—but recognizing key sections lets you speak the language of the tax system instead of just hoping your software gets it right.

J

- **Joint Tax Return**: a tax return filed together by a married couple that combines both spouses' income, deductions, and credits on one form. This status often gives access to wider tax brackets, larger standard deductions, and certain benefits that are not available when filing separately. For FLYers, filing jointly can be a powerful planning move when one spouse has high W-2 income and the other has real estate or business losses that can legally offset it.
- **Jumpstart Our Business Startups Act (JOBS) Act**: a U.S. law passed in 2018 to make it easier for startups and small businesses to raise money. It relaxed several securities regulations, allowing companies to raise capital through methods like crowdfunding, private placements, and "mini-IPOs" (Regulation A+).

K

- **Kiddie House**: a nickname for a rental property parents buy near their child's college or university, where the student lives in one room and rents out the others to classmates. Instead of paying dorms or landlords, the family's money goes into a house they own, often with help from 529 plans and co-signing parents. For FLYers, a Kiddie House turns "college housing" from a pure expense into a real-life business, tax-planning, and wealth-building lab.
- **Kiddie Tax**: a special tax rule that applies to a child's unearned income—like interest, dividends, or capital gains—above certain limits when they are under 18, or a full-time student under 24. Once that unearned income crosses the yearly threshold, part of it gets taxed at the parents' higher tax rate instead of the child's lower rate. For FLYers, understanding the Kiddie Tax is crucial when using UTMA accounts or gifting investments, so you do not accidentally trigger surprise taxes while trying to save for college or a first home.

L

- **Land**: the part of real estate that is the ground itself, not the building, improvements, or structures placed on it. For tax purposes, land is not depreciated because it does not wear out, even though its market value can rise or fall. For FLYers, separating land value from building value is critical when calculating depreciation and analyzing deals.

- **Late Fees**: extra charges a tenant pays when rent or other required payments are not made by the agreed-upon due date. They are meant to encourage on-time payment and compensate the landlord for added hassle and risk. For FLYers, clearly written and fairly enforced late-fee policies are part of running rentals like a business, not a hobby.
- **Lease Contract**: the written agreement between a landlord and tenant that spells out rent amount, due dates, rules, responsibilities, and what happens if either side breaks the terms. It protects both parties by turning expectations into legal language instead of verbal promises. For FLYers, a strong lease is your first line of defense—it prevents many conflicts before they start and gives you a roadmap when problems do arise.
- **Lender Credit**: money the lender gives you at closing to help cover costs like origination fees or other closing expenses, usually in exchange for accepting a slightly higher interest rate. It reduces the cash you need up front but may increase your total interest paid over time. For FLYers, lender credits can make a deal possible when cash is tight, as long as you run the numbers and understand the long-term trade-off between receiving a lender credit now and paying a slightly higher mortgage interest over years).
- **Leverage**: using borrowed money, such as a mortgage or line of credit, to control a larger asset than you can buy with cash alone. When an investment goes well, leverage magnifies your returns; when it goes badly, it also magnifies losses. For FLYers, responsible leverage—paired with reserves and conservative assumptions—is the engine that lets a small down payment control a six-figure property and turn modest appreciation into big gains.
- **Liability Insurance**: coverage that protects you if someone sues you for injuries or damage they say you caused, such as a slip-and-fall at your rental or a car accident. It pays for legal defense and, if needed, settlements up to the policy limit. For FLYers, solid liability and umbrella insurance are must-haves once you own property or run a business, because one lawsuit can be more dangerous than one bad deal.
- **Life Expectancy**: an estimate of how long a person is statistically expected to live based on age, gender, and health data. It is used by insurers and financial planners to design policies, pensions, and retirement plans. For FLYers, understanding life expectancy helps you see why starting early with investing, insurance, and real estate gives compound growth decades to work in your favor.
- **Liquid Assets**: resources you can turn into cash quickly with little or no loss in value, such as checking and savings accounts, money market funds, or certain short-term investments. They are what you rely on for emergencies, down payments, and unexpected opportunities. For FLYers, keeping a slice of your net worth in liquid assets is what keeps you from having to sell properties or investments at the wrong time. Given the stable returns of cash value whole life insurance and high credit ratings of some largest whole insurance companies, IBLOC is deemed liquidity assets with more flexibility and tax advantages than bank CDs or money market funds.
- **Living Benefits**: features of certain life insurance policies—especially cash value policies—that you can use while you are still alive, such as borrowing against cash value, accessing funds for chronic illness, or using riders for long-term care. They make the policy more than just a death benefit; it becomes a flexible financial tool. For FLYers, living benefits can support down payments, business funding, or medical needs without selling other investments.

- **Living Trust**: a legal arrangement you create during your lifetime that holds your assets and spells out who manages them if you become incapacitated and who receives them after you die. Unlike a simple will, a properly funded living trust can help your family avoid probate and keep your affairs more private. For FLYers, a living trust is part of treating your growing real-estate and investment portfolio like a real business that can outlive you.
- **LLC (Limited Liability Company)**: a flexible business entity that can own rentals, run a business, or hold investments while generally protecting the owners' personal assets from business-related lawsuits and debts. Income usually "passes through" to the owners' tax returns, avoiding corporate-level tax. For FLYers, using LLCs for rentals and side businesses is a core way to separate "you" from your properties and add a layer of asset protection.
- **Loan Estimate**: a standardized document your lender gives you early in the mortgage process that outlines the proposed loan's key terms—interest rate, monthly payment, closing costs, and whether amounts can change. It lets you compare offers from different lenders on an apples-to-apples basis before you commit. For FLYers, reading the Loan Estimate carefully is how you catch junk fees, understand your true cost, and negotiate better.
- **Long-Term Capital Gains**: profits from selling an asset you have held for more than one year, which are taxed at special, usually lower rates than ordinary income. These favorable rates reward patient investing rather than short-term trading. For FLYers, aiming for long-term gains—especially on stocks and investment properties—means more of your growth stays in your pocket instead of going to taxes.
- **Long-Term Rentals**: properties leased for extended periods, typically six months or more, to tenants who treat them as their main home rather than a vacation spot. They usually offer more stable cash flow, fewer turnovers, and less cleaning than short-term rentals. For FLYers balancing school or early career, long-term rentals near the "five golden geographies" (campuses, hospitals, military bases, big-box anchors, and AI hubs) can provide predictable income without daily hosting work.

M

- **Magnificent 7**: a nickname for the seven mega-cap U.S. tech-driven companies (Apple, Microsoft, Nvidia, Amazon, Alphabet, Meta, and Tesla) that now make up an outsized share of the S&P 500. When these giants move, they can swing the whole stock index, which increases concentration risk. For FLYers, the Magnificent 7 are a reminder that even "diversified" stock indexes can become tech-heavy, so adding real estate, cash value whole life insurance, and other assets keeps your overall portfolio balanced.
- **Maintenance**: the ongoing work and costs needed to keep a property safe, functional, and attractive, such as fixing leaks, servicing HVAC, painting, and yard care. Good maintenance prevents small issues from becoming expensive emergencies and keeps tenants happier and longer-term. For FLYers, budgeting realistically for maintenance—monthly or per-door—is non-negotiable if you want real cash flow, not surprise crises.
- **Market Timing**: trying to predict short-term ups and downs in stocks or real estate so you can buy at the "bottom" and sell at the "top." Even professionals struggle to do this consistently, and many investors lose money by waiting too long or panicking at the wrong moment. For FLYers, focusing on disciplined buying, long-term holding, using BBB strategy to buy the market dips, and smart tax timing usually beats chasing the perfect day on a chart.
- **Material Participation**: an IRS concept that measures whether you are actively involved enough in a business or rental activity to treat its income and losses as "non-passive." Tests include things like hours worked, decision-making, and being the primary person running the

show. For FLYers, qualifying for material participation—especially as a Real Estate Professional—can unlock powerful tax treatment where rental losses can offset your spouse's W-2, or your small business income.

- **Maturity**: both the date when a loan or investment comes due and the personal growth that comes from handling responsibility over time. A loan's maturity date is when you must have it fully repaid, while your own maturity shows in how you handle money, relationships, and risk. For FLYers, financial maturity means thinking beyond this month's wants and seeing how today's choices ripple through the next 10, 20, or 30 years.
- **Medical Power of Attorney**: a legal document that lets you name someone you trust to make medical decisions for you if you cannot speak for yourself. It kicks in if you are unconscious, seriously ill, or otherwise unable to decide, and it guides doctors based on your belief and wishes. For FLYers, setting up a medical power of attorney as part of basic estate planning is an act of love toward your family—they will know who is in charge and what you would have wanted.
- **Military Bases**: large installations where service members live, train, and work, often surrounded by strong and steady housing demand funded by government housing allowances. Rentals near major bases tend to have reliable tenants and lower default risk, though turnover can be tied to deployment cycles. For FLYers, buying near a stable military base can be a smart long-term rental strategy, especially when combined with good property management and local knowledge.
- **MLS Market Data**: information from the Multiple Listing Service, the professional database where licensed agents list properties for sale or rent and record details like price, days on market, and final sale terms. It is more complete and detailed than most public real estate sites. For FLYers who get a real-estate license or build a relationship with an agent, access to MLS data is like having x-ray vision on a market—crucial for pricing, offer strategy, and spotting trends early.
- **Mortgage Insurance**: a policy that protects the lender (not you) if you stop making mortgage payments and the home is foreclosed. It is often required when your down payment is below 20%, such as with many FHA or low-down conventional loans. For FLYers, mortgage insurance is a cost of using high leverage to get into the game early—but the goal is to refinance or build equity so you can eventually remove or reduce it.
- **Mutual Funds**: pooled investment vehicles where many investors' money is combined and managed by professionals who buy stocks, bonds, or other assets according to a stated strategy. Some are actively managed (trying to beat the market), while others simply track indexes, though ETFs now often do that more cheaply. For FLYers, mutual funds can be a starting point inside 401(k)s and IRAs, but paying attention to fees and choosing low-cost options makes a big difference over decades. For example, Fidelity S&P 500 index fund (FXAIX) has an expense ratio of 0.015%, the lowest in its peer group. For every $10,000 fund value in your retirement account, you only pay $1.5 expenses annually.

N

- **National Association of Realtors (NAR)**: the largest trade group for real estate agents and brokers in the U.S., which sets professional standards, influences housing policy, and historically influenced how commissions are structured. Court cases and new rules have recently pushed NAR and its members to become more flexible and transparent about fees and buyer-agent agreements. For FLYers, especially those who want to pursue a real estate license, understanding NAR's role explains why commission rules are changing in their favor and why having a savvy, ethics-driven agent still matters.

- **Net Investment Income Tax**: an extra federal tax—currently 3.8%—that applies to certain high-income taxpayers' investment income, such as interest, dividends, capital gains, and rental profits (if any). It kicks in only when your income rises above specific thresholds, layering on top of regular income or capital-gains taxes. For FLYers who eventually build large portfolios, planning around this tax (for example investing in zero-dividend broad based stocks, buying and hold, avoiding dividend paying stocks or bond funds, using BBB strategy, coupled with real-estate losses) can protect more of your passive income.
- **Network**: the web of people you know—and who know you—across school, work, church, community groups, and online spaces. A strong network includes mentors, peers, lenders, agents, contractors, and professionals who can share knowledge, deals, and opportunities. Your network is your net worth. For FLYers, your network is often more valuable than your net worth at the beginning, because the right introductions can accelerate learning and shorten the path to your first property or business.
- **New Builds**: brand-new construction properties that have never been lived in, often sold by builders with modern layouts, energy-efficient systems, and low initial repair needs. Builders sometimes offer incentives like closing-cost credits or rate buy-downs to attract early buyers in a community. For FLYers, new builds can be an easier, more predictable first purchase, as long as you still analyze HOA fees, taxes, and realistic rents—not just the shiny finishes.
- **Net Operating Income (NOI)**: the money a rental property earns from rent and other income after you subtract all operating expenses (like taxes, insurance, utilities you pay, repairs, and management fee) but before mortgage payments and income taxes. It is the key number used to calculate cap rate and value for many investment properties. For FLYers, focusing on growing NOI—by raising rents fairly and controlling expenses—is how you systematically increase both cash flow and property value over time.
- **Net Worth**: your total assets (cash, properties, investments, businesses) minus all your liabilities (mortgages, student loans, credit cards, car loans, and other debts). It is a simple but powerful measure of where you stand financially right now. For FLYers, tracking net worth yearly—rather than just income—keeps you focused on building ownership and equity, not just chasing a bigger paycheck.
- **Non-Correlation**: a relationship between two assets where they do not move up and down together, or only do so weakly, when markets change. For example, on your FLY vision board, housing, whole life insurance, stock indexes, and Bitcoin have shown different patterns over time, which helps smooth out overall results. For FLYers, mixing non-correlated assets is like building a team where each player shines in different seasons, reducing the chance that everything crashes at the same time.

O

- **One Big Beautiful Bill (OBBB)**: a major tax law package in your FLY world that extends and enhances many of the Trump-era tax cuts for families, small businesses, and young investors. It raises key thresholds, expands credits, introduces tools like Trump Accounts, and keeps bonus depreciation and high estate exemptions in place. For FLYers, OBBB is the legal "tailwind" that makes early real estate, Roth strategies, and family planning even more powerful over a lifetime.
- **Operating Agreement**: the internal rulebook for an LLC that explains who owns what percent, who makes decisions, how profits are shared, and what happens if someone leaves

or dies. Even in a single-member LLC, an operating agreement shows banks, courts, and the IRS that you are treating the business as a separate legal entity. For FLYers, a clear operating agreement is like pre-writing the answers to future arguments, keeping family and partners on the same page.

- **Opportunity Zone**: a specially designated geographic area—often in lower-income or redeveloping neighborhoods—where investors can get tax breaks for putting money into qualified real-estate or business projects. If you reinvest capital gains into an Opportunity Zone fund and hold long enough, you may defer or even reduce some taxes on those gains. For FLYers, Opportunity Zones show how tax law can reward both community improvement and long-term investing, if you do careful due diligence.
- **Ordinary and Necessary Expense**: a tax phrase for costs that are both common in your type of business and helpful or appropriate to running it, such as mileage, advertising, software, or reasonable professional fees. These expenses are generally deductible against your business or rental income. For FLYers, learning what counts as "ordinary and necessary" turns everyday work—like driving to a property, paying a CPA, or using management software—into legal tax savings.
- **Other People's Money (OPM)**: money you borrow from banks, lenders, or even family to control assets much larger than your own cash would allow. When used wisely in rentals and businesses, OPM can multiply your returns because you keep the upside after paying back the loan and interest. For FLYers, OPM is not an excuse for reckless debt; it is a disciplined tool that lets a small down payment command a big, appreciating asset.
- **Other People's Time (OPT)**: the idea of building systems and teams so you are not the only one doing the work—hiring property managers, contractors, virtual assistants, or student helpers. OPT frees you to focus on higher-level decisions and new opportunities instead of being stuck in every task. For FLYers, mastering OPT is how you scale from one house you manage yourself to a portfolio that runs even when you are in class, traveling, or with family.
- **Owner-Occupied Rental**: a property where you live in part of the home (like one bedroom or one unit) and rent out the rest to roommates or tenants. Because it is both your primary residence and a rental, you can often access better loan terms while still claiming rental deductions and depreciation on the rented portion. For FLYers, an owner-occupied rental is the classic house-hack: "my room, my rules, my rental" and a fast track to building equity while keeping housing costs low.
- **Over-withheld Taxes**: extra amounts your employer takes out of your paycheck for federal or state income tax that end up being more than you actually owe for the year. This usually leads to a big tax refund, which feels nice but really means you gave the government an interest-free loan. For FLYers, adjusting your W-4 so withholding matches your true tax—especially when you have rental losses or big deductions—puts more cash in your pocket each month to save, invest, and compound.

P

- **Paid-up Additions (PUA)**: extra chunks of whole life insurance that you buy inside the policy to increase both its cash value and death benefit faster. PUAs help your policy grow more like a high-octane savings engine instead of just basic coverage. For FLYers, loading policies with PUAs (like the 10-10-80 design of your life insurance policy: 10% money to pay whole life premium, 10% to buy a renewal one-year term life, and 80% as cash dump) turns cash value life insurance into a more powerful "family bank" you can borrow from later.

- **Partnership Return (1065)**: the tax return a multi-owner partnership or multi-member LLC files each year to report its income, expenses, and how profits or losses are split among partners. The partnership itself usually does not pay income tax; instead, it sends each partner a Schedule K-1 that flows onto their personal return. For FLYers, understanding Form 1065 matters when you start owning rentals or businesses with siblings, friends, or parents so everyone's share is reported correctly.
- **Passive Activity Loss**: a loss from an activity in which you do not materially participate, such as many rentals or limited partnerships, under IRS rules. These losses are usually limited and can only offset passive income unless you qualify for special exceptions like real estate professional status. For FLYers, managing passive losses wisely—through AGI planning and real-estate hours—can turn "on-paper" losses into real tax savings that fund more investments.
- **Passive Income**: money that keeps coming in with little day-to-day effort once the system is set up, such as rental income, certain royalties, or dividends. It still requires upfront work, capital, and good management, but it does not depend on you trading hours for dollars like a regular job. For FLYers, building multiple streams of true passive income is the heart of financial independence—the point where your money works harder than you do.
- **Point (Mortgage)**: a fee equal to 1% of the loan amount that you pay to the lender at closing, often in exchange for a lower interest rate (called "buying down" the rate). Paying points increases your upfront closing costs but can reduce your monthly payment and total interest over time. For FLYers, deciding whether to pay points is a math problem: if you will keep the loan long enough, the long-term savings can outweigh the extra cash at closing. If you anticipate mortgage interest rate will drop in future years and plan to refinance, paying points now may not be a good decision.
- **Post-nuptial Agreement**: a legal contract spouses sign after they are married that spells out how assets, debts, and support would be handled if they separate or divorce. It can update or replace what they would have put in a prenup and is often used when circumstances change—like starting a business, receiving an inheritance, or buying rentals. For FLYers, a well-designed post-nup is not about expecting failure; it is about clarity and protecting both parents and kids when money and real estate enter the picture.
- **Power of Attorney**: a legal document that authorizes someone you trust (your "agent") to act on your behalf in financial or legal matters if you are unavailable or unable. This can include signing closing documents, paying bills, or managing rentals when you are out of the country or incapacitated. For FLYers, having the right power of attorney in place is practical—especially if you study abroad, travel, or have deals closing while you are in class or training.
- **Prenuptial Agreement**: a contract signed before marriage that outlines how property, debts, and support will be handled if the marriage ends. It can protect pre-marital assets, business interests, and inheritance plans, and avoid ugly surprises later. For FLYers, a fair, well-communicated prenup is like an insurance policy for both spouses: it lets you talk about money openly and protect family real estate or businesses before emotions run high.
- **Primary Residence**: the main home where you live most of the time, receive mail, and register important things like your driver's license and voter registration. Tax rules give primary residences special benefits, such as the §121 exclusion that lets you exclude a large chunk of gain when you sell after living there long enough. For FLYers, choosing and documenting your primary residence correctly can make the difference between a tax-free win and a surprise bill when you sell.

- **Principal**: the original amount of money you borrow on a loan or the amount you have left to repay, not counting interest. With every mortgage payment, a portion goes to interest and a portion chips away at principal, slowly increasing your equity. For FLYers, watching the principal drop over time is a powerful motivator—you see that every payment is not just an expense, but a transfer from the bank's column to your net-worth column.
- **Privacy Protection**: the steps you take to keep your personal and financial information safe, such as using LLCs for property ownership, redacting addresses, and limiting what you share publicly. It also includes digital habits like strong passwords, two-factor authentication, and credit monitoring to avoid identity theft. For FLYers, good privacy protection is part of risk management—keeping your growing wealth and personal life shielded from scammers, stalkers, and unnecessary attention.
- **Probate**: the court process after someone dies to validate their will (if there is one), settle debts, and transfer assets to heirs. It can take months or years, cost legal fees, and turn family privacy into public record. For FLYers, using tools like living trusts and proper titling can help your future family avoid probate delays and keep your real-estate legacy moving smoothly to the next generation.
- **Property Appraisal**: an independent, professional opinion of what a property is worth, usually ordered by a lender before approving a mortgage or refinance. The appraiser compares your property to recent comparable sales and adjusts for things like size, condition, and location. For FLYers, the appraisal can be both a gatekeeper and a reality check—if it comes in low, you may need to renegotiate, bring more cash, or challenge the report with better comparables.
- **Property Appreciation**: the increase in a property's market value over time due to factors like demand, location improvements, inflation, and upgrades. Even modest annual appreciation, when combined with leverage, can produce very high returns on your original down payment. For FLYers, property appreciation is one of the main reasons to start young—the longer you hold, the more time you give this quiet wealth engine to work in the background.
- **Property Management**: the day-to-day handling of a rental—finding and screening tenants, collecting rent, handling maintenance, responding to issues, and enforcing the lease. You can self-manage or hire a professional manager who typically charges a percentage of monthly rent. For FLYers, learning the basics of property management early makes you a better landlord, even if you eventually outsource—and it can become a business of its own with low risk and recurring income.
- **Property Tax**: an annual tax charged by local governments based on the assessed value of land and buildings you own. It helps pay for schools, roads, police, fire services, and other community needs, and is usually added into your monthly mortgage payment via escrow. For FLYers, understanding property tax rates and trends is crucial when analyzing deals—high taxes can make a "cheap" house expensive, while tax-friendly areas can boost long-term cash flow.

Q

- **Qualified Business Income (QBI)**: the net profit from certain pass-through businesses—like sole proprietorships, partnerships, S-corps, and many LLCs—that may qualify for a special deduction (up to 20%) on your tax return. It is basically your business income after ordinary and necessary expenses, but before personal deductions. For FLYers with side hustles or real-estate agent income, understanding QBI turns everyday business profit into a built-in tax discount when structured and reported correctly.

- **Qualified Family-Owned Business Interest (QFOBI)**: a category in estate and inheritance planning where a closely held family business can receive special valuation or deduction treatment for estate-tax purposes. The goal is to let families pass operating businesses—like a real estate company or restoration shop—to the next generation without being forced to sell just to pay estate tax. For FLYers, QFOBI planning is part of thinking bigger than one lifetime: structuring family enterprises so they can be inherited intact.
- **Qualified Higher Education Expenses**: IRS-approved college and post-secondary costs for an eligible student at an eligible institution—usually including tuition, required fees, books, supplies, and in many cases room and board (if the student is at least half-time). Your transportation cost between home and campus, your health insurance cost in college, and your fraternity or sorority dues are most likely non-qualified. These expenses matter for tax tools like 529 plans and some education credits. For FLYers, aligning your spending with "qualified" definitions means you can tap 529 money tax-free while also possibly claiming credits where rules allow.
- **Qualified Medical Expenses**: health-care costs that count for tax-favored treatment in accounts like HSAs and FSAs—such as doctor visits, prescriptions, certain therapies, and some medical equipment. The IRS publishes detailed lists, and not every wellness purchase qualifies. For FLYers, keeping receipts and knowing what is "qualified" lets you use HSA funds tax-free and avoid surprises if the IRS ever asks for proof.
- **Qualified Tuition Program (QTP)**: another name for a 529 plan, a tax-advantaged savings program set up by states or schools to help families save and invest for education. Money you contribute grows tax-deferred, and withdrawals are tax-free when used for qualified education expenses like tuition, many fees, and sometimes room and board (if you are at least a part-time student). For FLYers, using a QTP is like running college savings through a turbocharger—especially when your state also gives a tax deduction for contributions.

R

- **Real Estate License**: a state-issued credential that allows you to legally represent buyers, sellers, landlords, or tenants in real estate transactions for a fee. Getting licensed usually requires pre-licensing education, passing an exam, and working under a broker at first. For FLYers, a real estate license can lower your own transaction costs, open extra income streams, and give you direct access to market data and deals.
- **Real Estate Mentor**: an experienced investor or agent who is willing to share real-world knowledge, mistakes, and strategies with you as you start your journey. A good mentor helps you shorten the learning curve, avoid common traps, and think bigger than one property. For FLYers, choosing the right mentor is like choosing a "flight instructor" for money—you still fly the plane, but you are not flying blind.
- **Real Estate Professional (REP)**: a special IRS status for people who spend enough hours and effort in real estate activities—like development, construction, acquisition, management, or brokerage—to be considered full-time in the field. When you qualify and materially participate, rental real-estate losses can offset your spouse's W-2 and your small business income instead of being trapped as passive. For FLYers, achieving REP status (or having a spouse who does) turns cost segregation and depreciation into a powerful tax shield.
- **Real Property**: land and anything permanently attached to it, such as buildings, houses, and certain fixed improvements like driveways and fences. It is different from "personal

property" like cars, furniture, or appliances that can be moved. For FLYers, understanding real property is important because tax rules, estate planning, and lending treat it very differently than movable stuff.

- **Recapture Depreciation Tax**: the tax you pay when you sell a property and the IRS "recaptures" some of the depreciation you claimed in prior years, often at a special maximum rate (your marginal tax bracket or 25%, whichever the lower) instead of regular capital-gains rates. It is basically the government saying, "We let you reduce your taxable income earlier, now we want part of that back when you sell." For FLYers, planning for depreciation recapture—through 1031 exchanges, timing, and loss harvesting—keeps a surprise bill from eating too much of your profit.
- **Recording Fees**: small charges paid to the local government to officially record documents like deeds, mortgages, and liens in the public records. Recording makes your ownership and loan terms legally recognized and searchable. For FLYers, these fees are part of closing costs and, while not huge by themselves, they matter when you are calculating total acquisition cost and future basis.
- **Recordkeeping**: the habit of keeping organized, accurate documentation of your income, expenses, contracts, mileage, and major decisions. Good records back up your tax deductions, protect you in audits or disputes, and make it easier to analyze your portfolio. For FLYers, strong recordkeeping is not optional—it is the backbone of treating your rentals and businesses like real companies instead of guesswork.
- **Refinancing**: replacing an existing mortgage with a new one—often to get a lower interest rate, change the loan term, remove a co-signer, or pull out equity. Done wisely, refinancing can cut monthly payments, reduce lifetime interest, or free up cash for the next investment. For FLYers, refis are a key tool in the "Buy, Borrow, and Build" cycle, but only when the numbers justify the closing costs and you keep enough cushion for rate and market risk.
- **Refundable Credit**: a type of tax credit that can reduce your tax liability below zero, meaning you can get money back even if you did not owe any tax. Examples include part of the American Opportunity Tax Credit, earned income tax credit (age 25 or above), and child tax credit. For FLYers, refundable credits can function like an annual "bonus" from the tax code, especially in college and early-career years when income is lower.
- **Remodeling**: making significant changes to the look, layout, or function of a property—like updating kitchens and bathrooms, adding bedrooms, or opening up walls. Good remodeling can increase rent, reduce vacancies, and boost property value, but it requires planning, permits, and solid budgets. For FLYers, remodeling is one of the fastest ways to gain appreciation, as long as you separate true value-add projects from flashy, low-ROI upgrades.
- **Rent-to-Income Ratio**: the percentage of a tenant's gross monthly income that goes toward rent, often used by landlords to judge affordability. A common guideline is that rent should not exceed about 30% of a tenant's income, though this can vary by market. For FLYers, checking rent-to-income helps you screen for tenants who can realistically pay on time without being constantly stressed or one emergency away from default.
- **Rental Deduction**: a tax write-off related to a rental property, such as mortgage interest, property taxes, insurance, repairs, utilities you pay, management fees, travel to the property, and depreciation. These deductions reduce the taxable income from your rental, sometimes even creating a loss on paper. For FLYers, maximizing legitimate rental deductions is how you let the tax code reimburse you for running your real-estate business.
- **Rental Questionnaire**: a form you give prospective tenants that asks about their income, employment, rental history, pets, move-in timing, and other key details. It helps you pre-

screen applicants before running background checks or scheduling showings. For FLYers, a good questionnaire saves time, filters out obvious mismatches, and shows that you run your rental like a professional, not casually.

- **Repairs and Maintenance**: the routine and corrective work needed to keep a property in good, safe, and rentable condition—like fixing leaks, patching drywall, replacing broken locks, or servicing HVAC. These costs are generally deductible in the year you pay them (unlike capital improvements, which are added to basis and depreciated over multiple years). For FLYers, separating repairs from improvements correctly keeps you compliant and ensures you get all the immediate deductions you are allowed.
- **Replacement Costs**: the amount it would take to rebuild or replace part or all of a property with similar materials and quality at today's prices. Insurers use replacement cost estimates to set coverage limits and premiums; investors use them to understand whether a property is under- or over-insured. For FLYers, making sure your coverage matches replacement cost—not just purchase price—helps you recover fully if disaster strikes.
- **Residential Rental Property**: real estate used primarily for people to live in, such as single-family houses, condos, duplexes, or small apartment buildings. It has its own set of tax rules, including the 27.5-year depreciation schedule and special passive-loss limitations. For FLYers, residential rentals are usually the first asset class you master, because they are easier to understand, finance, and manage than many commercial properties.
- **Retirement Accounts**: tax-advantaged accounts designed to help you save for later life, such as 401(k)s, 403(b)s, IRAs, Roth IRAs, Solo 401(k)s, and HSAs (for medical). Some give you a tax break now (traditional), while others give you tax-free withdrawals later (Roth), and all are built to harness compounding over decades. For FLYers, maxing out the best retirement accounts available—especially ones with employer match or Roth features—is non-negotiable fuel for your FLY Vision Board.
- **Return on Equity**: the annual profit you are earning on the actual equity you have in a property, not just on your original down payment. As your home appreciates and your loan balance drops, your equity grows—and if your cash flow stays the same, your return on equity often shrinks over time. For FLYers, watching return on equity helps you decide when to refinance, 1031 exchange, or re-deploy equity into better-performing assets.
- **Return on Investment (ROI)**: a basic measure of how much profit you earn compared with how much cash you put in, usually expressed as a percentage. For a rental, ROI might consider cash flow, principal pay-down, appreciation, and tax benefits relative to your down payment and closing costs. For FLYers, focusing on true, all-in ROI—rather than just one piece like appreciation—keeps you from chasing deals that look good on paper but do not actually grow your net worth.
- **Revocable Living Trust**: an estate-planning tool you create while alive that holds your assets and can be changed or revoked at any time. When you die or become incapacitated, a successor trustee you chose steps in to manage and eventually distribute those assets according to your instructions, usually without going through probate. For FLYers, putting rentals and key accounts into a revocable living trust is how you build a system that can protect your family and carry your wealth forward seamlessly.
- **Room and Board**: the combined cost of housing and food for a student living at or near school—such as dorm fees plus meal plans or rent plus groceries. For tax purposes, room and board sometimes count as qualified education expenses for 529 plans, up to certain limits and rules. For FLYers, understanding room-and-board rules is what makes strategies like the Kiddie House and 529-funded rent both tax-efficient and compliant.

- **Roth IRA and Roth 401(k)**: retirement accounts where you contribute after-tax dollars now and withdrawals in retirement (if rules are met) are completely tax-free, including all the investment growth. A Roth IRA is opened by you, while a Roth 401(k) is offered by employers; both are especially powerful when you are in a low tax bracket early in life. For FLYers, funding Roth accounts while young lets decades of compounding happen in a "never-taxed-again" zone.
- **Rule of 72**: a quick mental math trick to estimate how many years it will take for your money to double at a given annual rate of return. You divide 72 by the interest or growth rate—so at 8% per year, money roughly doubles in about 9 years. For FLYers, the Rule of 72 makes compounding feel real: it shows why starting at 18 or 20 can mean multiple doubles before age 40, while waiting a decade can cost you entire "doublings" of your wealth.

S

- **S&P 500 Index**: a stock market index that tracks 500 of the largest U.S. companies (measured by their stock market capitalization dollar amounts) across many industries, like Amazon, Berkshire Hathaway, Costco, Dell, and Exxon Mobil). Owning an S&P 500 index fund is like owning a tiny slice of the U.S. economy in one investment. For FLYers, it is one of the simplest ways to get broad, low-cost stock exposure inside brokerage, HSA, 529, and 401(k) accounts.
- **Sale Price**: the final amount a buyer agrees to pay and a seller agrees to accept for a property, as shown on the closing documents. It is the starting point for calculating things like real-estate commissions, transfer taxes, and capital gains. For FLYers, understanding the true sale price (after credits and adjustments) is key for tracking basis, ROI, and future tax planning.
- **School Districts**: geographic zones that determine which public schools serve a property and its residents. Strong school districts often drive higher demand and prices because families are willing to pay more to live there. For FLYers, paying attention to school districts—even if you do not have kids yet—matters because good schools can mean more stable rents and better long-term appreciation.
- **Section 121 Exclusion**: a tax rule that lets you exclude up to a large amount of profit (for example, $250,000 single / $500,000 married) when you sell your primary residence, if you meet the ownership and use tests. This means you can keep that portion of gain tax-free. For FLYers, planning moves around §121—like living in a house before or after renting it—can turn owner-occupant deals into tax-advantaged wealth jumps.
- **Securities-Backed Line of Credit (SBLOC)**: a line of credit you open using your investment portfolio (stocks, ETFs, and index funds) as collateral instead of selling those investments. You can borrow a percentage of the portfolio's value, often at competitive rates, while your assets stay invested. For FLYers, an SBLOC is a way to tap Other People's Money from your own brokerage account for down payments or opportunities—if you respect margin risk and do not over-borrow. It is advisable to have two SBLOCs: one backed by S&P 500 index fund; and the other by no-dividend broad-based stocks such as Berkshire Hathaway B Class (BRK.B), given the low correlation of these two investments. It is also advisable to have IBLOC as standby liquidity to address any margin calls, if both S&P 500 index and BRK.B fall significantly at the same time (the last occurrence was in 2008-2009 financial crisis).

- **Security Deposit**: money a tenant gives a landlord at the start of a lease as a safety cushion against unpaid rent or damage beyond normal wear and tear. If the tenant leaves the property in good condition and current on rent, most or all of the deposit is usually returned. For FLYers, handling security deposits correctly—and documenting move-in and move-out conditions—is essential for fairness, compliance, and avoiding disputes.
- **Self-Employment Tax**: the combined Social Security and Medicare tax (around 15.3%) that self-employed people pay on their business profits, covering both the "employee" and "employer" portions. It applies to net earnings from side hustles, independent contracting, and some LLC income. For FLYers, understanding self-employment tax keeps you from being surprised at filing time and motivates smart use of retirement plans and deductions to soften the hit.
- **Self-discipline**: the ability to control your actions, emotions, and habits in service of long-term goals, even when you do not feel like it. It shows up in consistent saving, careful spending, study time for licenses, and how you follow up with tenants, lenders, and partners. For FLYers, self-discipline is the bridge between your vision board and reality—it is how you turn "someday" into signed deeds and funded accounts.
- **Seller Credit**: money the seller agrees to put toward your closing costs, repairs, or other expenses as an incentive to close the deal. It reduces how much cash you need at the table but may affect the final agreed-upon price. For FLYers, negotiating smart seller credits can make a stretched budget work—especially on new builds or in slower markets—without faking affordability.
- **Settlement Date**: the day the property officially changes hands, when funds are exchanged, documents are signed, and the deed is recorded. It is often called "closing day," and after this date, you are legally the owner and responsible for the property. For FLYers, timing the settlement date matters for things like pro-rated taxes, first mortgage payment, and even where you live for school or work deadlines.
- **Short-Term Rentals**: properties rented for brief stays—often less than 7 at a time—through platforms like Airbnb or VRBO. They can produce higher gross income but require more hands-on work, cleaning, and careful attention to local laws and taxes. For FLYers, short-term rentals can be lucrative near beaches, campuses, hospitals, or event hubs, but they require strong systems and discipline to avoid burnout and legal trouble.
- **Side Hustle**: a small business or income activity you run in addition to your main job or school, such as tutoring, junk removal, flight instruction, or online freelancing. It can provide extra cash, business experience, and tax deductions, and sometimes grows into your full-time work. For FLYers, a well-run side hustle is often the engine that funds down payments, Roth contributions, and investments.
- **Single-Member LLC**: a limited liability company with only one owner, treated as a "disregarded entity" for tax purposes (unless you elect otherwise), so its income and expenses flow directly to your personal return. It can still provide legal separation between your personal assets and your business or rental activities. For FLYers, forming a single-member LLC is a common first step to giving your side hustle or rental a professional, protected structure.
- **Social Intelligence**: the ability to read people, understand interpersonal dynamics, and respond in ways that build trust and cooperation. It shows up when you interview tenants, negotiate with sellers, work with contractors, or speak with lenders and partners. For FLYers, social intelligence can turn average deals into great ones because people prefer to work with landlords and investors who listen, communicate clearly, and act with respect.

- **Solo 401(k)**: a retirement plan designed for self-employed individuals and small business owners with no full-time employees besides a spouse. It allows both "employee" and "employer" contributions, which can add up to very high annual limits and may include a Roth and loan feature. For FLYers with real-estate or business income, a Solo 401(k) is like a jumbo retirement rocket: big tax deductions now or big tax-free growth later, plus the option to borrow up to $50,000 for real estate deals. Research brokerage firms that offer loan feature in the Solo 401(k) program.
- **Standard Deduction**: a fixed dollar amount the IRS lets you subtract from your income instead of itemizing individual deductions like mortgage interest and charity. Its size depends on your filing status and is adjusted over time, and many taxpayers now use it because it is higher than their total itemized deductions. For FLYers, knowing your standard deduction helps you decide whether to itemize and reminds you that even low-income years can be completely tax-free with the right planning.
- **State 529 Plan**: a tax-favored education savings program run by a state that lets you invest for future college and, in some cases, K-12 costs. While federal tax benefits are similar across states, many states also give their residents an income-tax deduction or credit for contributions. For FLYers and their parents, picking a strong, low-fee state 529 plan turns education dollars into tax-efficient, compounding assets instead of just cash out the door.
- **State Income Tax**: the tax some states charge on your income in addition to federal income tax, with rates and rules that vary widely. A few states have no income tax, while others have high rates but also rich deductions and credits. For FLYers, where you live—and sometimes where you claim residency—can make a big difference in your after-tax income and how quickly you reach financial independence.
- **Step-Up in Basis**: a tax rule that resets an inherited asset's cost basis to its fair market value at the original owner's death. This often wipes out decades of capital gains for the heirs, so they can sell with little or no capital-gains tax on past appreciation. For FLYers, the step-up in basis explains why families often "swap 'til they drop" with 1031 exchanges and then hold until death—so the next generation can start with a clean slate.
- **Stock Index Funds**: funds that are built to track a specific market index—like the S&P 500 or a total stock market index—by holding all or most of its components. They offer instant diversification and usually have very low expense ratios, making them ideal core holdings. For FLYers, stock index funds are the simplest way to own hundreds or thousands of companies at once while keeping costs and guesswork low.
- **Straight-Line Depreciation**: a method of depreciation where you spread the cost of an asset evenly over its useful life—such as 27.5 years for residential rental buildings. Each year, you deduct the same depreciation amount from your rental income. For FLYers, straight-line depreciation is the default baseline; cost segregation and bonus depreciation are how you legally "bend" that line to pull more deduction into earlier years.
- **Street Smart**: practical, real-world savvy about how people and systems work, especially outside of textbooks and formal rules. It includes reading non-verbal cues, spotting scams, negotiating, and quickly assessing risk in new situations. For FLYers, being street smart complements being book smart—you need both to navigate tenants, contractors, and deals in the real-world financial jungle.
- **Student Loans**: money borrowed to pay for education costs, typically from federal or private lenders, that must be repaid with interest after school. They can be helpful tools but become heavy chains if taken on without a plan, especially if balances are large and degrees do not lead to strong earning power. For FLYers, the goal is to keep student loans as low as

possible and pair them with real-estate, business, and tax strategies so they do not delay homeownership or investing for decades.

- **Successor Trustee**: the person or institution you name in a living trust to take over management of the trust's assets if you die or become incapacitated. They follow the instructions you left for handling, protecting, and eventually distributing your property. For FLYers, choosing a wise and trustworthy successor trustee is part of designing a legacy that will actually work the way you intended when you are no longer in the cockpit.
- **Swap and Drop**: a nickname for a long-term strategy where an investor repeatedly "swaps" properties through 1031 exchanges during life (deferring capital gains and depreciation recapture each time) and then "drops" the final property to heirs at death, who receive a step-up in basis. The result is decades of tax deferral followed by a potential reset that erases much of the built-up tax liability. For FLYers, swap-and-drop shows how real estate plus smart timing can turn tax rules into a multi-generation advantage, not just a yearly headache.

T

- **Tangible Assets**: physical things you can see and touch that have value, such as real estate, cars, equipment, gold, or even certain collectibles. They differ from purely digital or paper assets like bank balances or stock entries, even though those also represent value. For FLYers, owning solid tangible assets—especially well-chosen properties—is a key way to anchor your wealth in the real world, not just on a screen.
- **Target Date Funds**: mutual funds or ETFs that automatically adjust their mix of investments over time based on a specific "target" year, like 2055 or 2060, when you might retire. They start more aggressive (more stocks) and gradually move toward more conservative holdings (more bonds) as the target date approaches. For FLYers, target date funds are a by-default option in employer-sponsored 401(k)s. But pay close attention to their fees and long term performances, because most target date funds have much higher fees (0.2-0.5%) than S&P 500 index fund (as low as 0.015%), and have long term performance lagging behind the S&P 500 index fund due to the dragging factor by bond portfolio.
- **Tax-Advantaged Accounts**: special accounts where the government gives you a tax break either when you put money in, when it grows, or when you take it out—examples include 401(k)s, IRAs, ESAs, HSAs, and 529 plans. They are designed to encourage saving for goals like retirement, health care, and education. For FLYers, filling these buckets early and consistently is like building secret tunnels under the tax code so more of your growth stays yours.
- **Tax Code**: the giant set of laws and rules that decides how income, investments, businesses, and estates are taxed in the United States. It is organized into sections (like §121, §1031, or §469) and backed up by regulations and court cases that interpret what those sections mean in real life. For FLYers, you do not have to memorize the code, but learning the most useful sections turns tax from something that "happens to you" into something you can plan around.
- **Tax-Deferred Accounts**: accounts where you postpone paying taxes on contributions and growth until you withdraw the money later, usually in retirement—like traditional 401(k)s, traditional IRAs, and some annuities. Your money can grow faster in the meantime because you are investing dollars that have not yet been taxed. For FLYers, using tax-deferred accounts in your high-earning years, and then managing withdrawals carefully later, is one more lever in your lifetime tax strategy.

- **Tax Efficiency**: the practice of arranging your investments, accounts, and transactions so you legally pay the least reasonable amount of tax over your whole life—not just this year. It includes things like using Roth IRA and HSA accounts, harvesting losses, timing sales, and placing the right assets in the right accounts. For FLYers, tax efficiency is like adding a silent 1–2% to your returns just by being intentional about where and how you invest.
- **Tax Filing**: the yearly process of reporting your income, deductions, credits, and payments to the government using tax forms (like Form 1040) so they can calculate whether you owe more or get a refund. Filing correctly and on time keeps you compliant and avoids penalties, but filing strategically is where planning pays off. For FLYers, doing your own return at least once—ideally with a mentor—helps you really understand how the numbers connect to your day-to-day choices.
- **Tax-Free Cash Flow**: income that you receive without owing income tax on it, such as certain distributions from Roth accounts, HSA reimbursements for qualified medical expenses, or Augusta Rule rent within the 14-day limit. In real estate, some or all of your rental cash flow may also be sheltered by depreciation. For FLYers, building tax-free or tax-sheltered cash flow means you keep more from each dollar of passive income, accelerating the path to independence.
- **Tax-Free Loans**: borrowed money that is not treated as taxable income when you receive it, such as loans from banks, HELOCs, SBLOCs, IBLOCs, or 401(k) loan. You still must repay the loan with interest, but the IRS does not count loan proceeds as income as long as the agreement is real. For FLYers, carefully structured tax-free loans let you access capital for investments while keeping your assets growing and your reported income lower.
- **Tax-Free Real Estate Legacy**: a plan where properties are bought, managed, and passed down using strategies like 1031 exchanges, trusts, and the step-up in basis so that most appreciation is never heavily taxed. The goal is for the next generation to receive valuable properties with minimal debt and minimal built-in tax liability. For FLYers, designing a tax-free legacy is about thinking beyond "my house" to "our family portfolio" that can last for decades.
- **Tax-Free Withdrawals**: money you take out of certain accounts or strategies that the IRS does not tax, such as qualified Roth IRA/401(k) withdrawals, HSA funds used for medical expenses, or some life-insurance living benefits from critical illness rider, chronical illness rider or terminal illness rider. You already paid the tax upfront, or the law gives that treatment as a special incentive. For FLYers, stacking multiple sources of tax-free withdrawals in the future gives you huge flexibility to control your tax bracket year by year.
- **Tax Loophole**: a term people use for gaps, quirks, or special rules in the tax law that can be used to reduce taxes in ways the average person does not know about. Some loopholes were deliberate policy choices; others are side-effects of complex legislation. For FLYers, the key is not chasing sketchy tricks, but learning solid, legal strategies—like 121, 1031, REP status, short-term rental, and self-rental—that may look like loopholes to people who never bothered to read the rules.
- **Tax Loss Harvesting**: selling investments that have dropped in value so you can lock in the loss for tax purposes and use it to offset current or future capital gains, and sometimes a small amount of ordinary income. You can then reinvest in a similar, but not "substantially identical," asset to stay in the market. For FLYers, disciplined tax-loss harvesting in brokerage and even crypto can turn market dips into long-term tax savings. At the time the book is published, crypto investment is not subject to the wash sale rule, making crypto a powerful loss harvesting tool.

- **Tax Planning**: the proactive process of arranging your finances, investments, and business activities throughout the year to legally minimize taxes over time. It involves choosing account types, timing income and deductions, deciding when to sell or exchange properties, and coordinating with your CPA or advisor. For FLYers, tax planning is not something you do in April; it is something you build into every big financial decision all year.
- **Tax Return**: the full set of forms you file each year (like Form 1040 and attached schedules) that tells the government what you earned, what you can deduct, what credits you claim, and how much tax you already paid. It is both a report card and a receipt for your financial year. For FLYers, reading your own tax return line by line teaches you where your money actually went and what levers you can pull next year.
- **Tax Savings**: the difference between what you would have paid in tax without planning and what you actually pay after using legal strategies like deductions, credits, and smart account choices. Tax savings can be redirected into investments, debt payoff, or building your First Home Fund. For FLYers, every dollar tax saved and reinvested is like a quiet employee that works for you for the rest of your life.
- **Tenant Screening**: the process of evaluating potential renters using applications, rental questionnaires, credit checks, references, and sometimes background reports. The goal is to find tenants who can pay on time, treat the property well, and follow the lease agreement. For FLYers, strong tenant screening is the cheapest insurance you can buy—it prevents most "nightmare tenant" stories before they ever start.
- **Traditional 401(k)**: an employer-sponsored retirement plan where your contributions are made with pre-tax dollars, reducing your taxable income today. The money grows tax-deferred, and you pay income tax when you withdraw it in retirement. For FLYers, taking full advantage of employer matches in a traditional 401(k) is like accepting free pay raises that compound for decades. You can do Roth conversion at market downturns, so called Roth the Dip.
- **Traditional IRA**: an individual retirement account you open yourself, where contributions may be tax-deductible depending on your income and whether you or a spouse are covered by a workplace plan. Growth is tax-deferred, and withdrawals in retirement are taxed as ordinary income. For FLYers, a traditional IRA can be a useful tool in high-income years or as part of a future Roth conversion strategy.
- **Trump Account**: a special tax-advantaged savings account introduced in the One Big Beautiful Bill, designed for children under 18 to build long-term investment capital. Contributions are limited each year, grow tax-favored, and are meant to support future education, entrepreneurship, or first-home goals. For FLYers, the Trump Account is another dedicated bucket where family dollars can compound for the next generation instead of being spent on short-term consumption.
- **Trustee**: the person or institution responsible for managing the assets inside a trust according to the rules and wishes laid out in the trust document. They owe a legal duty to act in the best interests of the beneficiaries, not themselves. For FLYers, choosing a wise, organized, and trustworthy trustee—often a parent now and eventually a financially mature child—helps ensure your real-estate and investment legacy is handled with care when you are not at the controls.

U

- **Umbrella Insurance**: a low-cost liability policy that sits on top of your other insurance (auto, home, rental) and gives you extra protection if a big claim or lawsuit goes beyond those basic limits. It typically adds $1–2 million of coverage for a few hundred dollars a year. For FLYers, an umbrella policy is an affordable peace of mind once you own property, drive regularly, or have meaningful assets to protect.

- **Unrealized Gain**: the increase in value of an investment you still own, where the price has gone up but you have not sold yet. On paper you are richer, but you have not locked in the profit or triggered tax. For FLYers, paying attention to unrealized gains helps you decide when to hold, when to harvest, and when to use BBB strategies instead of knee-jerk selling.
- **Underwriting**: the lender's detailed review process where they verify your income, credit, debts, assets, and the property itself before deciding whether to approve your loan and on what terms. It is where your file is checked against guidelines to judge risk. For FLYers, strong preparation—clean documents, honest applications, and good credit—makes underwriting smoother and helps you secure better rates and faster approvals.
- **Utility Costs**: the ongoing expenses for services that keep a property livable and functional—such as electricity, water, gas, trash, sewer, and sometimes internet. Depending on your strategy, these may be paid by the landlord, the tenant, or split between them. For FLYers, choosing who pays which utilities is a key part of structuring leases and analyzing true cash flow.
- **Uniform Transfers to Minors Act (UTMA)**: a law that allows adults to gift money or investments to a minor through a custodial account, where an adult manages the assets until the child reaches a specified age (often 18 or 21, depending on the state). The money legally belongs to the child and must be used for their benefit. For FLYers, well-funded UTMA accounts—invested in long-term, zero-dividend, broad-based stocks—can grow into serious college or first-home capital, but you must also plan around Kiddie Tax.

V

- **Vacancy**: the period when a rental unit is empty and not producing rent, either between tenants or because the market is soft or the property is mis-priced. Every vacancy month reduces your annual cash flow and return. For FLYers, planning for some vacancy in your numbers—and working hard to minimize it through good marketing and management—is essential to staying solvent and calm.
- **VA Loans**: home loans backed by the U.S. Department of Veterans Affairs, available to eligible veterans, active-duty service members, and some surviving spouses. They often require no down payment, have competitive interest rates, and do not require private mortgage insurance. For FLYers with military ties, VA loans can be one of the most generous and powerful tools for buying a first home or house hack.
- **Valuation**: the process of estimating what a property or business is worth, using methods like comparable sales, income (NOI and cap rate), or replacement cost. Accurate valuation matters for buying, selling, refinancing, insurance, and tax planning. For FLYers, learning how valuation works gives you confidence to recognize a real deal—and to walk away when the numbers don't make sense.
- **VRBO**: short for "Vacation Rentals by Owner," an online platform where property owners list homes, condos, or rooms for short-term stays. It connects hosts with travelers and handles marketing, bookings, and payments for a fee. For FLYers running short-term rentals, listing on VRBO (alongside similar platforms) can turn a well-located property into a flexible, high-income asset—if you stay on top of reviews, rules, and guest service.
- **Variable Interest Rate**: a loan interest rate that can change over time based on a benchmark, such as the prime rate (the interest rate banks charge their most credit worthy

clients) or an index like secured overnight financing rate (SOFR, an overnight borrowing rate of U.S. treasury securities). Your payment may go up or down as rates move, which adds uncertainty compared with a fixed-rate loan. For FLYers, variable rates can start lower and look attractive, but you must stress-test your budget and cash flow to be sure you can handle higher payments if the rate rises.

- **Verified Proof of Income**: documentation that confirms how much money you actually earn, such as pay stubs, W-2s, tax returns, or bank statements showing deposits. Lenders, landlords, and even some schools or aid offices use it to decide whether you qualify for loans, rentals, or assistance. For FLYers, keeping clean, organized proof of income makes mortgage approvals, leases, and financial aid applications much smoother—and signals that you are serious and reliable.

W

- **W-2 Income**: money you earn as an employee, reported each year on a Form W-2 from your employer. It includes wages, salaries, tips, and bonuses before taxes and other payroll deductions are taken out. For FLYers, W-2 income is often your starting fuel for building credit, saving for a down payment, and funding tax-advantaged accounts like 401(k)s and HSAs.
- **W-4 Form**: the form you give your employer when you start a job (or when your situation changes) to tell them how much tax to withhold from each paycheck. It asks about your filing status, dependents, and any expected deductions or extra income. For FLYers, filling out the W-4 thoughtfully—especially when you have rental losses or big deductions—helps you avoid being over-withheld or owing a big bill in next April.
- **W-9 Form**: a form you fill out to give your name, address, and taxpayer ID (SSN or EIN) to someone who will pay you as an independent contractor, landlord, or vendor. They use it to prepare forms like 1099-NEC or 1099-MISC for tax reporting. For FLYers, using an EIN instead of your SSN on W-9s can protect your privacy and make your business look more professional.
- **Wash Sale Rule**: a tax rule that disallows a capital loss on a stock or security if you sell it at a loss and then buy the same or a "substantially identical" investment within 30 days before or after the sale. The disallowed loss is not gone forever; it is added to the cost basis of the new shares. For FLYers, understanding the wash sale rule keeps your tax-loss harvesting legal and effective, especially when rotating between similar index funds. Crypto is not subject to wash sale rule at the time this book is published.
- **Wealth Transfer**: the movement of assets—like real estate, investments, and businesses—from one generation to the next through gifts, inheritances, and trusts. Done wisely, it minimizes taxes, avoids family conflict, and passes on both money and wisdom. For FLYers, planning for wealth transfer early means thinking about how your future kids will receive assets, not just how you will accumulate them.
- **Whole Life Insurance**: a type of permanent life insurance that provides lifelong coverage and builds cash value that grows over time at a relatively stable rate. Premiums are higher than term insurance, but the policy can pay dividends and allow policy loans against the cash value. For FLYers, properly structured whole life with strong companies can serve as a "financial safety vault" and part of a family bank strategy alongside real estate and index funds.
- **Written Leases**: formal, signed rental agreements that spell out rent, term, responsibilities, rules, and consequences in clear language. They protect both landlord and tenant far better

than verbal promises, especially if a dispute ends up in court. For FLYers, always using written leases—no matter how friendly the tenant—turns your rental into a professional, enforceable business.

- **Witness of Living Trust**: a person who observes the signing of a living trust (and often related documents) and then signs to confirm that the grantor signed willingly and was of sound mind. The exact requirements vary by state and may sometimes overlap with notarization. For FLYers, choosing reliable, disinterested witnesses helps ensure your trust will stand up legally when it is needed most.
- **Wealth Management**: the integrated process of planning, investing, tax strategy, risk management, and estate planning to grow and protect your net worth over time. It looks at the whole picture—real estate, securities portfolios, businesses, insurance, and family goals—rather than just one account or year. For FLYers, thinking in wealth-management terms means you stop chasing random tips and start building a coordinated lifelong plan.
- **Wealth Circle**: a small, intentional community of people—family, friends, mentors, or peers—who meet regularly to share knowledge, hold each other accountable, and collaborate on financial and business goals. It might study deals, books, tax strategies, and personal habits together. For FLYers, joining or creating a wealth circle turns the journey from solo to shared—you grow faster when you surround yourself with others who are serious about building, not just spending.

X

- **Cross-Generational Building**: the intentional process of using today's money, skills, and structures to strengthen not just your own life, but your children's and grandchildren's as well. It means involving younger family members early in real decisions, such as managing rentals, learning tax strategies, and serving on a family LLC or family foundation, so they gain hands-on experience instead of just inheriting checks. For FLYers, cross-generational building turns wealth into a family project: each generation learns, invests, and adds to the foundation, instead of starting over from scratch.

Y

- **Yield**: the income you earn from an investment over a period of time—such as interest from bonds, dividends from stocks, or net rent from property—expressed as a percentage of what you invested or the asset's current value. It focuses on cash coming out of the investment, not on price changes or capital gains. For FLYers, comparing yields helps you see which assets are really paying you now versus which ones are mainly long-term appreciation plays.
- **Youth Entrepreneurship**: starting and running real businesses while you are still in your teens or early 20s, such as tutoring, junk removal, flight instruction, e-commerce, or small service companies. It teaches you to solve real problems, manage money, work with clients, and take smart risks long before a "traditional" career begins. For FLYers, youth entrepreneurship is more than extra cash—it is a training ground for leadership, financial literacy, and building assets instead of just chasing jobs.

Z

- **Zero Is Hero**: a principle that says your goal in key parts of your financial life is to drive certain tax, fee, or risk numbers as close to zero as possible. It shows up in ideas like aiming for zero consumer debt, zero or super low fees, and near-zero tax on major gains through smart planning. For FLYers, "Zero Is Hero" is a reminder that every percentage point you avoid in tax or interest can be re-routed into compounding assets that work for you.

- **Zero Dividends Stocks**: stocks that choose not to pay out cash dividends, instead reinvesting profits back into the business to fuel growth. Because they do not send you taxable dividend checks each year, most of the gain shows up later as capital appreciation, which you control the timing of by deciding when to sell. For FLYers, owning broad-based, zero-dividend stocks in taxable accounts can be a tax-smart way to build long-term wealth with less yearly tax drag.
- **Zoning Codes**: local laws that dictate how land and buildings can be used—such as whether a lot can hold single-family homes, multi-family units, commercial buildings, or mixed-use spaces. They also cover details like setbacks, height limits, parking requirements, and rules for additions like ADUs or short-term rentals. For FLYers, understanding zoning codes turns you from a passive buyer into a strategist who can see what a property could become, not just what it is today.
- **Zillow**: a widely used real-estate website and app where you can search homes and rentals, see estimated values ("Zestimates"), view photos and past sale prices, and gauge neighborhood trends. It provides quick, free access to comparable listings and rent ranges, though its estimates are not always perfectly accurate. For FLYers, Zillow is a helpful first-pass research tool, but serious offers still need your own analysis, local data, and sometimes professional advice.

Index

Made in the USA
Monee, IL
14 June 2026

54113358R00162